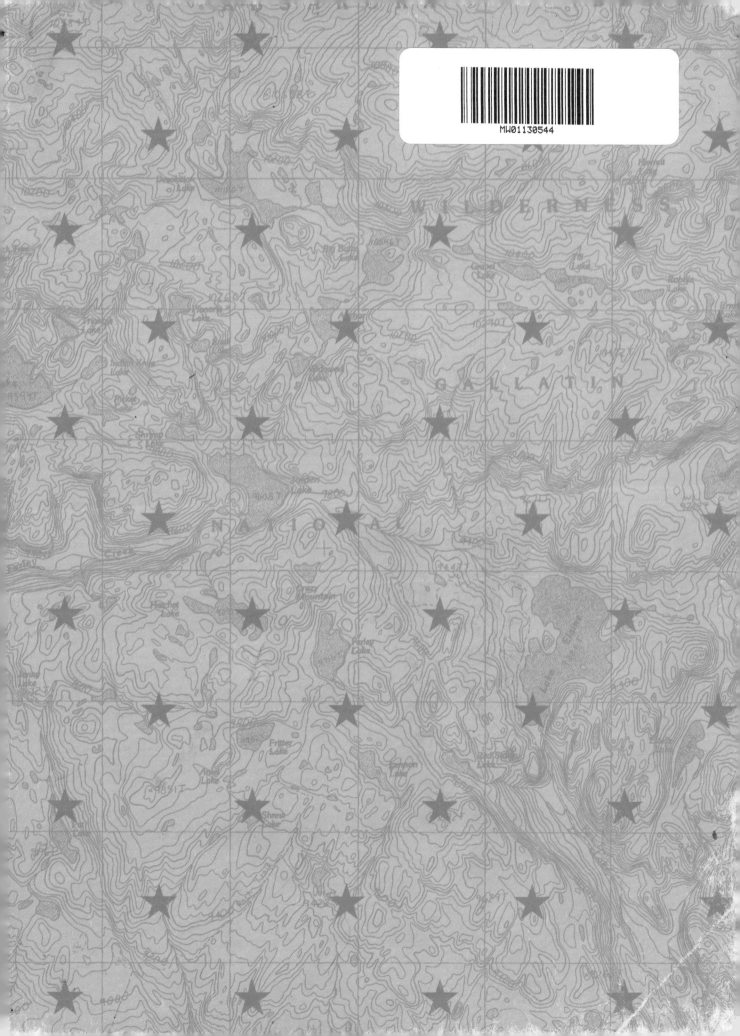

HOUGHTON MIFFLIN
SOCIAL STUDIES

⋆ PENNSYLVANIA STUDIES ⋆

Visit *Education Place*®
www.eduplace.com/kids

 HOUGHTON MIFFLIN   BOSTON

PENNSYLVANIA

Pennsylvania Databank

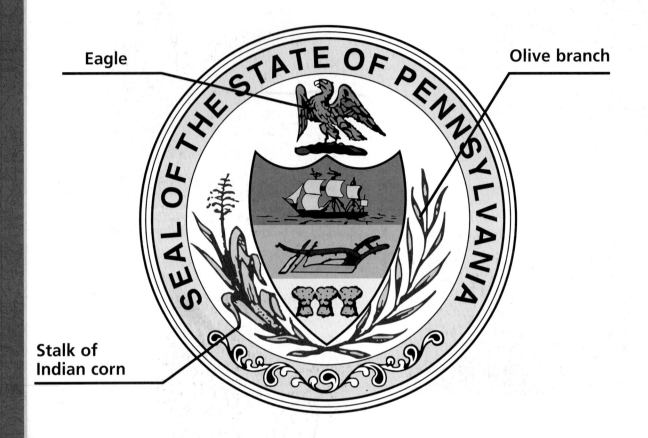

Eagle

Olive branch

Stalk of
Indian corn

SEAL OF THE STATE OF PENNSYLVANIA

Pennsylvania Facts

Population, 2000	12,281,054
Land Area	45,308 square miles (117,348 square kilometers)
Economy	**Agriculture:** Milk, beef cattle, mushrooms, greenhouse and nursery products, corn, hay **Industry:** Service industry, tourism, banking, health care, food products, chemicals, machinery, printed materials
Song	"Pennsylvania"
Motto	"Virtue, Liberty, and Independence"
State Nickname	The Keystone State

Pennsylvania Symbols

State Flower
Mountain Laurel

State Animal
Whitetail Deer

State Fish
Brook Trout

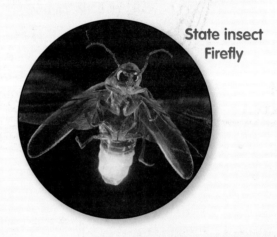

State insect
Firefly

State Bird
Ruffed Grouse

State Tree
Hemlock

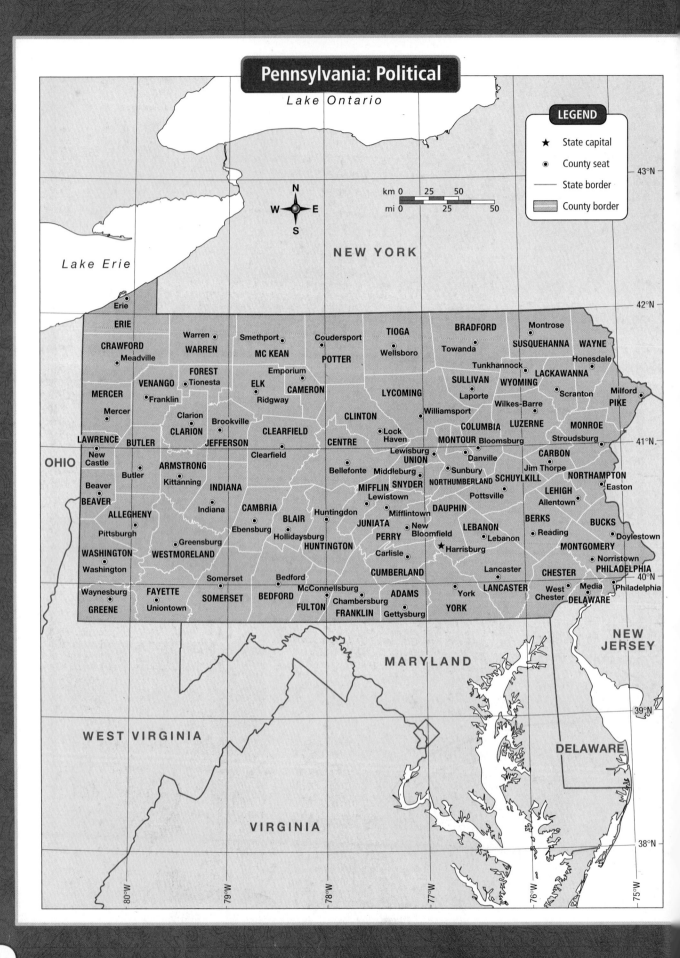

Pennsylvania: Political

Lake Ontario

NEW YORK

LEGEND

★ State capital

◉ County seat

— State border

▦ County border

43°N

Lake Erie

42°N

Erie

ERIE

CRAWFORD
Meadville

Warren
WARREN

Smethport
MC KEAN

Coudersport

POTTER

TIOGA
Wellsboro

BRADFORD
Towanda

Montrose

SUSQUEHANNA

Tunkhannock

WAYNE
Honesdale

FOREST
Tionesta

Emporium

ELK
Ridgway

CAMERON

LYCOMING
Williamsport

SULLIVAN
Laporte

WYOMING
Wilkes-Barre

LACKAWANNA
Scranton

Milford
PIKE

VENANGO
Franklin

MERCER
Mercer

Clarion
CLARION

Brookville

CLEARFIELD

CLINTON

Lock
Haven

COLUMBIA
Bloomsburg

LUZERNE

MONROE
Stroudsburg

41°N

LAWRENCE
New
Castle

BUTLER
Butler

JEFFERSON

Clearfield

CENTRE

Lewisburg
UNION
Bellefonte Middleburg

MONTOUR

Danville

CARBON
Jim Thorpe

Beaver

ARMSTRONG
Kittanning

INDIANA

MIFFLIN
Lewistown

SNYDER

Sunbury
NORTHUMBERLAND

SCHUYLKILL
Pottsville

NORTHAMPTON
Easton

BEAVER

ALLEGHENY
Pittsburgh

Indiana

CAMBRIA
Ebensburg

BLAIR
Hollidaysburg

Huntingdon

JUNIATA
Mifflintown

PERRY

New
Bloomfield

DAUPHIN

LEBANON
Lebanon

LEHIGH
Allentown

BERKS
Reading

BUCKS
Doylestown

WASHINGTON
Washington

Greensburg
WESTMORELAND

HUNTINGTON

Carlisle

★ Harrisburg

MONTGOMERY
Norristown

PHILADELPHIA

40°N

Waynesburg

FAYETTE
Uniontown

SOMERSET

Somerset

BEDFORD

Bedford

McConnellsburg

FULTON

CUMBERLAND

Chambersburg

FRANKLIN Gettysburg

ADAMS

York

YORK

Lancaster

LANCASTER

CHESTER
West
Chester

Media
DELAWARE

Philadelphia

GREENE

MARYLAND

NEW
JERSEY

39°N

WEST VIRGINIA

DELAWARE

VIRGINIA

38°N

80°W   79°W   78°W   77°W   76°W   75°W

km 0   25   50
mi 0   25   50

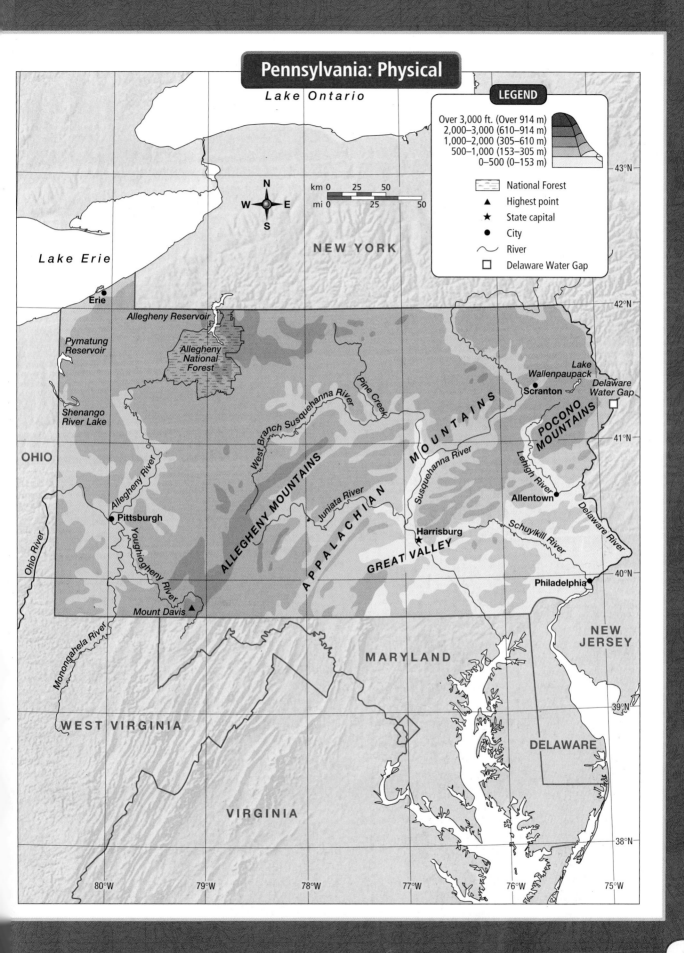

Pennsylvania: Physical

Lake Ontario

LEGEND

Over 3,000 ft. (Over 914 m)
2,000–3,000 (610–914 m)
1,000–2,000 (305–610 m)
500–1,000 (153–305 m)
0–500 (0–153 m)

National Forest
▲ Highest point
★ State capital
● City
〜 River
▢ Delaware Water Gap

Lake Erie

NEW YORK

● Erie

Allegheny Reservoir

Pymatung Reservoir

Allegheny National Forest

Pine Creek

West Branch Susquehanna River

Lake Wallenpaupack

● Scranton

Delaware Water Gap

POCONO MOUNTAINS

Shenango River Lake

ALLEGHENY MOUNTAINS

A P P A L A C H I A N   MOUNTAINS

Susquehanna River

Lehigh River

Delaware River

OHIO

Allegheny River

Juniata River

● Allentown

● Pittsburgh

Youghiogheny River

Ohio River

Harrisburg ★

GREAT VALLEY

Schuylkill River

Mount Davis ▲

● Philadelphia

Monongahela River

MARYLAND

NEW JERSEY

WEST VIRGINIA

DELAWARE

VIRGINIA

km 0   25   50
mi 0   25   50

43°N
42°N
41°N
40°N
39°N
38°N

80°W   79°W   78°W   77°W   76°W   75°W

Pennsylvania: Precipitation

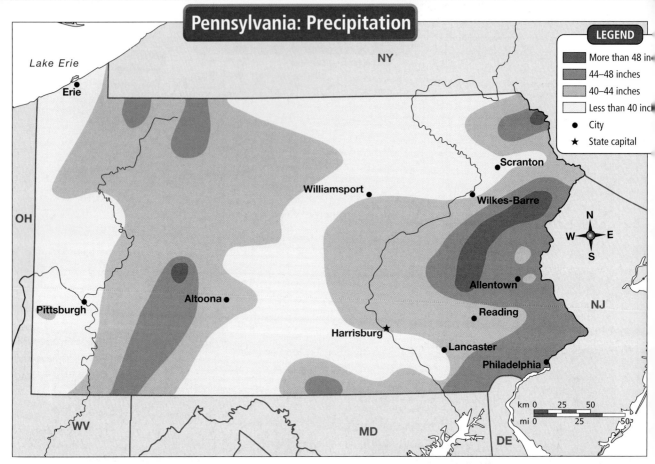

LEGEND
- More than 48 in
- 44–48 inches
- 40–44 inches
- Less than 40 inc
- ● City
- ★ State capital

NY

Lake Erie

Erie

OH

Scranton

Williamsport

Wilkes-Barre

N
W • E
S

Altoona

Allentown

NJ

Pittsburgh

Reading

Harrisburg

Lancaster

Philadelphia

km 0   25   50
mi 0   25   50

WV

MD

DE

Average January Temperature

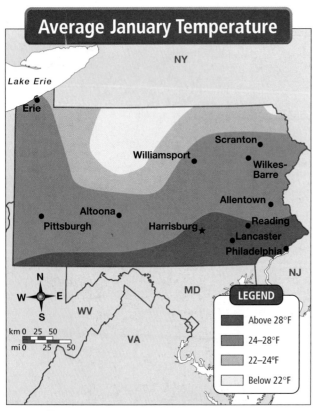

NY

Lake Erie

Erie

Scranton

Williamsport

Wilkes-Barre

Allentown

Altoona

Reading

Pittsburgh

Harrisburg

Lancaster

Philadelphia

NJ

N
W • E
S

km 0 25 50
mi 0   25   50

WV

MD

VA

LEGEND
- Above 28°F
- 24–28°F
- 22–24°F
- Below 22°F

Average July Temperature

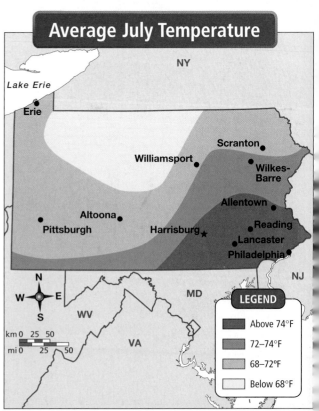

NY

Lake Erie

Erie

Scranton

Williamsport

Wilkes-Barre

Allentown

Altoona

Reading

Pittsburgh

Harrisburg

Lancaster

Philadelphia

NJ

N
W • E
S

km 0 25 50
mi 0   25   50

WV

MD

VA

LEGEND
- Above 74°F
- 72–74°F
- 68–72°F
- Below 68°F

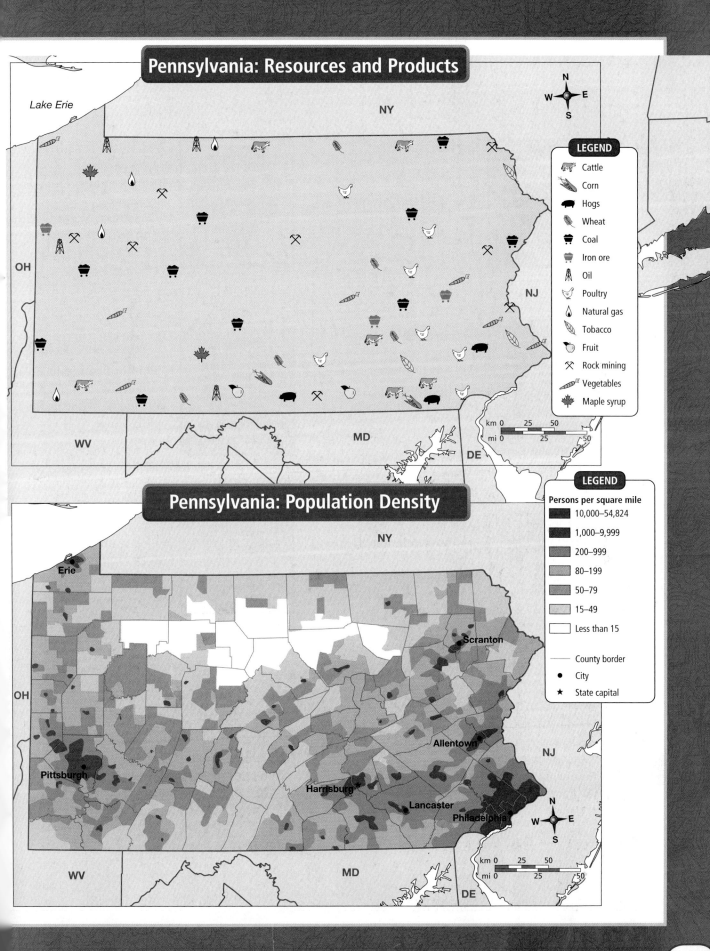

Pennsylvania: Resources and Products

Lake Erie

NY

OH

NJ

WV

MD

DE

LEGEND

Cattle
Corn
Hogs
Wheat
Coal
Iron ore
Oil
Poultry
Natural gas
Tobacco
Fruit
Rock mining
Vegetables
Maple syrup

km 0   25   50
mi 0   25   50

Pennsylvania: Population Density

NY

Erie

Scranton

OH

Allentown

NJ

Pittsburgh

Harrisburg

Lancaster

Philadelphia

WV

MD

DE

LEGEND

Persons per square mile
10,000–54,824
1,000–9,999
200–999
80–199
50–79
15–49
Less than 15

— County border
● City
★ State capital

km 0   25   50
mi 0   25   50

★ AUTHORS ★

Senior Author
Dr. Herman J. Viola
Curator Emeritus
Smithsonian Institution

Dr. Cheryl Jennings
Project Director
Florida Institute of
  Education
University of North Florida

Dr. Sarah Witham
Bednarz
Associate Professor,
  Geography
Texas A&M University

Dr. Mark C. Schug
Professor and Director
Center for Economic
  Education
University of Wisconsin,
  Milwaukee

Dr. Carlos E. Cortés
Professor Emeritus, History
University of California,
Riverside

Dr. Charles S. White
Associate Professor,
School of Education
Boston University

Consulting Authors

Dr. Dolores Beltran
Assistant Professor
Curriculum Instruction
California State University, Los Angeles
(Support for English Language Learners)

Dr. MaryEllen Vogt
Co-Director
California State University Center for
the Advancement of Reading
(Reading in the Content Area)

HOUGHTON MIFFLIN

SOCIAL STUDIES

PENNSYLVANIA STUDIES ★

HOUGHTON MIFFLIN   BOSTON

PENNSYLVANIA

Consultants

Philip J. Deloria
Associate Professor
Department of History
    and Program in
    American Studies
University of Michigan

Lucien Ellington
UC Professor of Education
    and Asia Program,
    Co-Director
University of Tennessee,
Chattanooga

Thelma Wills Foote
Associate Professor
University of California,
Irvine

Stephen J. Fugita
Distinguished Professor
Psychology and Ethnic
    Studies
Santa Clara University

Charles C. Haynes
Senior Scholar
First Amendment Center

Ted Hemmingway
Professor of History
The Florida Agricultural &
    Mechanical University

Douglas Monroy
Professor of History
The Colorado College

Lynette K. Oshima
Assistant Professor,
Department of Language,
    Literacy and
Sociocultural Studies
    and Social Studies
    Program Coordinator
University of New Mexico

Jeffrey Strickland
Assistant Professor, History
University of Texas Pan
    American

Clifford E. Trafzer
Professor of History and
    American Indian Studies
University of California,
Riverside

Teacher Reviewers

Michelle Light
Cornwall Elementary School
Cornwall, PA

John Thomas
McIntyre Elementary
Pittsburgh, PA

Printed in the U.S.A.

ISBN: 0-618-55278-2

23456789-VH-13-12 11 10 09 08 07

Contents

Contents... vi–xv

▶ About Your Textbook xvi

▶ Reading Social Studies xvi

Bringing the world to your classroom!

UNIT 1

Pennsylvania's Land and First People

Preview 1

CHAPTER 1 — The First Pennsylvanians

Vocabulary Preview   Reading Strategy: Predict and Infer 2

Lesson 1   Core   **Land and Water** 4

Map and Globe Skills Review Map Skills 8

Lesson 2   Core   **People Arrive** 10
Lesson 3   Core   **Early Cultures** 14

Chapter 1 Review and Test Prep 18

CHAPTER 2 — Colonial Period

Vocabulary Preview   Reading Strategy: Monitor and Clarify 20

Lesson 1   Core   **Explorers and Early Settlers** 22
Lesson 2   Core   **William Penn's Colony** 26

Map and Globe Skills Use Latitude and Longitude 30

Lesson 3   Core   **The Colony Grows** 32
Lesson 4   Core   **Life in the New Colony** 36

Chapter 2 Review and Test Prep 40

Unit 1 Review   **WR**   Connect to Today 42

UNIT 2 A New Nation and State

Preview 44

CHAPTER 3 Creating a New Nation

Vocabulary Preview   Reading Strategy: Summarize 46

Lesson 1   Core   The French and Indian War 48
Lesson 2   Core   Declaring Independence 52
Lesson 3   Core   The Revolution 56
Lesson 4   Core   A New Nation 60

Graph and Chart Skills Make a Timeline 66

Chapter 3 Review and Test Prep 68

CHAPTER 4 Growth and Expansion

Vocabulary Preview   Reading Strategy: Question 70

Lesson 1   Core   Keystone State 72

Reading and Thinking Skill
Distinguishing Fact from Opinion 76

Lesson 2   Core   Transportation and Trade 78
Lesson 3   Core   Industry Changes 82

Chapter 4 Review and Test Prep 86

Unit 2 Review WR   Connect to Today 88

UNIT 3 Growth and Change

Preview 90

CHAPTER 5 The Civil War

Vocabulary Preview   Reading Strategy: Predict and Infer 92

Lesson 1 Core   **Divided States** 94

Citizenship Skill Understand Point of View 98

Lesson 2 Core   **Civil War** 100

Study Skill Identify Primary and Secondary Sources 104

Lesson 3 Core   **The War and Pennsylvania** 106

Chapter 5 Review and Test Prep 110

CHAPTER 6 Into the 20th Century

Vocabulary Preview   Reading Strategy: Question 112

Lesson 1 Core   **Manufacturing and Business** 114
Lesson 2 Core   **Making Steel** 118
Lesson 3 Core   **Immigration and Reform** 122

Citizenship Skill Make a Decision 126

Lesson 4 Core   **Changing Times** 128

Reading and Thinking Skill Identify Cause and Effect 134

Chapter 6 Review and Test Prep 136

Unit 3 Review WR Connect to Today 138

UNIT 4 Pennsylvania Today

Preview 140

CHAPTER 7 Government in Pennsylvania

Vocabulary Preview   Reading Strategy: Summarize 142

Lesson 1   Core   United States Government 144
Lesson 2   Core   State Government 148

Citizenship Skill Resolve Conflicts 152

Lesson 3   Core   Rights and Responsibilities 154

Chapter 7 Review and Test Prep 158

CHAPTER 8 People and the Economy

Vocabulary Preview   Reading Strategy: Question 160

Lesson 1   Core   People of Pennsylvania 162

Graph and Chart Skill Read a Circle Graph 166

Lesson 2   Core   Working in Pennsylvania 168
Lesson 3   Core   Connections to the World 172

Chapter 8 Review and Test Prep 176
Unit 4 Review WR   Connect to Today 178

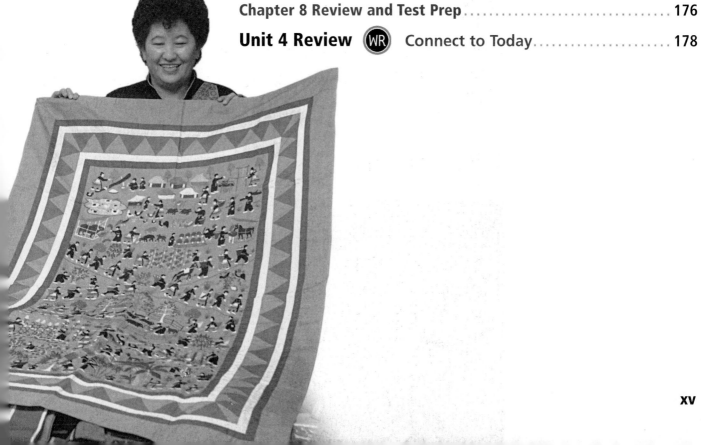

UNIT 5 · The East

UNIT 5 — The East

Preview **180**

CHAPTER 9 — Exploring the East

Vocabulary Preview Reading Strategy: Summarize **182**

Lesson 1 Core   Land and Climate **184**
Lesson 2 Core   Resources and Economy **188**

Study Skills Use Reference Materials **194**

Lesson 3 Core   The Mid-Atlantic **196**

Chapter 9 Review and Test Prep **200**

Unit 5 Review WR Connect to Today **202**

References

Citizenship Handbook

Pledge of Allegiance R2

Character Traits R4

Pennsylvania Governors R6

Pennsylvania Counties R8

Pennsylvania Databank R10

Biographical Dictionary R16

Resources

Geographical Terms R20

Atlas R22

Gazetteer R31

Glossary R37

Index R43

Credits R51

Skill Lessons

Take a step-by-step approach to learning and practicing key social studies skills.

Map and Globe Skills

Review Map Skills   8
Use Latitude and Longitude   30
Skill Practice: Map Skill
5, 129
Skill Practice: Reading Maps
49, 57, 80, 163, 169

Graph and Chart Skills

Make a Timeline   66
Read a Circle Graph   166
Skill Practice: Reading Charts
146, 148, 149, 189, 198

Study Skills

Identify Primary and Secondary Sources   104
Use Reference Materials   194
Skill Practice: Reading Visuals
192

Citizenship Skills

Understand Point of View   98
   Apply Critical Thinking
Make a Decision   126
Resolve Conflicts   152
Skill Practice: Make a Decision
170

Reading and Thinking Skills

Distinguish Fact from Opinion	76
Identify Cause and Effect	134
Apply Critical Thinking	

Reading Skills/Graphic Organizer

Cause and Effect
10, 26, 48, 72, 114, 122, 172

Compare and Contrast
14, 60, 82, 100, 148, 196

Sequence
56, 128

Problem and Solution
78, 144

Main Idea and Details
4, 22, 25, 36, 94, 118, 184

Draw Conclusions
162

Predict Outcomes
32, 52, 106

Categorize
168

Classify
154, 188

About Your Textbook

① How It's Organized

Units The major sections of your book are units.

Each starts with a big idea. ——

Get ready for reading.

Chapters Units are divided into chapters, and each opens with a vocabulary preview.

Four important concepts get you started. ——

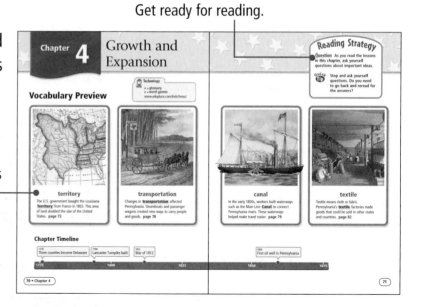

❷ Core

Lessons Lessons bring social studies to life and help you meet your state's standards.

Core Lesson

Vocabulary strategies help with word meanings.

Before you read, use your prior knowledge.

Reading skills support your understanding of the text.

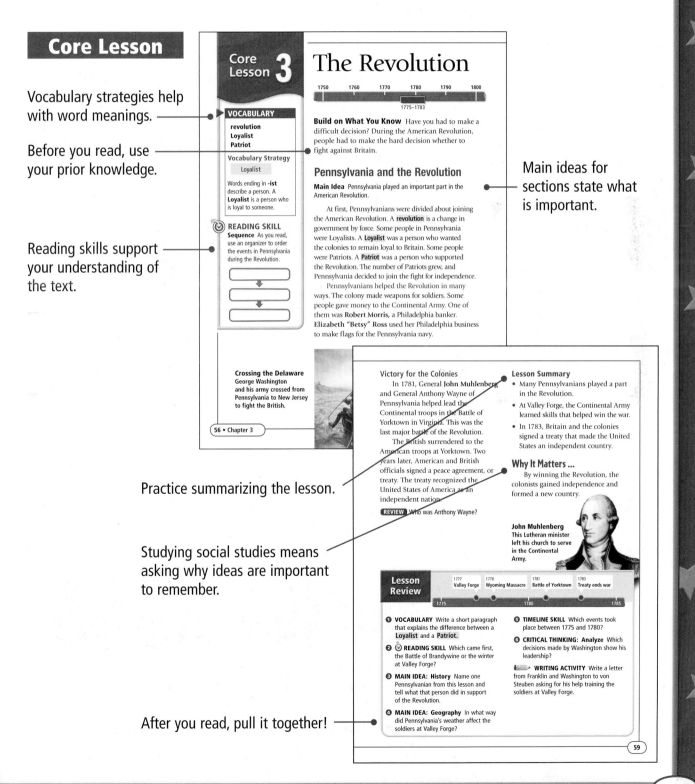

Core Lesson 3

The Revolution

1750 1760 1770 1780 1790 1800

1775–1783

Build on What You Know Have you had to make a difficult decision? During the American Revolution, people had to make the hard decision whether to fight against Britain.

VOCABULARY
revolution
Loyalist
Patriot

Vocabulary Strategy
Loyalist

Words ending in **-ist** describe a person. A **Loyalist** is a person who is loyal to someone.

READING SKILL
Sequence As you read, use an organizer to order the events in Pennsylvania during the Revolution.

Pennsylvania and the Revolution

Main Idea Pennsylvania played an important part in the American Revolution.

At first, Pennsylvanians were divided about joining the American Revolution. A **revolution** is a change in government by force. Some people in Pennsylvania were Loyalists. A **Loyalist** was a person who wanted the colonies to remain loyal to Britain. Some people were Patriots. A **Patriot** was a person who supported the Revolution. The number of Patriots grew, and Pennsylvania decided to join the fight for independence.

Pennsylvanians helped the Revolution in many ways. The colony made weapons for soldiers. Some people gave money to the Continental Army. One of them was **Robert Morris**, a Philadelphia banker. **Elizabeth "Betsy" Ross** used her Philadelphia business to make flags for the Pennsylvania navy.

Crossing the Delaware
George Washington and his army crossed from Pennsylvania to New Jersey to fight the British.

56 • Chapter 3

Main ideas for sections state what is important.

Victory for the Colonies
In 1781, General **John Muhlenberg** and General Anthony Wayne of Pennsylvania helped lead the Continental troops in the Battle of Yorktown in Virginia. This was the last major battle of the Revolution.

The British surrendered to the American troops at Yorktown. Two years later, American and British officials signed a peace agreement, or treaty. The treaty recognized the United States of America as an independent nation.

REVIEW Who was Anthony Wayne?

Lesson Summary
• Many Pennsylvanians played a part in the Revolution.
• At Valley Forge, the Continental Army learned skills that helped win the war.
• In 1783, Britain and the colonies signed a treaty that made the United States an independent country.

Why It Matters ...
By winning the Revolution, the colonists gained independence and formed a new country.

John Muhlenberg
This Lutheran minister left his church to serve in the Continental Army.

Practice summarizing the lesson.

Studying social studies means asking why ideas are important to remember.

Lesson Review

1777 Valley Forge   1778 Wyoming Massacre   1781 Battle of Yorktown   1783 Treaty ends war

1775   1780   1785

❶ **VOCABULARY** Write a short paragraph that explains the difference between a **Loyalist** and a **Patriot.**

❷ **READING SKILL** Which came first, the Battle of Brandywine or the winter at Valley Forge?

❸ **MAIN IDEA: History** Name one Pennsylvanian from this lesson and tell what that person did in support of the Revolution.

❹ **MAIN IDEA: Geography** In what way did Pennsylvania's weather affect the soldiers at Valley Forge?

❺ **TIMELINE SKILL** Which events took place between 1775 and 1780?

❻ **CRITICAL THINKING: Analyze** Which decisions made by Washington show his leadership?

WRITING ACTIVITY Write a letter from Franklin and Washington to von Steuben asking for his help training the soldiers at Valley Forge.

59

After you read, pull it together!

3 Skills

Skill Building Learn map, graph, and study skills, as well as citizenship skills for life.

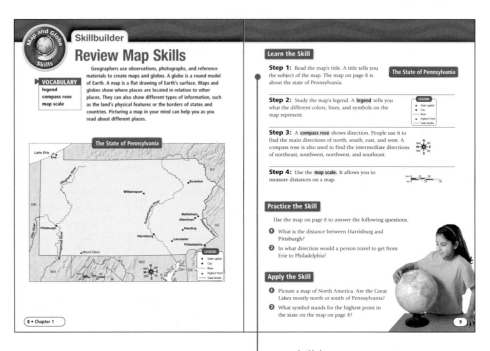

Skill lessons step it out.

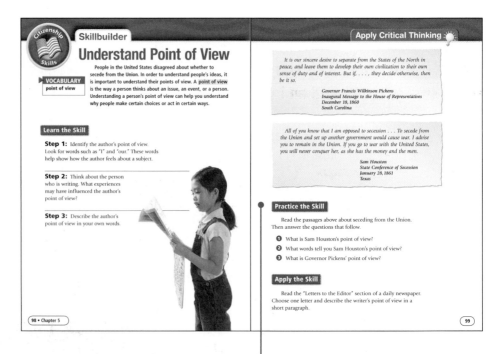

Practice and apply a social studies skill.

❹ References

Citizenship Handbook

The back of your book includes sections you'll refer to again and again.

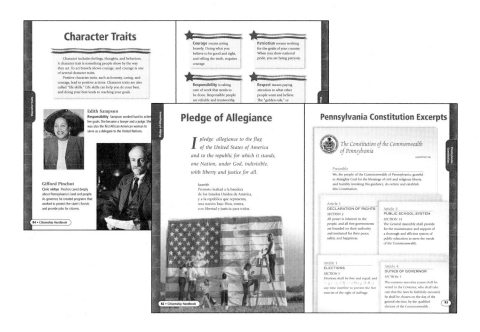

Resources

Look for atlas maps, a glossary of social studies terms, and an index.

Reading Social Studies

Your book includes many features to help you be a successful reader. Here's what you will find:

VOCABULARY SUPPORT

Every chapter and lesson helps you with social studies terms. You'll build your vocabulary through strategies you're learning in language arts.

Preview
Get a jump start on four important words from the chapter.

Vocabulary Strategies
Focus on word roots, prefixes, suffixes, or compound words, for example.

Vocabulary Practice
Reuse words in the reviews, skills, and extends. Show that you know your vocabulary.

READING STRATEGIES

Look for the reading strategy and quick tip at the beginning of each chapter.

Predict and Infer
Before you read, think about what you'll learn.

Monitor and Clarify
Check your understanding. Could you explain what you just read to someone else.

Question
Stop and ask yourself a question. Did you understand what you read?

Summarize
After you read, think about the most important ideas of the lesson.

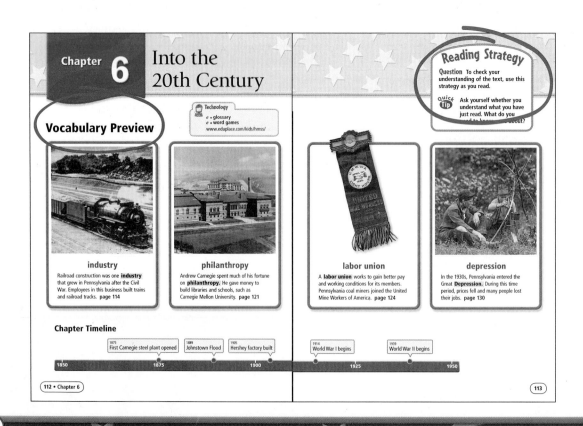

Chapter **6** Into the 20th Century

Technology
e • glossary
e • word games
www.eduplace.com/kids/hmss/

Reading Strategy
Question To check your understanding of the text, use this strategy as you read.
quick Tip Ask yourself whether you understand what you have just read. What do you...

Vocabulary Preview

industry
Railroad construction was one **industry** that grew in Pennsylvania after the Civil War. Employees in this business built trains and railroad tracks. **page 114**

philanthropy
Andrew Carnegie spent much of his fortune on **philanthropy**. He gave money to build libraries and schools, such as Carnegie Mellon University. **page 121**

labor union
A **labor union** works to gain better pay and working conditions for its members. Pennsylvania coal miners joined the United Mine Workers of America. **page 124**

depression
In the 1930s, Pennsylvania entered the Great **Depression**. During this time period, prices fell and many people lost their jobs. **page 130**

Chapter Timeline

| 1875 First Carnegie steel plant opened | 1889 Johnstown Flood | 1905 Hershey factory built | 1914 World War I begins | 1939 World War II begins |

1850   1875   1900   1925   1950

112 • Chapter 6

113

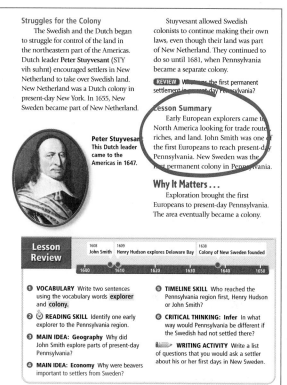

READING SKILLS

As you read, organize the information.
These reading skills will help you:

Sequence

Cause and Effect

Compare and Contrast

Problem and Solution

Draw Conclusions

Predict Outcomes

Categorize (or) Classify

Main Idea and Details

COMPREHENSION SUPPORT

Build on What You Know
Check your prior knowledge. You may already know a lot!

Review Questions
Connect with the text. Did you understand what you just read?

Summaries
Look for three ways to summarize—a list, an organizer, or a paragraph.

UNIT 1

Pennsylvania's Land and First People

The Big Idea

Why do you think people move to a new land?

" I make no doubt this place will at some future day be one of the most populous and delightful seats on earth."

William Bartram, American author who studied plants and nature, late 1700s

Henry Hudson
1565?–1611

How do people discover new lands? Hudson found new waterways that later explorers used to reach present-day Pennsylvania.
page 23

History Makers

Armegott Printz
1627–1676

Unlike most women of her time, Armegott Printz was able to read and write. She was involved in struggles between Dutch and Swedish settlers. **page 24**

Lappawinsoe
1700s

Lappawinsoe was a leader of the Lenni Lenape Indians in Pennsylvania in the 1700s. He agreed to the Walking Purchase, which gave American Indian land to colonists. **page 34**

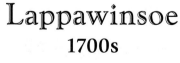

Chapter 1

The First Pennsylvanians

Technology

e • **glossary**
e • **word games**
www.eduplace.com/kids/hmss/

Vocabulary Preview

climate

Long ago, Pennsylvania's **climate** was much colder than it is today. When people first arrived in Pennsylvania, the land was probably covered in ice and snow. **page 6**

migrate

People in ancient times often had to **migrate,** or move, from one region to another in search of food. They often migrated to follow animals. **page 10**

Chapter Timeline

About 12,000 years ago
Paleo-Indians

About 10,000 years ago
Archaic people

12,000 years ago

8,000 years ago

Reading Strategy

Predict and Infer Use this strategy before you read each lesson in this chapter.

Look at the pictures in the lesson to guess what it will be about. What do the images show?

artifact

An **artifact** is an item used by a group of people in daily life. These items help scientists figure out what the lives of ancient people were like. **page 11**

culture

Each American Indian group in what is present-day Pennsylvania had its own **culture.** These groups had their own arts, languages, and belief systems. **page 14**

About 500 years ago
Eastern Woodland groups

4,000 years ago   Today

Land and Water

VOCABULARY

region
landform
elevation
climate

Vocabulary Strategy

landform

When you read a compound word, think about the meanings of the two smaller words that make the word. A **landform** is a certain **form,** or type, of **land.**

READING SKILL

Main Idea and Details
Write the main idea about Pennsylvania regions, and add details to support it.

Build on What You Know How would you describe the land where you live? Is it flat or hilly? Different areas of Pennsylvania look different, depending on the features that make up the land.

Pennsylvania's Land

Main Idea Pennsylvania is located in the eastern part of the United States and has five major land regions.

Pennsylvania is a state in the Mid-Atlantic region in the eastern part of the United States. A **region** is an area of land that has one or more features in common. Sometimes regions are based on physical features, such as landforms. A **landform** is a certain type of land, such as a mountain or a valley.

The land in northwest Pennsylvania is near sea level, or the level of the surface of the world's oceans. If you traveled across the state's mountains, forests, and rocky plateaus, you would see that Pennsylvania's elevation changes across the state. A plateau is a high, mostly flat area. **Elevation** is the height of a landform above sea level. Pennsylvania's elevation changes from 0 feet to more than 3,000 feet.

Susquehanna River This river flows through the eastern part of the state.

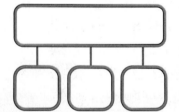

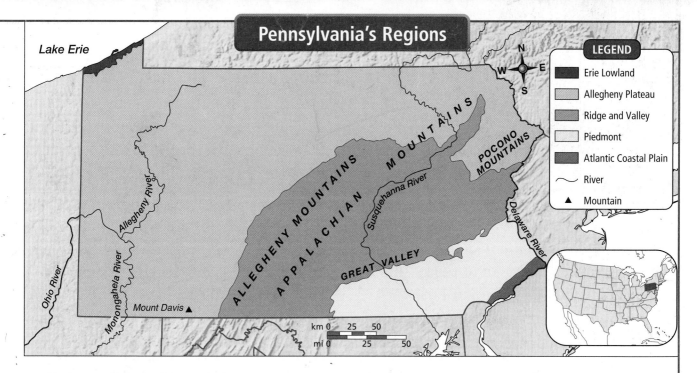

Pennsylvania's Regions Pennsylvania's five regions have different landforms and bodies of water.

SKILL **Map Skill** Through which three regions does the Susquehanna River flow?

Pennsylvania's Regions

Pennsylvania consists of five regions: Allegheny Plateau, Erie Lowland, Ridge and Valley, Piedmont, and Atlantic Coastal Plain.

The Allegheny Plateau is the largest region in Pennsylvania. It covers about half of the state. The Allegheny Plateau has deep valleys, flat-topped ridges, and hardwood forests. The Pocono Mountains are located in this region. Mt. Davis is also in this region. It is the highest point in the state at 3,213 feet above sea level.

The Erie Lowland region borders Lake Erie. A long time ago this narrow strip of land was part of the lakebed. Now it is a level, sandy plain.

The Ridge and Valley region is a wide strip of land that lies in the center of the state. The Allegheny and Appalachian mountains are located here. This region has forests, ridges, valleys, and rolling hills. The Great Valley is found in this region.

The Piedmont region is found in the southeastern portion of the state. It has hills and valleys. South Mountain and Reading Prong are found in the Piedmont region.

The Atlantic Coastal Plain is a narrow strip of land located in the far southeastern portion of the state. It is a low, flat, sandy plain.

REVIEW Describe the landforms and other features of the Allegheny Plateau.

5

Pennsylvania's Climate

Main Idea Pennsylvania's climate is influenced by its location and landforms.

Most of Pennsylvania has a continental climate. **Climate** is the typical weather of a place over a long period of time. Places with a continental climate have temperatures that are cold in the winter and warm in the summer.

Pennsylvania's climate varies from region to region. Location and elevation affect each region's climate.

Regions with higher elevations usually have cooler temperatures and more precipitation than regions with lower elevations. Precipitation is water that falls to earth as rain, hail, sleet, or snow. In the mountains of Pennsylvania's Ridge and Valley region, the temperatures are cooler than in regions with lower elevations.

Summer During the summer months, temperatures in Pennsylvania can climb as high as 100°F.

The Allegheny Plateau also has a cooler climate. This area is usually humid in the summer.

The Piedmont and Atlantic Coastal Plain regions in southeast Pennsylvania have the warmest climate of the state's five regions. Winter is usually mild in these two regions.

The Erie Lowland has a mild climate. This is because the waters of Lake Erie warm the shores of this region.

Winter Pennsylvania averages between 30 and 54 inches of snow each year.

The Water Cycle

Each of Pennsylvania's regions is affected by the water cycle. The water cycle is the movement of water from the Earth to the atmosphere and back again. This cycle has been occurring throughout the Earth's history.

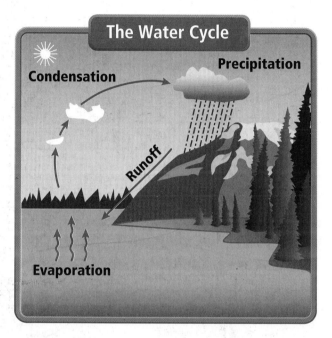

The Water Cycle

Condensation

Precipitation

Runoff

Evaporation

Water in Pennsylvania About three percent of Pennsylvania is covered by water.

Water changes form several times during this cycle. The sun causes water to evaporate. The evaporated water later returns to Earth as precipitation.

REVIEW In what way are the climates of the Erie Lowland region and the Ridge and Valley region different?

Lesson Summary

Pennsylvania has five regions. Each region's landforms and location influence its climate.

Why It Matters . . .

Throughout history, the state's geography and climate have affected where Pennsylvanians live and what they do.

Lesson Review

❶ **VOCABULARY** Fill in the blank with the correct word.

climate   elevation   region

Pennsylvania is located in the Mid-Atlantic _____ of the United States.

❷ 🔄 **READING SKILL** Name two **details** that tell about this **main idea:** Pennsylvania has five main land regions.

❸ **MAIN IDEA: Geography** What landforms do Pennsylvania's regions have?

❹ **MAIN IDEA: Geography** Name two factors that affect Pennsylvania's climate.

❺ **CRITICAL THINKING: Compare and Contrast** Choose two Pennsylvania land regions. Explain how they are alike and how they are different.

✏️ **WRITING ACTIVITY** Write a short description of the water cycle. Tell how it affects the climate of the place where you live.

Skillbuilder

Review Map Skills

Geographers use observations, photographs, and reference materials to create maps and globes. A globe is a round model of Earth. A map is a flat drawing of Earth's surface. Maps and globes show where places are located in relation to other places. They can also show different types of information, such as the land's physical features or the borders of states and countries. Picturing a map in your mind can help you as you read about different places.

VOCABULARY
legend
compass rose
map scale

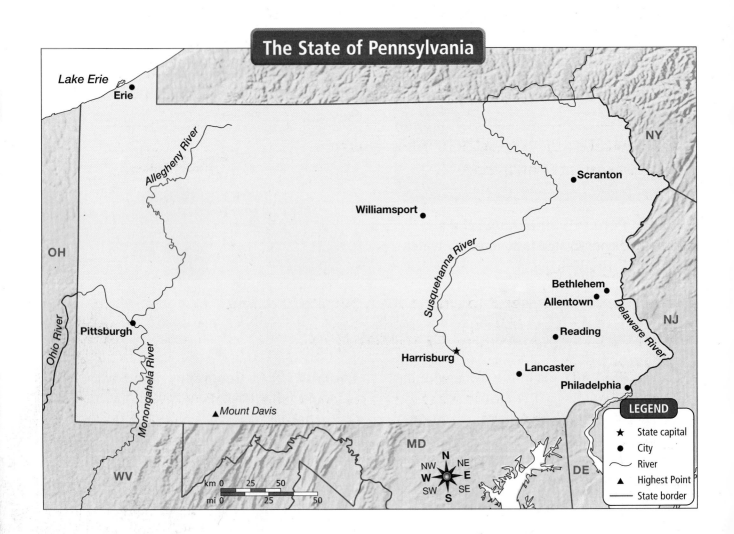

The State of Pennsylvania

LEGEND
★ State capital
● City
〜 River
▲ Highest Point
— State border

Learn the Skill

Step 1: Read the map's title. A title tells you the subject of the map. The map on page 8 is about the state of Pennsylvania.

Step 2: Study the map's legend. A **legend** tells you what the different colors, lines, and symbols on the map represent.

LEGEND
★ State capital
● City
∼ River
▲ Highest Point
— State border

Step 3: A **compass rose** shows direction. People use it to find the main directions of north, south, east, and west. A compass rose is also used to find the intermediate directions of northeast, southwest, northwest, and southeast.

Step 4: Use the **map scale.** It allows you to measure distances on a map.

km 0   25   50
mi 0   25   50

Practice the Skill

Use the map on page 8 to answer the following questions.

1. What is the distance between Harrisburg and Pittsburgh?

2. In what direction would a person travel to get from Erie to Philadelphia?

Apply the Skill

1. Picture a map of North America. Are the Great Lakes mostly north or south of Pennsylvania?

2. What symbol stands for the highest point in the state on the map on page 8?

People Arrive

| 12,000 years ago | 8,000 years ago | 4,000 years ago | Today |

12,000 years ago–3,000 years ago

Build on What You Know You may have noticed that the way your neighborhood looks can change over time. Geography also changes over time.

Pennsylvania in the Ice Age

Main Idea Scientists believe people first came to Pennsylvania thousands of years ago when the land was very different.

Thousands of years ago, Earth experienced a period called the Ice Age. During this time, Earth looked very different than it does today. Glaciers, or huge sheets of moving ice, covered parts of the earth. Many scientists believe early people migrated from Asia or Europe to the Americas at that time. To **migrate** is to move from one place to another. Some scientists think that people in search of food crossed a land bridge that long ago connected Asia to North America. Others suggest that people traveled by sea. Scientists continue to make discoveries about the first Americans.

VOCABULARY

migrate
adapt
artifact

Vocabulary Strategy

artifact

An **artifact** is an object made by people. Scientists study these objects to learn **facts** about the way people lived.

READING SKILL

Cause and Effect As you read, list the ways that a warming climate affected Pennsylvania and its first people.

Causes	Effects

Ice Age Pennsylvania
People migrated to hunt large animals, such as these woolly mammoths.

The Climate Warms

Many scientists agree that the first people arrived in present-day Pennsylvania at least 12,000 years ago. Early people followed and hunted herds of animals such as mammoths. These animals no longer exist. The Ice Age ended when the climate warmed. This warming took place over thousands of years.

As the climate changed, so did the land. Melted ice created new streams and rivers. This water helped shape Pennsylvania's landforms. It also covered the land bridge between Asia and North America. People could no longer use this bridge to migrate.

New animals and plants appeared during this time, but some animals and plants died out. Some scientists think the huge Ice Age mammals died out because early people hunted them too much. Others think the animals could not adapt to the warmer climate. To **adapt** means to change in order to live in a new environment. Early people adapted to the changes by hunting smaller animals and eating wild plants.

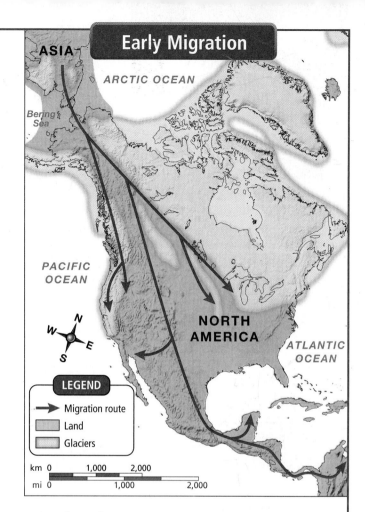

People Migrate People in prehistoric times may have come to North America by crossing a land bridge over the Bering Sea.

Paleo-Indians

The earliest people to live in North America were the Paleo-Indians. Paleo-Indians moved from place to place, following herds of animals for food. They gathered nuts and berries to eat. Caves and tents served as shelters.

Scientists learn about people who lived in the past by studying artifacts from the past. An **artifact** is an object made by human hands. Scientists have found Paleo-Indian artifacts in southwestern and central Pennsylvania.

REVIEW In what way did melting glaciers affect North America's land?

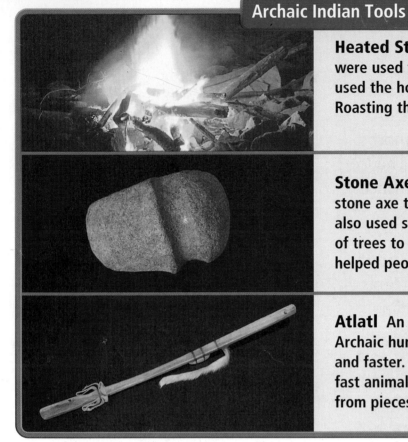

Archaic Indian Tools

Heated Stones Stones heated in fires were used to boil water. The Archaic people used the hot stones to roast meat in pits. Roasting the meat helped it last longer.

Stone Axe The Archaic Indians used a stone axe to cut down trees. They also used stone axes to dig out the inside of trees to make canoes. Dugout canoes helped people travel on rivers.

Atlatl An atlatl was a tool that helped the Archaic hunters throw their spears harder and faster. The atlatl allowed them to catch fast animals like deer. Atlatls were made from pieces of stone and wood.

Other Prehistoric People

Main Idea Over time, ancient people changed and learned to use the land in new ways.

About 10,000 years ago, the Archaic Indians lived in present-day Pennsylvania. The Archaic Indians found new ways to use the area's rich land and resources.

Like the Paleo-Indians, the Archaic Indians hunted animals and gathered plants, nuts, and berries for food. They also began to grow their own food. They grew sunflowers for seeds and gourds for containers.

The Archaic Indians spent less time moving around in search of food because they grew crops. They were able to settle in small villages.

Archaic Indians used spears, hammers, and fishhooks made from bone, shell, stone, and wood. They also made important discoveries. For example, they learned to use stones heated in fire to cook food. They also used stones to grind tools such as the axe. The Archaic Indians also created a tool called an atlatl (aht LAHT uhl). This tool allowed the Archaic Indians to throw spears faster and farther.

Woodland Indians

Over time, American Indian groups changed. About 3,000 years ago, Woodland Indian groups lived in Pennsylvania. Woodland Indians in Pennsylvania hunted animals and gathered some wild plants for food. They also grew their own food. They discovered new foods that had not been grown by the Paleo and Archaic Indians, such as corn and squash. They settled for long periods of time in order to grow and harvest crops.

REVIEW Why did Woodland Indians settle for long periods of time?

Pottery Woodland people probably used artifacts such as this bowl to store food.

Lesson Summary

The first people in Pennsylvania lived thousands of years ago in a time called prehistory. Early peoples adapted their ways of life to changes in the environment.

Why It Matters . . .

American Indians were the first people to settle in Pennsylvania and to grow their own food.

Lesson Review

| 10,000 years ago | 3,000 years ago |
| **Archaic Indians** | **Woodland Indians** |

| 12,000 years ago | 8,000 years ago | 4,000 years ago | Today |

① **VOCABULARY** Write a sentence that tells why a person who would **migrate** might need to **adapt.**

② 🔄 **READING SKILL** What **effect** did climate change have on Pennsylvania's land?

③ **MAIN IDEA: History** When do scientists believe the first people came to present-day Pennsylvania?

④ **MAIN IDEA: Technology** What tools were made by the Archaic Indians?

⑤ **TIMELINE SKILL** About how many years ago did Archaic Indians live in present-day Pennsylvania?

⑥ **CRITICAL THINKING: Generalize** Describe the ways American Indian groups used Pennsylvania's plants and animals.

RESEARCH ACTIVITY Choose one of the American Indian groups you have studied in this lesson. Use the library or the Internet to learn more about the lives of these ancient peoples. Write a few paragraphs reporting your results.

Early Cultures

12,000 years ago	8,000 years ago	4,000 years ago	Today

500 years ago–300 years ago

VOCABULARY

culture
wigwam
longhouse
wampum

Vocabulary Strategy

longhouse

When you read a compound word, think about the meaning of the two smaller words. A **longhouse** is a long building in which several families live.

READING SKILL

Compare and Contrast
Chart the ways that the Haudenosaunee and Algonquian Indians were similar and different.

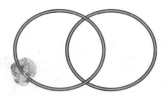

Build on What You Know Do you speak the same language as the people near you? Most of the early American Indians in present-day Pennsylvania spoke the same language as the people near them. They spoke one of two main languages.

Early Pennsylvania Indians

Main Idea Early American Indian groups shared similar cultures within language groups.

The northeastern part of the present-day United States has long been home to American Indian groups. This area is called the Eastern Woodlands. By 1500, many groups of people had settled in this area. Each group had its own culture. A **culture** is a way of life that people share. Most of these peoples spoke one of two types of languages. Some spoke an Algonquian (ahl GONG kwi uhn) language. Others spoke a Haudenosaunee (hah den oh SAW nee) language. Haudenosaunee groups also have been called Iroquois (IHR uh kwoi).

Eastern Woodlands
Trees such as maple and oak grow in this area.

Algonquian

Main Idea Algonquian groups in Pennsylvania included the Lenni Lenape and the Shawnee.

One of the earliest Algonquian groups to live in what is present-day Pennsylvania was the Lenni Lenape (leh NEE leh nah PEH). Lenni Lenape means "original people." The Lenni Lenape also were called the Delaware because they lived along the Delaware River.

Most Lenni Lenape settled in one place for a long period of time. They lived in communities of related families. Women were very important in Lenni Lenape communities. When a man married, he moved into his wife's home. Lenni Lenape communities usually included several houses called wigwams. A **wigwam** was a small round house made of bark with a dome-shaped roof.

Lenni Lenape grew crops such as beans, corn, and squash. They sometimes ground and boiled corn to make soup, bread, and dumplings.

Wigwams Wigwams were seasonal homes that the Algonquians used during different times of the year.

They hunted animals such as ducks, bears, turkeys, and deer. The Lenni Lenape also gathered nuts, berries, and mushrooms.

Religion was an important part of Lenni Lenape life. They believed in a creator who made the universe.

In the late 1600s, an Algonquian group called the Shawnee moved into present-day Pennsylvania. The Shawnee did not settle in one place for long. They lived in temporary villages. In warm months, the Shawnee planted and harvested corn, pumpkins, and other crops. In colder months, the Shawnee set up villages in forests.

Many Algonquian peoples held festivals related to the harvest or to religion. These celebrations included dancing, singing, drumming and story-telling.

REVIEW What does the name Lenni Lenape mean?

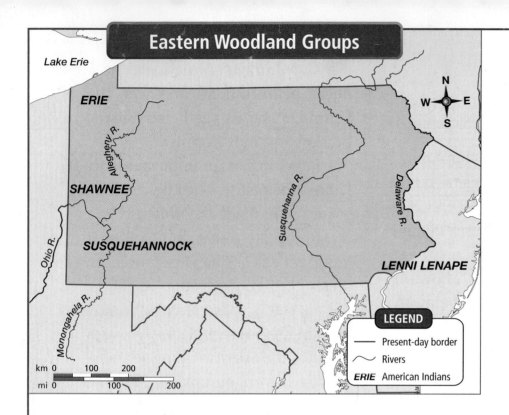

Eastern Woodland Groups

Lake Erie

ERIE

Allegheny R.

SHAWNEE

Susquehanna R.

Delaware R.

SUSQUEHANNOCK

Ohio R.

Monongahela R.

LENNI LENAPE

N
W E
S

km 0   100   200
mi 0   100   200

LEGEND
— Present-day border
∿ Rivers
ERIE American Indians

Early Settlement
The Algonquian and Haudenosaunee cultures lived in different areas of what is now present-day Pennsylvania.

SKILL Reading Maps
Who lived in the eastern part of the state?

Haudenosaunee

Main Idea Haudenosaunee groups included the Erie and the Susquehannock.

Haudenosaunee means "people of the longhouse." A **longhouse** was a long, bark-covered building. Many families lived in one longhouse. Like Algonquian peoples, Haudenosaunee men went to live with their wives' families after marriage.

The Erie were one of the earliest Haudenosaunee groups to settle in what is present-day Pennsylvania. This group lived along the shores of Lake Erie. Little is known about them, except that they fought wars with other Haudenosaunee groups. Because of this, the Erie culture disappeared in the mid-1600s.

About 500 years ago, several Haudenosaunee groups to the north of present-day Pennsylvania joined together. They often battled other American Indian groups in the area. These conflicts caused several groups to migrate to what is present-day Pennsylvania in the 1600s. One of these groups was the Susquehannock (sus kwuh HAH nuk).

The Susquehannock grew corn, squash, and beans. They also hunted and fished. The Susquehannock settled in one place for several years and moved when the soil no longer produced good crops.

They made clothing from deerskin and the fur of beavers, foxes, wolves, and bears. The Susquehannock peoples used shells, feathers, and fringe to decorate their clothes. Like the Erie, the Susquehannock culture disappeared because of conflict with other groups.

Trade

American Indian groups in the 1500s and 1600s sometimes traded with one another. Through trade, they could gain items that they could not make or gather themselves. The Lenni Lenape made bags and baskets of woven grass that they exchanged for food or other goods.

Many groups, including the Susquehannock, traded using wampum. **Wampum** is an Algonquian word that describes pieces of carefully shaped and cut seashell. Wampum could be strung like beads and used as money.

REVIEW What is wampum?

Lesson Summary

Algonquian	Haudenosaunee
Wigwams, grew crops, hunted and fished, festivals celebrated the harvest or religion, traded goods	Longhouses, grew crops, hunted and fished, wore clothing made from deerskin or animal fur, traded goods

Why It Matters . . .

Early American Indian culture is still practiced by some groups today.

Wampum Belt This belt was made by the Lenni Lenape in Pennsylvania.

Lesson Review

About 350 years ago **Erie disappeared**   About 325 years ago **Shawnee in Pennsylvania**

500 years ago   400 years ago   300 years ago

1. **VOCABULARY** A _____ is a way of life that a group of people share.

   culture   wigwam   longhouse

2. 📖 **READING SKILL** Write a paragraph in which you **contrast** Algonquian and Haudenosaunee villages.

3. **MAIN IDEA: Culture** In what ways did the Lenni Lenape prepare corn?

4. **MAIN IDEA: History** What caused the disappearance of the Erie culture?

5. **TIMELINE** How many years ago did the Erie disappear?

6. **CRITICAL THINKING: Analyze** In what way did American Indian groups adapt to their life in Pennsylvania?

HANDS ON **ART ACTIVITY** Choose one of the American Indian groups discussed in the lesson. Make a fact file on the life of that group. Illustrate their food, housing, and festivals.

Visual Summary

1 – 4. Write a description of each item named below.

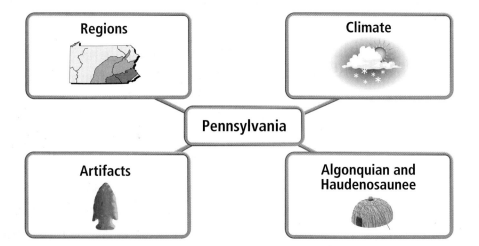

Regions

Climate

Pennsylvania

Artifacts

Algonquian and Haudenosaunee

Facts and Main Ideas

✔ **TEST PREP** Answer each question below.

5. **Geography** Describe the Atlantic Coastal Plain.

6. **History** Who were the first people to live in Pennsylvania?

7. **Geography** In what ways did Pennsylvania's land and people change as the Ice Age ended?

8. **History** Describe the clothing made by the Susquehannock.

Vocabulary

✔ **TEST PREP** Choose the correct word from the list below to complete each sentence.

elevation, p. 4
adapt, p. 11
wampum, p. 17

9. People and animals _____ to a changing environment.

10. American Indians used _____ during trade.

11. Pennsylvania's climate is affected by _____.

CHAPTER SUMMARY TIMELINE

| 12,000 years ago **Paleo-Indians** | 10,000 years ago **Archaic Indians** | | 500 years ago **Eastern Woodland groups** |

| 12,000 years ago | 8,000 years ago | 4,000 years ago | Today |

Apply Skills

✓ **TEST PREP** **Map Skill** Study the map of Pennsylvania below. Then use what you have learned about reading a map to answer each question.

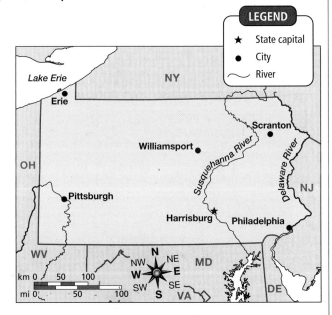

LEGEND
★ State capital
● City
⌒ River

12. In which direction would you travel from Scranton to Pittsburgh?

A. northeast

B. southeast

C. southwest

D. northwest

13. How far would you travel if you drove from Williamsport to Harrisburg?

A. about 10 miles

B. about 25 miles

C. about 70 miles

D. about 150 miles

Critical Thinking

✓ **TEST PREP** Write a short paragraph to answer each question below.

14. Synthesize Describe how landforms affect Pennsylvania's regions.

15. Draw Conclusions Why did conflict cause American Indian groups to settle in Pennsylvania?

Timeline

Use the Chapter Summary Timeline to answer the question.

14. About how long after the Paleo-Indians did the Archaic peoples live?

Activities

HANDS ON **Speaking Activity** Prepare a guided tour of the landforms of Pennsylvania as you might view them from an airplane.

Writing Activity Write a description of a prehistoric artifact that might be found in Pennsylvania. Explain what it was used for and what it tells about prehistoric life.

Technology
Writing Process Tips
Get help with your description at
www.eduplace.com/kids/hmss/

Chapter 2

Colonial Period

Technology

e • **glossary**
e • **word games**
www.eduplace.com/kids/hmss/

Vocabulary Preview

explorer

Henry Hudson was an **explorer** who arrived in what is now Pennsylvania in the early 1600s. Explorers came to find resources in the new land. **page 22**

charter

The king of England signed a **charter** that made Pennsylvania an English colony. This official document gave William Penn control of Pennsylvania. **page 26**

Chapter Timeline

1608	1638	1681
John Smith in Pennsylvania	Swedish settle in Pennsylvania	Penn granted colony

1600   1650   1700

Reading Strategy

Monitor and Clarify As you read, use this strategy to check your understanding.

Quick Tip Ask yourself whether what you are reading makes sense. Reread if you need to.

economy

As more people moved to Pennsylvania, the colony's **economy** grew. Many Pennsylvanians worked in jobs such as shipbuilding and ironworking. **page 34**

rural

Many Pennsylvania colonists lived in **rural** areas. People in these areas farmed the land using plows and other tools. **page 36**

1737
Walking Purchase signed

1755
College of Philadelphia

1750

1800

Explorers and Early Settlers

1600   1650   1700   1750   1800

1609–1681

Build on What You Know When you go to a new place, do you bring something from home to make you feel comfortable? Europeans who came to Pennsylvania brought their culture and customs with them.

VOCABULARY

explorer
settlement
colony

Vocabulary Strategy

explorer

Explore means to travel through unknown lands in search of something. An **explorer** is someone who does this.

READING SKILL

Main Idea and Details
Provide details that support the main idea about European exploration.

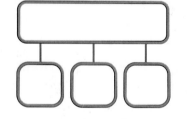

Europeans Reach North America

Main Idea People in Europe began traveling to North America and present-day Pennsylvania about 500 years ago.

European explorers began traveling to North America in the 1400s. An **explorer** is a person who travels in search of something. Some explorers were looking for new routes to travel to other lands. Others were looking for valuable goods such as silk and spices.

Over time, more explorers began to travel to North America to claim land or find wealth. Others came looking for a place where they could practice their religion freely. The first explorers probably set foot in what is now Pennsylvania in the 1600s.

Half Moon This ship is a copy of the one that European explorers sailed to the Delaware Bay.

Explorers in Pennsylvania

In 1608, an Englishman named **John Smith** became one of the first explorers to come to present-day Pennsylvania. Smith had helped set up a community in present-day Virginia in the early 1600s. When the community needed food, Smith left to find it. He sailed on the Chesapeake Bay and up the Susquehanna River. He met the Susquehannock Indians there.

In 1609, the Dutch hired English explorer **Henry Hudson** to find a direct water route to Asia across the Atlantic Ocean. Although Hudson did not find such a route, he did explore the Delaware Bay. His voyage made way for later Dutch explorers in this region, such as **Cornelius Hendrickson.** By 1623, the Dutch had set up a trading post in the Schuylkill River area.

REVIEW Why did early European explorers travel to North America?

Exploring North America Both the English and the Dutch traveled waterways that led to present-day Pennsylvania.

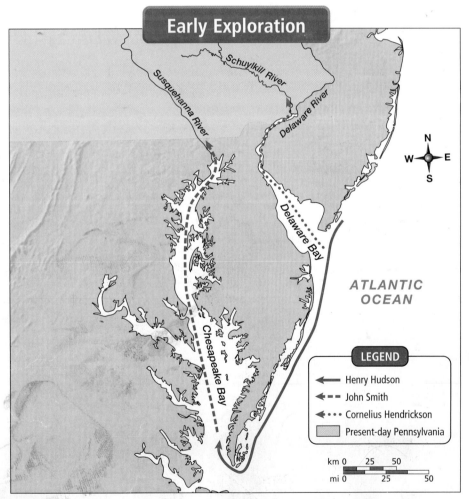

Early Exploration

Schuylkill River

Susquehanna River

Delaware River

Delaware Bay

Chesapeake Bay

ATLANTIC OCEAN

N W E S

LEGEND
- ← Henry Hudson
- ◄ - - - John Smith
- ◄ ···· Cornelius Hendrickson
- Present-day Pennsylvania

km 0   25   50
mi 0   25   50

First Settlement

Main Idea New Sweden was the first community in what is present-day Pennsylvania.

In 1638, people from Sweden became the first Europeans to make a permanent settlement around the Delaware River. A **settlement** is a community of people living in a new place. The colony of New Sweden included what is present-day Pennsylvania, New Jersey, and Delaware. A **colony** is a settlement ruled by a distant country.

People who came to New Sweden hunted the wildlife in the area, particularly beaver. Beaver skins were used to make hats that were very popular in Europe.

A Swedish military leader named **Johan Printz** (YO hahn PRIHNZ) became governor of New Sweden. Printz worked to set up boundaries for the colony. He also set up the capital of New Sweden at Tinicum (TIH nih kuhm) Island. Tinicum Island is now part of present-day Pennsylvania. Printz's daughter, **Armegott** (AHR meh gaht) **Printz,** helped her father buy the island from the Dutch.

Swedish settlers in the new land brought with them the culture and customs of their homeland. For example, many settlers built traditional Swedish log cabins. These buildings had sloped roofs, small windows, and walls made of logs stacked on top of one another. Several early Swedish log cabins remain in Pennsylvania today.

Log Cabin This Pennsylvania cabin was built in 1640 by Swedish colonists near present-day Clifton Heights.

Fur Trade People in New Sweden sold beaver skins for high prices. Europeans used the skins to make top hats.

Struggles for the Colony

The Swedish and the Dutch began to struggle for control of the land in the northeastern part of the Americas. Dutch leader **Peter Stuyvesant** (STY vih suhnt) encouraged settlers in New Netherland to take over Swedish land. New Netherland was a Dutch colony in present-day New York. In 1655, New Sweden became part of New Netherland.

Peter Stuyvesant
This Dutch leader came to the Americas in 1647.

Stuyvesant allowed Swedish colonists to continue making their own laws, even though their land was part of New Netherland. They continued to do so until 1681, when Pennsylvania became a separate colony.

REVIEW What was the first permanent settlement in present-day Pennsylvania?

Lesson Summary

Early European explorers came to North America looking for trade routes, riches, and land. John Smith was one of the first Europeans to reach present-day Pennsylvania. New Sweden was the first permanent colony in Pennsylvania.

Why It Matters . . .

Exploration brought the first Europeans to present-day Pennsylvania. The area eventually became a colony.

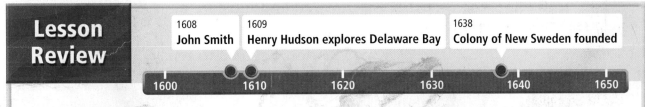

Lesson Review

1608	1609	1638
John Smith	Henry Hudson explores Delaware Bay	Colony of New Sweden founded

1600   1610   1620   1630   1640   1650

① **VOCABULARY** Write two sentences using the vocabulary words **explorer** and **colony.**

② **READING SKILL** Identify one early explorer to the Pennsylvania region.

③ **MAIN IDEA: Geography** Why did John Smith explore parts of present-day Pennsylvania?

④ **MAIN IDEA: Economy** Why were beavers important to settlers from Sweden?

⑤ **TIMELINE SKILL** Who reached the Pennsylvania region first, Henry Hudson or John Smith?

⑥ **CRITICAL THINKING: Infer** In what way would Pennsylvania be different if the Swedish had not settled there?

WRITING ACTIVITY Write a list of questions that you would ask a settler about his or her first days in New Sweden.

25

William Penn's Colony

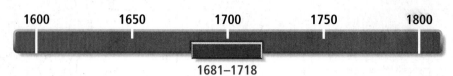

1681–1718

Build on What You Know You know that religion is important to many people. It can affect the choices they make. Religion was very important to many of the first settlers in Pennsylvania.

A New Colony Forms

Main Idea William Penn established the Pennsylvania colony as a place where Quakers could freely practice their religion.

In the late 1600s, **William Penn,** a man from a wealthy English family, asked **King Charles II** to grant him land in North America. The king owed a debt to Penn's father. A **debt** is money that is borrowed and must be paid back.

King Charles II agreed to repay the debt by granting Penn this land. The king signed the Charter of 1681, establishing a new colony. A **charter** is an official document that tells how something should be done. The new colony was called Pennsylvania, which means "Penn's woods."

William Penn Penn's colony was officially established by King Charles II on March 4, 1681.

VOCABULARY

debt
charter
tolerance
assembly
veto

Vocabulary Strategy

tolerance

The suffix **-ance** means "the act of doing something." **Tolerance** is the act of accepting different beliefs.

READING SKILL
Cause and Effect Fill in the organizer below to show why William Penn founded the Pennsylvania colony.

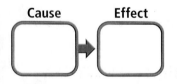

Cause   Effect

Quaker Meeting House In the colony, Quakers held religious services, or meetings, in buildings like this one in Buckingham.

Religious Freedom

As a young man, William Penn had joined a religious group known as the Society of Friends, or Quakers. He hoped to establish a safe home for Quakers in the Pennsylvania colony. Quakers dressed and spoke plainly and believed that all people were equal. In England, Quakers were often not treated fairly because their religion was different from the Church of England.

Penn wanted the Pennsylvania colony to be a place of religious tolerance. **Tolerance** means allowing beliefs that are different from one's own. Pennsylvania colonists believed that people of different religions should live together in peace. They believed in religious tolerance.

REVIEW Why did William Penn want tolerance in colonial Pennsylvania?

Pennsylvania's Government

Main Idea Pennsylvania colonists were given many important rights.

William Penn once wrote, "Governments, like clocks, go from the motion men give them." He meant that he wanted colonists to be a part of their government. Penn set up an assembly of representatives. This type of **assembly** is a group of people who come together to make laws.

Colonists elected people to represent them in the assembly. The representatives could approve or veto suggested laws. **Veto** means to reject, or not to approve.

In 1682, the assembly created a series of laws known as the Great Law. The Great Law outlined the rules Pennsylvanians would be expected to follow. It allowed colonists to choose their own religion and to worship freely.

In 1701, Penn wrote the Charter of Privileges. The Charter of Privileges allowed the assembly to suggest new laws.

Penn also worked to build a new city, which he named Philadelphia. The word *Philadelphia* comes from a Greek word meaning "brotherly love." He organized the city streets as a grid. A grid is a series of straight lines that criss-cross one another and form squares. This plan influenced the design of many cities throughout the colonies.

Treaties with American Indians

Penn wanted to gain more land for his colony. He also wanted to maintain peaceful relations with American Indians in Pennsylvania. Much of the land in Pennsylvania was controlled by the Lenni Lenape.

Between 1682 and 1701, Penn signed a number of treaties with Lenni Lenape groups. He also purchased some land from the Lenni Lenape. The treaties stated which land belonged to the American Indians and the price colonists would pay them to buy land.

Penn's Treaties Treaties with Lenni Lenape groups gave the colonists more land in Pennsylvania.

Hannah Penn

William Penn's second wife, **Hannah Callowhill Penn,** became an important leader of the colony. When Penn became ill in 1712, Hannah Penn took over many of his responsibilities. These included governing the colony. She led the colony for many years after her husband's death in 1718. Hannah Penn is considered to be the first woman leader of Pennsylvania.

REVIEW What rights did Penn's government give to the colonists?

Hannah Penn This Pennsylvania leader lived in Bucks County. People can visit a re-creation of the Penn family home, Pennsbury, today.

Lesson Summary

- Pennsylvania became a colony in 1681.
- William Penn wanted people in the colony to have religious freedom and be a part of their new government.
- Penn made agreements with American Indians that gave the colonists more land.

Why It Matters . . .

Penn's ideas of government influenced the governments of other colonies.

Lesson Review

1681 Charter of 1681		1712 Hannah Penn leads colony	1718 William Penn dies
1680	1690	1700	1710	1720

① **VOCABULARY** Explain how the **debt** owed to William Penn's father was related to the **charter** given to him by King Charles II.

② **READING SKILL** What **caused** William Penn to want to start a colony in North America?

③ **MAIN IDEA: Government** What rights did people have under Penn's government?

④ **MAIN IDEA: History** What was the Great Law?

⑤ **TIMELINE SKILL** In what year did Hannah Penn begin to lead the colony?

⑥ **CRITICAL THINKING: Fact and Opinion** Write one fact about Penn's treaties with American Indians. Then write an opinion about that fact.

WRITING ACTIVITY Write a letter encouraging a friend to settle in Pennsylvania. List reasons that explain why Pennsylvania is a good place to settle.

Skillbuilder

Use Latitude and Longitude

> **VOCABULARY**
> lines of latitude
> lines of
>   longitude

Where in the world is Pennsylvania? One way to answer that question is to use lines of latitude and longitude. These imaginary lines cross one another to form a grid over the Earth's surface. Lines of latitude run east and west. Lines of longitude run north and south.

Learn the Skill

Step 1: Find the labels for the lines of latitude. Lines of latitude, or parallels, measure distance north and south of the equator. The equator is located at 0° latitude. Pennsylvania lies north of the equator, so its lines of latitude are labeled N. They tell how many degrees north of the equator Pennsylvania lies.

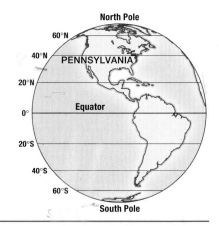

Step 2: Find the labels for the lines of longitude. Lines of longitude, or meridians, measure distance east and west of the prime meridian. Pennsylvania lies west of the prime meridian, so its lines of longitude are labeled W. They tell how many degrees west of the prime meridian Pennsylvania lies.

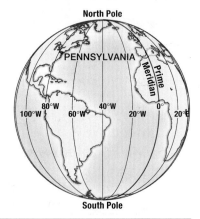

Step 3: Use crossing lines of latitude and longitude to name the location of a place.

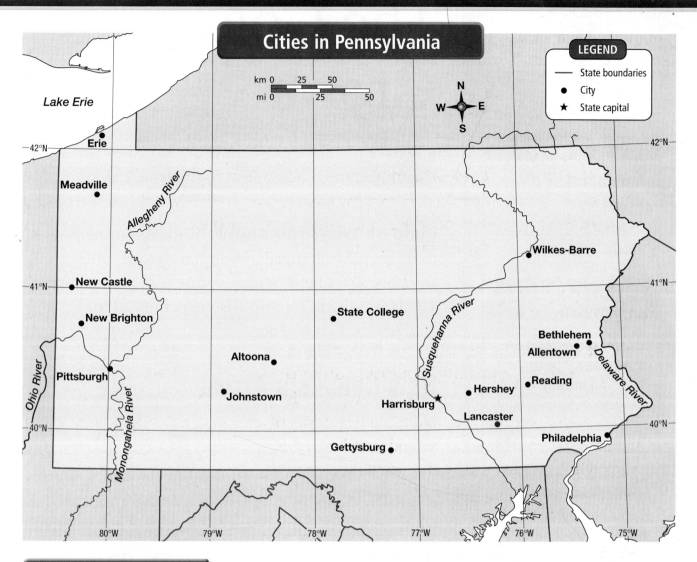

Cities in Pennsylvania

LEGEND
— State boundaries
• City
★ State capital

Lake Erie

42°N — Erie
Meadville
Allegheny River
Wilkes-Barre
41°N — New Castle
New Brighton
State College
Susquehanna River
Bethlehem
Allentown
Altoona
Pittsburgh
Ohio River
Monongahela River
Johnstown
Hershey
Reading
Delaware River
Harrisburg
Lancaster
40°N —
Gettysburg
Philadelphia

80°W   79°W   78°W   77°W   76°W   75°W

Practice the Skill

Use the map of Pennsylvania to answer the following questions.

1 What line of longitude runs through the city of Pittsburgh?

2 Which Pennsylvania city is located near 40°N, 75°W?

3 Which Pennsylvania city is on about the same line of latitude as Philadelphia?

Apply the Skill

Use the grid on this map of Pennsylvania. List three points at which a line of longitude crosses a line of latitude. Next to each point, label the nearest city. For example, the city nearest to 41°N, 78°W is State College.

The Colony Grows

1600   1650   1700   1750   1800

1683–1737

Build on What You Know Think about the ways that you have changed as you have grown older. You have become bigger, stronger, and more independent. The Pennsylvania colony also experienced many changes as it grew older.

New Colonists Arrive

Main Idea Pennsylvania grew quickly as many people came to live in the colony.

After William Penn established the Pennsylvania colony in the early 1700s, many immigrants traveled from Europe to live in North America. An **immigrant** is a person who moves to a new country.

Settling Pennsylvania

Immigrants came to Pennsylvania from many countries, including England, Germany, the Netherlands, Scotland, and Ireland. These people chose to live in Pennsylvania for different reasons. Some of them wanted religious freedom. Others wanted to escape war in their homelands.

Immigrants settled in different parts of Pennsylvania. They often stayed near others who had come from the same country. People from the same country could speak their language and keep their customs if they lived close together.

English settlers stayed mainly in the southeastern part of the colony. Cities such as Philadelphia began to grow there.

Small groups of Irish and Welsh immigrants settled around Philadelphia. It eventually became the largest city in England's North American colonies.

German immigrants settled in the central part of the colony as well as in the southeast. They built communities such as Germantown, north of Philadelphia, and began farming the land.

Many of the people who came to Pennsylvania were Scots-Irish. These immigrants were Scots who came from Ireland. The Scots-Irish traveled farther west than other groups. They settled Pennsylvania's western frontier, which was land that had not yet been explored.

REVIEW From what countries did immigrants come to settle in Pennsylvania?

Philadelphia, 1720 This city, located along the Schuylkill and Delaware rivers, grew quickly in the early 1700s.

The Economy Grows

Main Idea Pennsylvanians farmed and worked in many industries.

Settlers in the Pennsylvania colony did different kinds of work to build a strong economy. **Economy** describes the goods and services that a community uses and produces.

Farming was an important part of Pennsylvania's economy. Farmers grew wheat and corn. They sold these crops to people in Pennsylvania and in other colonies. Farm products provided food for the thousands of colonists living in Philadelphia and other growing cities.

Industries also helped Pennsylvania's economy. An **industry** is a business that makes goods or provides services. Pennsylvania's industries included shipbuilding, iron production, and printing. Colonists also worked in the lumber, fabric, and crafts industries.

Trade was another important part of Pennsylvania's economy. **Trade** means buying or selling goods. Philadelphia became a trading center because its river ports connected to the Atlantic Ocean. Colonists used the river ports to ship goods from Pennsylvania to sell in other colonies and countries.

Shipbuilding Many workers were needed to cut the wood and build the large ships that were made in Pennsylvania along the Delaware River.

Ship

Ramp

Wood

Saw

Trouble for American Indians

As more settlers came to Pennsylvania, colonists needed more land. Sometimes, settlers ignored the treaties that William Penn had made with Pennsylvania Indians and took land from American Indians.

In 1737, some colonial leaders claimed to find an old treaty. The treaty said colonists could purchase "as much land as could be walked in a day and a half." Some Lenni Lenape leaders, including Lenape **Chief Lappawinsoe**, believed the agreements had been made years before. They signed the treaty, known as the Walking Purchase.

The colonists chose three of their fastest runners to measure land. Because of this, colonists took more land than the Lenni Lenape intended to sell.

REVIEW What kinds of crops did farmers grow in the early Pennsylvania colony?

Lesson Summary

> Immigrants came to live in Pennsylvania.

> European immigrants lived in different parts of Pennsylvania.

> As Pennsylvania grew, the economy developed. Colonists took more land from American Indians.

Why It Matters . . .

The culture of European immigrants has influenced the culture of Pennsylvania and the United States.

Lesson Review

	1700s European immigration	**1737** Walking Purchase signed
1600	1700	1800

1 **VOCABULARY** Choose the word that completes this sentence: _____s from Europe came to settle in the Pennsylvania colony.

trade   economy   immigrant

2 ↻ **READING SKILL** Write a sentence **predicting** what might have happened if colonial leaders had honored Penn's treaties with the American Indians.

3 **MAIN IDEA: Geography** In what area of the Pennsylvania colony did Scots-Irish immigrants settle?

4 **MAIN IDEA: Economy** What industries began to develop in colonial Pennsylvania?

5 **TIMELINE SKILL** In what year did the Walking Purchase take place?

6 **CRITICAL THINKING: Generalize** Write a statement that tells why immigrants came to Pennsylvania.

✏ **WRITING ACTIVITY** Write the first paragraph of an early 1700s newspaper article that tells about Pennsylvania's growing economy.

Life in the New Colony

| 1600 | 1650 | 1700 | 1750 | 1800 |

1728–1780

Build on What You Know Think about your community. Do you live in a large city, in a small town, or on a farm? In colonial times, cities were just beginning to grow.

Colonial Life

Main Idea In colonial times, people did many different kinds of work.

Pennsylvania cities grew quickly during colonial times as Europeans continued to immigrate to the American colonies. Most people lived in rural areas rather than in urban areas. A **rural** area is in the country. An **urban** area is in the city.

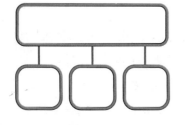
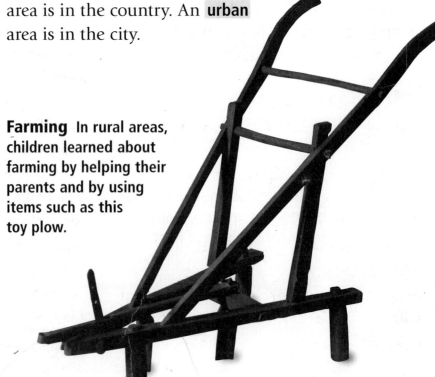

Farming In rural areas, children learned about farming by helping their parents and by using items such as this toy plow.

Cooking

Baking

Smoked Sausages

Colonial women This drawing was created in the early 1800s by Pennsylvanian Lewis Miller to show some of the work done by colonial women.

Work and the Economy

Colonists who lived in rural areas were usually farmers. They grew crops to feed their families and sold what was left to people in cities and other colonies. Men in rural areas usually raised crops. Women did many of the household chores. They also did some farm work, such as milking cows and gathering eggs.

People who lived in urban areas usually practiced a trade or worked in Pennsylvania's growing shipyards. Some worked in industries that produced goods, such as iron or paper.

Wealthy people in the colonies were usually merchants. Merchants owned stores where people could buy and trade goods. Some merchants used ships to buy and sell goods in other colonies.

Some colonists lived as indentured servants. An **indentured servant** was someone who agreed to work for a wealthy colonist for a period of time in order to pay off a debt. This debt was often the cost of traveling to Pennsylvania.

Some enslaved people also lived in the colony. An enslaved person is forced to work for someone else without pay, sometimes for their entire lives. Enslaved persons were bought and sold as property.

Some Pennsylvanians believed slavery was wrong. Still, slavery existed in Pennsylvania. Some wealthy Europeans kept slaves as servants in their homes. By 1730, about 4,000 enslaved persons lived in Pennsylvania.

REVIEW Explain the difference between rural and urban life in Pennsylvania.

New Ideas in the Colonies

Main Idea Pennsylvanians made new discoveries that benefited all colonists.

Some colonists in the 1700s developed new ideas and inventions that benefited many people. One Pennsylvanian, **Benjamin Franklin,** introduced many inventions and ideas that made life easier.

In about 1740, Franklin invented a stove that provided more warmth and less smoke than a fireplace. In 1752, Franklin did an experiment to learn more about lightning. As a result, he invented a lightning rod to protect buildings from lightning strikes. He also invented bifocal glasses. They had two different parts to help people see better both close up and far away.

John Bartram This Pennsylvania scientist, pictured at right with General George Washington, grew more than 200 kinds of plants on his 102-acre farm.

Franklin Stove These stoves were shaped like fireplaces but could be set in the middle of a room to provide more heat.

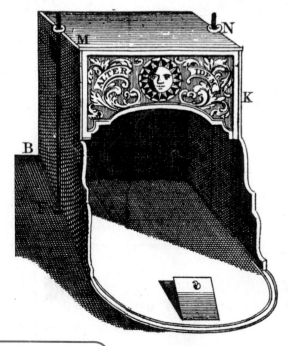

Pennsylvania colonist **John Bartram** was a scientist. He focused on botany, which is the study of plants. Bartram planted a garden along the Schuylkill (SKUL kihl) River. There, he studied the plants that grew in North America. Colonists learned about North American plants through Bartram's work. He is known as the "father of American botany."

Sybilla Masters lived in Philadelphia in the early 1700s. She invented a machine that ground corn into cornmeal. She is remembered as the first known woman inventor in North America.

Learning in the Colony

Most children in Pennsylvania did not attend school. Schools cost money to attend. Many colonists could not send their children to school. In rural areas, children worked on family farms. In urban areas, children may have learned a trade by helping their parents.

Pennsylvania led the colonies in other areas of learning. The first library in the colonies opened in Pennsylvania in 1731. The College of Philadelphia held its first classes in 1740 and became an official college in 1755. It was the first nonreligious college in the colonies.

REVIEW What inventions and ideas did Pennsylvanians introduce to the colonies?

Lesson Summary

Work in the Pennsylvania colony included farming and industry trades. Some people developed new ideas that benefited all colonists.

Why It Matters ...

The inventions and ideas of colonists made way for other inventions in later years.

College of Philadelphia Today, this school is known as the University of Pennsylvania.

Lesson Review

about 1740
Franklin stove invented

1755
College of Philadelphia founded

1725   1750   1775

① **VOCABULARY** Write a sentence that explains why a person would work as an **indentured servant.**

② **READING SKILL** Name one **detail** that supports the idea that the Pennsylvania colony was a leader in new ideas.

③ **MAIN IDEA: Economics** What kind of work did people do in Pennsylvania's rural and urban areas?

④ **MAIN IDEA: Culture** Why did some Pennsylvania leaders believe colonists should not own slaves?

⑤ **TIMELINE SKILL** In what year was the College of Philadelphia founded?

⑥ **CRITICAL THINKING: Draw Conclusions** In what way might colonial children have been affected by not attending school?

WRITING ACTIVITY Write a journal entry about a day in the life of a person in colonial Pennsylvania.

Visual Summary

1 – 3. Write a description of each of the Pennsylvanians pictured below.

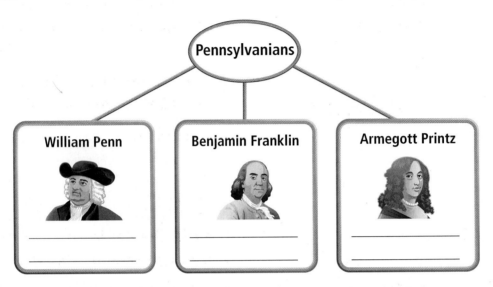

Pennsylvanians

William Penn

Benjamin Franklin

Armegott Printz

Facts and Main Ideas

✔ **TEST PREP** Answer each question below.

4. **History** What European country founded Pennsylvania's first permanent settlement?

5. **History** Why did King Charles give William Penn the land that would be Pennsylvania?

6. **Culture** Explain how tolerance is related to religious freedom.

7. **Economics** What were some of Pennsylvania's early industries?

8. **History** What was the Walking Purchase?

Vocabulary

✔ **TEST PREP** Choose the correct word from the list below to complete each sentence.

explorer, p. 22
economy, p. 34
urban, p. 36

9. The opposite of rural is _____.

10. The work done by immigrants helped strengthen Pennsylvania's _____.

11. John Smith was an early _____ of the Pennsylvania region.

| 1623 Dutch on Schuylkill River | 1681 Penn granted colony | 1701 Charter of Privileges | 1737 Walking Purchase signed |

1600   1700   1800

Apply Skills

 **TEST PREP Review Map
Skills** Study the Pennsylvania map below. Then use your map skills to answer each question.

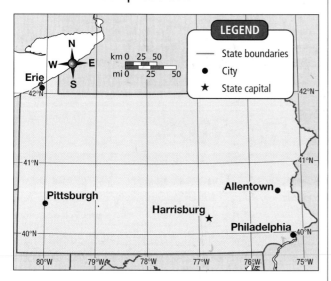

12. What line of latitude forms most of Pennsylvania's northern border?

A. 40°S
B. 75°W
C. 42°N
D. 80°E

13. What line of longitude is nearest to Harrisburg?

A. 77°W
B. 40°N
C. 80°W
D. 41°N

Critical Thinking

 TEST PREP Write a short paragraph to answer each question below.

14. Cause and Effect Why did people immigrate to Pennsylvania?

15. Summarize Describe William Penn's idea of Pennsylvania.

Timeline

Use the Chapter Summary Timeline above to answer the question.

16. When did King Charles II grant William Penn the Pennsylvania colony?

Activities

Research Activity Research one of Benjamin Franklin's inventions. Write a report to share with the class. Illustrate your work with a photograph or drawing.

Writing Activity Write a paragraph describing the Great Law.

 Technology
Writing Process Tips
Get help with your paragraph at www.eduplace.com/kids/hmss/

41

Review and Test Prep

Vocabulary and Main Ideas

✓ **TEST PREP** Write a sentence to answer each item below.

1. How does the **elevation** of different Pennsylvania regions affect their **climate?**

2. Name two **landforms** found in Pennsylvania.

3. What do scientists use **artifacts** for?

4. Describe Pennsylvania's first permanent European **settlement.**

5. What attracted early explorers and settlers to the **colony** of New Sweden?

6. Name two **industries** that supported the **economy** of early Pennsylvania.

Critical Thinking

✓ **TEST PREP** Write a short paragraph to answer each question. Use details to support your answer.

7. **Summarize** Write a summary of how people may have adapted to the warming climate in prehistoric Pennsylvania.

8. **Evaluate** Explain how the Walking Purchase affected American Indians.

Apply Skills

✓ **TEST PREP** Use this map of Pennsylvania and what you have learned about latitude and longitude to answer each question.

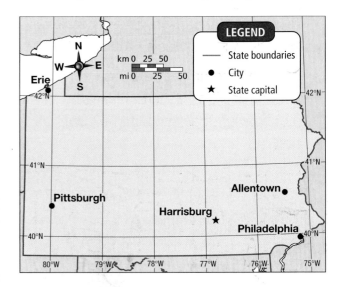

9. Which of the following best describes the location of Harrisburg?

    A. about 40°S, 76°W
    B. about 40°N, 80°E
    C. about 41°N, 76°W
    D. about 40°N, 77°W

10. Which Pennsylvania city is located at about 42°N, 80°W?

    A. Allentown
    B. Philadelphia
    C. Erie
    D. Harrisburg

Unit Activity

Make a Brochure

- William Penn has asked you to design a brochure that will encourage people to come live in Pennsylvania.

- Think about what might attract people to settle in Pennsylvania.

- Create a brochure that illustrates Pennsylvania's attractions. Make sure your brochure contains both text and pictures.

Pennsylvania's fertile farmland makes it a good place to live.

Pennsylvania's beaver pelt hats

At the Library

You may find this book at your school or public library.

Pennsylvania Indians: A Kid's Look at Our State's Chiefs, Tribes, Reservations, Powwows, Lore & More from the Past & the Present by Carol Marsh
Presents facts and history on American Indians in Pennsylvania.

Connect to Today

- Create a display that shows the importance of land, climate, and resources.

- Look for information about a harvest or seasonal festival.

- Write a description that tells what the festival celebrates.

- Find pictures to show why land, climate, or resources are important to the festival.

- Create a display with the information and pictures you find.

Technology

Weekly Reader online offers social studies articles. Go to: **www.eduplace.com/kids/hmss/**

A New Nation and State

The Big Idea

How did the United States become an independent nation?

" *All men are born equally free and independent. . . .* "

The Pennsylvania Constitution
Declaration of Rights, 1776

Elizabeth "Betsy" Ross
1752–1836

How did Pennsylvania women support the American Revolution? Ross owned an upholstery business and made flags for the Pennsylvania navy.
page 56

History Makers

Oliver Hazard Perry
1785–1819

He is remembered as a hero in the War of 1812. Captain Perry defeated the British in a battle on Lake Erie.
page 74

Jane Grey Swisshelm
1815–1884

She was determined to improve the lives of women. She wrote newspaper articles that helped convince the government to give women more rights. **page 84**

Chapter 3

Creating a New Nation

Technology

e • **glossary**
e • **word games**
www.eduplace.com/kids/hmss/

Vocabulary Preview

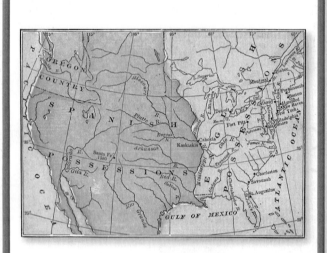

treaty

The **Treaty** of Paris officially ended the French and Indian War. This agreement gave Britain control of nearly all of France's land in North America. **page 50**

tax

Britain made the colonists pay a **tax** on items such as paper and tea. Colonists who did not want to pay this extra money threw tea off of ships **page 52**

Chapter Timeline

1754	1763	1765
French and Indian War begins	French and Indian War ends	Stamp Act passed

1750   1760

Reading Strategy

Summarize Use this strategy to better understand information in the text.

Quick Tip A summary includes only the most important information. Use main ideas to help you.

independence

On August 2, 1776, colonial leaders signed the Declaration of **Independence.** This document stated that the colonies intended to be free from Great Britain. **page 54**

constitution

In 1788, the **Constitution** of the United States was officially accepted. The Constitution was a written plan for how the new country's government would work. **page 61**

1775
American Revolution begins

1776
Declaration of Independence

1770 — 1780

Core Lesson 1

The French and Indian War

VOCABULARY

ally

treaty

proclamation

Vocabulary Strategy

> treaty

When you read the word **treaty,** think about the word **treat.** A treaty is a plan that tells how nations that have been at war will treat each other after the war.

 READING SKILL

Cause and Effect Use this chart to explain what caused Britain and France to go to war.

Build on What You Know It can be hard to share something that someone else also wants. In the same way, France and Britain had difficulty sharing land in North America.

Conflicts Over Territory

Main Idea France and Britain fought for control of North America.

In the early 1700s, settlers from Britain lived mostly along the Atlantic coast. Over time, British settlers began to move west.

The French trapped animals and traded goods on the land west of the Appalachian Mountains. They did not want British settlers to live on land where the French traded. The French built forts in western Pennsylvania to keep British settlers out of the Ohio River valley. One of the most important forts in the area was Fort Duquesne (doo KAYN). It was built near what is now Pittsburgh. Fort Duquesne protected the French as they traveled and traded along the Ohio and Monongahela rivers.

George Washington As a young military leader, Washington led British troops in several early battles with the French.

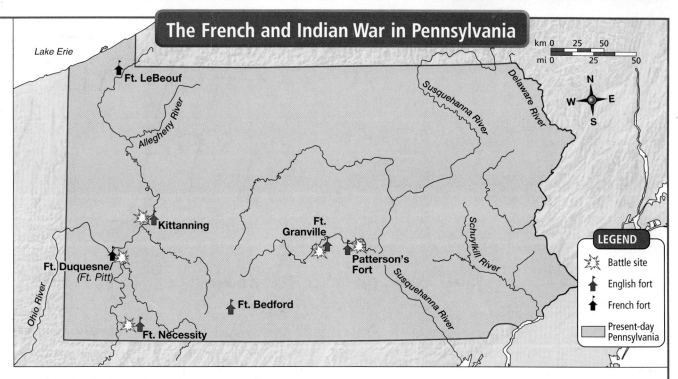

The French and Indian War in Pennsylvania

Battles in Pennsylvania Several forts in Pennsylvania, including Fort Necessity, were important battle sites during the French and Indian War.

SKILL Which Pennsylvania fort was located the farthest north?

War Begins

In 1754, Britain and France began to battle over land in North America. The conflict was called the French and Indian War. The war got its name because American Indian groups were also involved in it.

Many American Indian groups in the East became allies with either the French or the British. An **ally** is a person or group that joins another as a partner in a battle. Some American Indian groups, such as the Algonquian, sided with the French. The two groups already traded with each other.

Other American Indian groups, such as the Iroquois, sided with the British. The Iroquois, also known as the Haudenosaunee, were unhappy that French explorers traded on Iroquois land.

The French and their American Indian allies won many battles against the British early in the war. In July 1754, **George Washington** led British troops in a battle against the French at Fort Necessity in southwest Pennsylvania. Washington's troops lost the battle.

In 1755, the French defended Fort Duquesne in Pennsylvania from a British attack. In time, the British began to capture French forts, including Fort Duquesne in Pennsylvania. The British renamed it Fort Pitt. The British also captured several other French forts in 1758.

REVIEW Why did the French want to keep the British out of the lands west of the Appalachians?

Victory for the British This drawing shows George Washington, on the white horse, looking on as British soldiers raise their flag at Fort Duquesne after defeating the French.

The War Ends

Main Idea The British won the French and Indian War and gained land in North America.

The British continued to win battles during the war. The French lost more forts and realized they could not win. The war ended in 1763 with the Treaty of Paris. A **treaty** is an agreement between countries or rulers. France lost nearly all of its North American land in this treaty.

Even after the war ended, conflicts over land continued between the American Indians and the British. The American Indians did not want the British to settle on their lands.

An American Indian leader named **Pontiac** led members of several American Indian groups in attacks against settlements like Fort Pitt. Their attacks were known as Pontiac's Rebellion. They captured eight colonial forts, but the British continued to fight back. After months of fighting, many American Indians had lost their lives. Many of those who remained no longer wished to fight. In 1766, Pontiac agreed to sign a treaty that ended the rebellion.

Pontiac A city in Michigan and Lake Pontiac are named after this leader.

The Proclamation of 1763

Britain wrote the Proclamation of 1763 to prevent further conflicts between the colonists and American Indians. A **proclamation** is an official announcement.

In the Proclamation of 1763, the British agreed that American Indians would still control all land west of the Appalachians. The proclamation ordered settlers in this area to return to the eastern part of the colonies.

Colonists were angry about the proclamation. Some had supported the French and Indian War because they thought that it would allow them to move west. Many settlers continued to battle American Indians over land.

REVIEW Why did some American Indians fight the British during Pontiac's Rebellion?

Lesson Summary

> The French, British, and some American Indian groups fought the French and Indian War.

> The British won the conflict and gained control of much of North America.

> Britain wrote the Proclamation of 1763 after Pontiac's Rebellion.

Why It Matters . . .

The land the British gained in North America would eventually become part of a new, independent nation.

Proclamation of 1763 This document said settlers would not live on American Indian land west of the Appalachians.

By the KING.
A PROCLAMATION.
GEORGE R.

Lesson Review

1750   1760   1770

1754 **French and Indian War begins**

1763 **French and Indian War ends**

1. **VOCABULARY** What **conflict** led to the signing of the **Treaty** of Paris in 1763?

2. **READING SKILL** What **caused** the French and the British to go to war?

3. **MAIN IDEA: History** Why was Fort Duquesne important to the French?

4. **MAIN IDEA: Economics** What effect did the end of the French and Indian War have on France?

5. **TIMELINE SKILL** How long did the French and Indian War last?

6. **CRITICAL THINKING: Analyze** What was the purpose of the Proclamation of 1763?

HANDS ON

RESEARCH ACTIVITY Use library media to learn more about the goods settlers and American Indians traded in Pennsylvania. Make an illustrated chart to show your findings.

Declaring Independence

| 1750 | 1760 | 1770 | 1780 | 1790 | 1800 |

1765–1776

Build on What You Know Think about a time when you wanted to help make an important decision that affected you. Colonists also wanted a say in the decisions Britain made that affected the colonies.

Problems After the War

Main Idea The British government and the colonists disagreed about taxes after the French and Indian War.

Britain spent a large amount of money fighting the French and Indian War. The government needed more money. British leaders ordered colonists to pay new taxes. A **tax** is money that people or businesses pay to support the government. In 1765, a law called the Stamp Act required colonists to pay a tax on almost all printed paper, such as newspapers and playing cards. Britain also passed taxes on everyday items such as cloth, glass, and tea.

New Taxes Colonists used items, such as this teapot, to show their unhappiness with Britain's taxes.

Boston Tea Party During this protest, some colonists disguised themselves as American Indians while they dumped tea from British ships into the Boston Harbor.

The Colonists React

Colonists did not like the new taxes. They were unhappy because they could not take part in making the tax laws. They wanted their local leaders to represent them in Britain's government. The government of Britain did not allow the colonists to have any say in their taxes.

In 1767 and 1768, Philadelphia lawyer **John Dickinson** published several essays called *Letters from a Farmer in Pennsylvania*. Newspapers published these essays, which criticized new British laws and taxes.

Many colonists signed petitions protesting the taxes. A **petition** is a written request for action, signed by many people. Colonists also agreed to boycott goods produced in Britain. During a **boycott,** people refuse to use or buy certain goods or services.

In Boston, Massachusetts, people protested the tea tax by dumping tea in the harbor. This event became known as the Boston Tea Party. In Philadelphia, colonists warned British ship captains not to unload their goods because people would not buy them. The ships had to take their goods back to Britain.

REVIEW Why did colonists sign petitions?

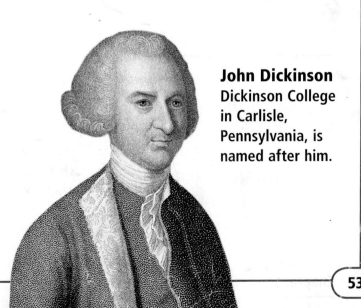

John Dickinson Dickinson College in Carlisle, Pennsylvania, is named after him.

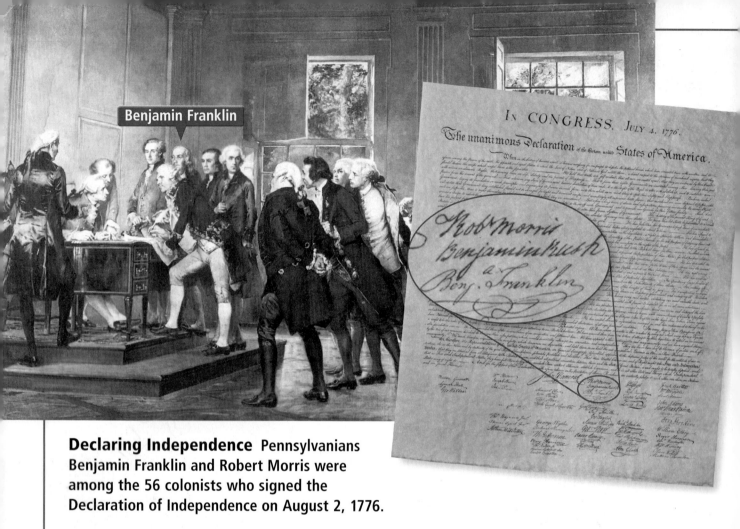

Benjamin Franklin

Declaring Independence Pennsylvanians Benjamin Franklin and Robert Morris were among the 56 colonists who signed the Declaration of Independence on August 2, 1776.

Meetings in Philadelphia

Main Idea Colonists wanted to become a separate nation from Britain.

Britain passed laws to punish the Massachusetts colony. In 1774, leaders from every colony met in Philadelphia to decide how to respond to these laws. The meeting became known as the First Continental Congress. Leaders at this meeting wrote a letter to the British government and the colonists. The letter said that colonists should have the same rights as people in Britain. More colonists began to support the idea of independence from Britain. **Independence** is freedom from the control of another person or government.

Moving Toward Independence

In April 1775, fighting broke out in Massachusetts between colonists and British soldiers. This early battle was the beginning of the war for independence.

In May 1775, leaders from the 13 colonies came together again at the Second Continental Congress in Philadelphia. There, colonial leaders organized the Continental Army. They chose George Washington to lead the colonial army.

At first, many colonists still hoped they could settle their problems without more fighting. But as battles continued in the Northeast, more colonists began to favor independence.

In January 1776, **Thomas Paine** published a booklet called *Common Sense* while he was living in Philadelphia. In the booklet, Paine encouraged colonists to declare independence from Britain.

In the summer of 1776, the Congress wrote a document declaring the colonies were a separate country from Britain. The document is called the Declaration of Independence.

REVIEW In what way was the Declaration of Independence a sign of a change?

Lesson Summary

The British tried to force the colonies to pay more taxes. The colonists protested the taxes. In 1776, the colonies decided to become independent of Britain.

Why It Matters . . .

The colonists wanted to make their own laws and have a role in their own government. The Declaration of Independence contains ideas about our country's values, such as freedom and equality.

First Battle This painting shows the first battle between the colonists and the British, which led to war.

Lesson Review

1770 — 1775 — 1780

1774
First Continental Congress meets

1776
Declaration of Independence written

❶ **VOCABULARY** Explain how a tax by the British made American colonists want independence.

❷ **READING SKILL** What was John Dickinson's reaction to British taxes?

❸ **MAIN IDEA: Economics** What was the Stamp Act?

❹ **MAIN IDEA: History** What was the purpose of Thomas Paine's booklet, *Common Sense?*

❺ **TIMELINE SKILL** Did the First Continental Congress meet before or after the Declaration of Independence was written?

❻ **CRITICAL THINKING: Analyze** What might have happened if the colonies had been allowed to elect representatives to the British government?

WRITING ACTIVITY Write a newspaper article describing important events of the Second Continental Congress.

The Revolution

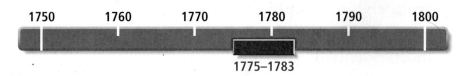

1750   1760   1770   1780   1790   1800

1775–1783

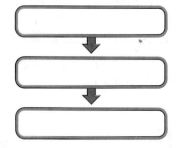

Build on What You Know Have you had to make a
difficult decision? During the American Revolution,
people had to make the hard decision whether to
fight against Britain.

Pennsylvania and the Revolution

Main Idea Pennsylvania played an important part in the
American Revolution.

At first, Pennsylvanians were divided about joining
the American Revolution. A **revolution** is a change in
government by force. Some people in Pennsylvania
were Loyalists. A **Loyalist** was a person who wanted
the colonies to remain loyal to Britain. Some people
were Patriots. A **Patriot** was a person who supported
the Revolution. The number of Patriots grew, and
Pennsylvania decided to join the fight for independence.

Pennsylvanians helped the Revolution in many
ways. The colony made weapons for soldiers. Some
people gave money to the Continental Army. One of
them was **Robert Morris**, a Philadelphia banker.
Elizabeth "Betsy" Ross used her Philadelphia business
to make flags for the Pennsylvania navy.

Crossing the Delaware
George Washington
and his army crossed from
Pennsylvania to New Jersey
to fight the British.

Washington's Army in Pennsylvania

At the start of the war, many battles took place near the Atlantic coast. But in 1776 and 1777, British troops began moving into Pennsylvania. In late 1776, George Washington and the Continental Army set up camp along the Delaware River in eastern Pennsylvania. On December 25, they crossed the river and surprised the British in Trenton, New Jersey. Patriots were overjoyed at the victory.

British soldiers began to march to Philadelphia, which was the capital of the colonies. Washington and his troops wanted to prevent the British from taking control of Philadelphia. They tried to block the British at the Battle of Brandywine, but were defeated.

The Capture of Philadelphia

People in Philadelphia feared that the British would attack soon. The members of the Continental Congress left the city.

Pennsylvania General **Anthony Wayne** was sent to lead a surprise attack on British troops. Instead, the British surprised Wayne and his soldiers with an ambush, or surprise attack, at Paoli. Many soldiers lost their lives during the ambush. This event came to be known as the Paoli Massacre.

British troops continued their march toward Philadelphia. They captured the city in late September 1777.

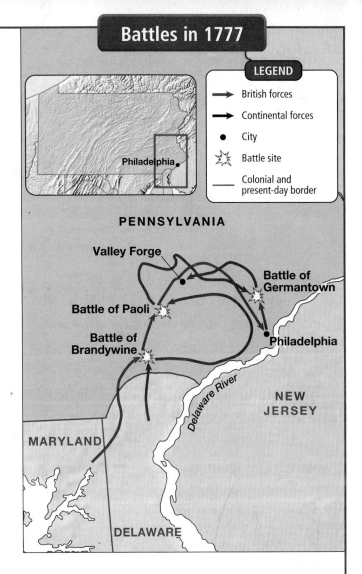

Battles in 1777

LEGEND
→ British forces
→ Continental forces
● City
✵ Battle site
— Colonial and present-day border

PENNSYLVANIA
Valley Forge
Battle of Germantown
Battle of Paoli
Battle of Brandywine
Philadelphia
Delaware River
NEW JERSEY
MARYLAND
DELAWARE

March Across Pennsylvania British troops traveled through Pennsylvania, winning several battles and capturing Philadelphia.

SKILL **Reading Maps** Which Pennsylvania battle was closest to Philadelphia?

In early October, Washington's soldiers attacked the British camp at Germantown, but they were defeated. The Continental Army had failed to stop the British in Pennsylvania. The American soldiers were tired but did not want to give up.

REVIEW Why did members of the Continental Congress leave Philadelphia?

Valley Forge

Main Idea The training of troops at Valley Forge helped lead the colonies to victory.

Washington's troops spent the winter of 1777–1778 at a camp in Valley Forge, Pennsylvania. The winter was very cold. Most soldiers did not have shoes or warm clothes. They ran out of supplies and had little to eat.

The British had a well-trained, skilled army. Many of Washington's soldiers were farmers. Washington and Benjamin Franklin hired a German military leader, **Frederick von Steuben** (vahn SHTOY buhn), to train the troops at Valley Forge. Von Steuben taught the soldiers skills that helped prepare them for battle.

The Conflict Continues

In the summer of 1778, a group of Loyalists and Iroquois Indians attacked a town in the Wyoming Valley in eastern Pennsylvania. The Iroquois believed the Patriots might try to take their land. Hundreds of colonists lost their lives in what became known as the Wyoming Massacre. This was the last fighting to take place in Pennsylvania during the Revolution.

By this time, most of the fighting had moved to the southern colonies. Benjamin Franklin and other colonial leaders were able to convince France and Spain to join the Patriot cause. The support from these nations helped the colonies win the war.

Valley Forge George Washington (third from left) led around 11,000 soldiers through a long, hard winter at this camp. **SKILL** **Reading Visuals** What might the man on the far right be doing with the bundle of sticks?

Victory for the Colonies

In 1781, General **John Muhlenberg** and General Anthony Wayne of Pennsylvania helped lead the Continental troops in the Battle of Yorktown in Virginia. This was the last major battle of the Revolution.

The British surrendered to the American troops at Yorktown. Two years later, American and British officials signed a peace agreement, or treaty. The treaty recognized the United States of America as an independent nation.

REVIEW Who was Anthony Wayne?

Lesson Summary

- Many Pennsylvanians played a part in the Revolution.
- At Valley Forge, the Continental Army learned skills that helped win the war.
- In 1783, Britain and the colonies signed a treaty that made the United States an independent country.

Why It Matters ...

By winning the Revolution, the colonists gained independence and formed a new country.

John Muhlenberg
This Lutheran minister left his church to serve in the Continental Army.

Lesson Review

1777	1778	1781	1783
Valley Forge	Wyoming Massacre	Battle of Yorktown	Treaty ends war

1775 — 1780 — 1785

1 **VOCABULARY** Write a short paragraph that explains the difference between a **Loyalist** and a **Patriot.**

2 **READING SKILL** Which came first, the Battle of Brandywine or the winter at Valley Forge?

3 **MAIN IDEA: History** Name one Pennsylvanian from this lesson and tell what that person did in support of the Revolution.

4 **MAIN IDEA: Geography** In what way did Pennsylvania's weather affect the soldiers at Valley Forge?

5 **TIMELINE SKILL** Which events took place between 1775 and 1780?

6 **CRITICAL THINKING: Analyze** Which decisions made by Washington show his leadership?

WRITING ACTIVITY Write a letter from Franklin and Washington to von Steuben asking for his help training the soldiers at Valley Forge.

A New Nation

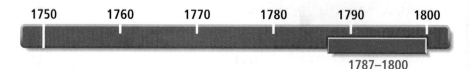

| 1750 | 1760 | 1770 | 1780 | 1790 | 1800 |

1787–1800

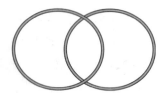

Build on What You Know When you begin a new school year, your teacher probably starts by telling you the rules of the classroom. One of the first things the new United States did was make rules about how the country should be run.

A National Government

Main Idea After winning the American Revolution, the people of the United States created a government for their new nation.

The people of the new United States needed to figure out how the country's government was going to work. The Continental Congress created a plan for the United States government called the Articles of Confederation. A **confederation** is a group of states that together form one country. The Articles of Confederation defined the different responsibilities that would be held by state governments and the national government. The national government could make decisions but its power under the Articles of Confederation was weak.

Independence Hall
Representatives signed the United States Constitution in this Philadelphia building.

The United States Constitution

Some people thought that the Articles of Confederation were too weak. The national government did not have the power to tax the states or make them work together.

In 1787, a group of delegates, or representatives, met in Philadelphia to write a new plan of government, called a constitution. A **constitution** is a document that outlines the laws of a government. Eight delegates from Pennsylvania, including Benjamin Franklin, attended this meeting.

The delegates worked for several months to create this document. They did not always agree on what it should say, and worked hard to reach an agreement. In September, the Constitution of the United States was finally written. It made the national government stronger. The document also explained the limits of the national government's powers.

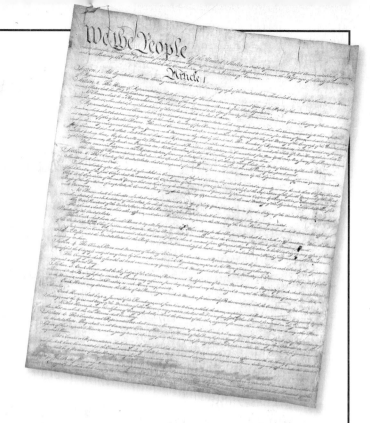

The Constitution The first four pages of this document are displayed at the National Archives Building in Washington, D.C.

Representatives in each state were asked to ratify the Constitution. **Ratify** means to approve something officially.

Some of the representatives wanted to make amendments to the Constitution before they would agree to ratify it. An **amendment** is a change or correction to improve something. These first amendments were called the Bill of Rights. They described certain rights that every person would have under the new system of government. These rights included freedom of speech and freedom of religion.

Pennsylvania became the second state to ratify the Constitution on December 12, 1787. Delaware had signed first, just a few days earlier.

REVIEW What is the Bill of Rights?

Independence Hall Today Delegates met in this room to write the Constitution. Today, many tourists visit Independence Hall.

A New State

Main Idea Pennsylvania developed a constitution, and the new state continued to grow.

In addition to the United States Constitution, each state also had its own constitution. Pennsylvania's first constitution was ratified in 1776.

Pennsylvania's constitution gave voting rights to men over 21 years of age who paid taxes, except enslaved men. It also set limits on the length of time representatives could serve in government. This rule was created to keep any one Pennsylvanian from becoming too powerful.

Pennsylvania's constitution gave certain rights to all Pennsylvanians. This section was called the Declaration of Rights. It gave Pennsylvanians the right to free speech and the right to practice their own religion.

In 1790, leaders in the state wrote a new constitution. This constitution made Pennsylvania's government more like that of the United States. Over the years, Pennsylvania has ratified a total of four different constitutions. The Declaration of Rights has remained part of each of these documents.

Pennsylvania Grows

After the American Revolution, more people moved to Pennsylvania. Between 1790 and 1800, the number of people in the state increased by almost one-third. This pattern continued for the next 60 years.

New developments, such as the Conestoga wagon, helped the state grow. The earliest Conestoga wagons were used in Lancaster County, Pennsylvania. Horses pulled these wagons, so people could travel longer distances in shorter periods of time. They also used wagons to haul heavy loads.

Conestoga Wagon This wagon was named for the Conestoga Creek region in Lancaster County, where it was developed by German settlers.

Bow

State leaders also helped Pennsylvania grow by giving away land in areas of the state where few people lived. In 1783, they gave land in the areas north and west of the Allegheny and Ohio rivers to soldiers who served in the Revolutionary War.

New towns began to appear across central and western Pennsylvania as more people moved there. These towns included Erie, Greensburg, Lock Haven, and Williamsport. Many Pennsylvanians still lived in the state's rural regions.

REVIEW In what way did Pennsylvania's constitution change in 1790?

Growth in the State

Number of People in Pennsylvania

1,600,000
1,400,000
1,200,000
1,000,000
800,000
600,000
400,000

1790 1800 1810 1820

Year

The State Grows Between 1790 and 1820, Pennsylvania's population grew more than three times larger.

SKILL About what year did the number of people in Pennsylvania grow to more than one million?

Bonnet

Sideboard

Curved floor to keep contents inside

Jockey Box to hold tools

Ending Slavery

In the late 1700s, Pennsylvanians were working to end slavery in the state. Before the Revolution, many of the African Americans living in Pennsylvania were slaves. In 1780, Pennsylvania passed a law called the Gradual Abolition of Slavery Act. It said that slaves must be freed when they reached the age of 28. The law began to end slavery in the state. By the beginning of the 1800s, most slaves in Pennsylvania had been freed.

Leaders such as **Absalom Jones** and **Richard Allen** helped free African Americans in Pennsylvania create their own churches and communities. In 1794, Richard Allen founded the Bethel African Methodist Episcopal Church in Philadelphia. It was the first independent African American church in the nation.

Bethel Church Absalom Jones (left) helped Richard Allen to set up the Bethel African American Methodist Episcopal Church. The first services were held in an old blacksmith's shop. Members built the church building below in 1841.

New Challenges

Some Pennsylvanians were unhappy about the taxes they had to pay to the U.S. government. Farmers in western Pennsylvania were unhappy about a tax on whiskey. They turned their grain into whiskey and sold it. They did not want to pay this tax. In 1794, farmers attacked government workers sent to collect the whiskey tax. This became known as the Whiskey Rebellion. Soldiers stopped the attacks.

The national government also placed a tax on homes and other property. Some Pennsylvanians refused to pay this tax and went to jail. In 1799, a group of people in the state demanded their release. This became known as the Fries Rebellion. Once again, soldiers stopped the rebellion.

In both cases, the national government stopped the rebellions. This showed the states that the national government had the ability to carry out its laws.

REVIEW What was the Whiskey Rebellion?

Lesson Summary

After the Revolution, the United States and Pennsylvania developed their governments. Pennsylvania's population grew. People worked to end slavery in the state.

Why It Matters ...

The United States and Pennsylvania constitutions put into law many of the freedoms enjoyed by Pennsylvanians today.

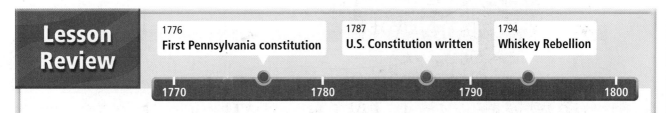

Lesson Review

1776 **First Pennsylvania constitution**

1787 **U.S. Constitution written**

1794 **Whiskey Rebellion**

1770   1780   1790   1800

❶ **VOCABULARY** Explain the way an **amendment** affects the **Constitution.**

❷ **READING SKILL** In what way is Pennsylvania's constitution similar to the U.S. Constitution?

❸ **MAIN IDEA: Government** What did delegates do in 1787 to make the nation's government stronger?

❹ **MAIN IDEA: Government** Identify one law outlined in Pennsylvania's first constitution.

❺ **TIMELINE SKILL** How many years after the U.S. Constitution was written did the Whiskey Rebellion take place?

❻ **CRITICAL THINKING: Fact and Opinion** State a fact and an opinion about Pennsylvania's constitution.

✏ **WRITING ACTIVITY** Write a news bulletin about the rebellions over taxes in Pennsylvania.

Skillbuilder

Make a Timeline

A timeline shows events in the order in which they happened. You can organize and remember information by making a timeline of important events and dates.

Learn the Skill

Step 1: List the important events and their dates. This list shows three events from Lesson 2.

> 1774–The First Continental Congress met in Philadelphia
>
> 1775–The war for independence began with fighting in Massachusetts
>
> 1776–Thomas Paine published Common Sense

Step 2: Decide how many years you will show on the timeline. The listed events cover a time period of two years, from 1774 to 1776. Draw the timeline so that each section stands for the same number of years. In this example, each section stands for one year.

1773	1774	1775	1776	1777

Step 3: Write each event above its listed year. Add a title.

Pennsylvania and the American Revolution

The First Continental Congress met in Philadelphia	The war for independence began with fighting in Massachusetts	Thomas Paine published Common Sense
1773	1774	1775	1776	1777

Practice the Skill

Read the paragraph below. It tells about events after the French and Indian War. Answer the questions. Then make a timeline of the events.

When the French and Indian War ended in 1763, the British wanted American colonists to pay new taxes. The taxes would help pay for the costs of the war. The British passed the Sugar Act of 1764. This law put a tax on molasses. In 1765, the British passed the Stamp Act. This law forced American colonists to pay a tax on most printed paper. The tax made colonists so angry that they organized protests. In 1766, the British government ended the Stamp Act.

1 What events and dates would you show on a timeline?

2 How many years would be covered on the timeline?

Apply the Skill

Reread the paragraph under "Practice the Skill." Make a timeline to show when important events occurred.

Review and Test Prep

Visual Summary

1 – 3. 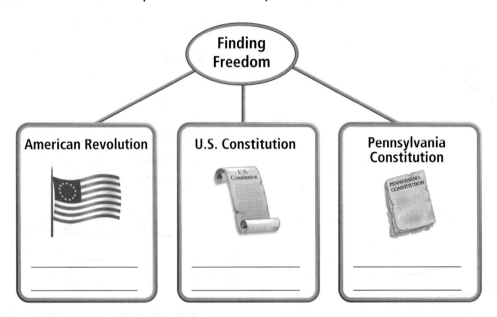 Write a description of each topic listed below.

Finding Freedom

American Revolution

U.S. Constitution

Pennsylvania Constitution

Facts and Main Ideas

✓ **TEST PREP** Answer each question below.

4. **History** What was the cause of the French and Indian War?

5. **History** Describe Pontiac's role in conflicts between American Indians and the British.

6. **Geography** Why did the Proclamation of 1763 anger some colonists?

7. **Government** What is the Bill of Rights?

Vocabulary

✓ **TEST PREP** Choose the correct word from the list below to complete each sentence.

treaty, p. 50
tax, p. 52
independence, p. 54

8. The _____ of Paris officially ended the French and Indian War.

9. The colonists fought the American Revolution to gain _____ from Britain.

10. Colonists objected to the Stamp Act because it put a(n) _____ on most printed paper.

CHAPTER SUMMARY TIMELINE

1754	1765	1776	1787
French and Indian War begins	Britain passes Stamp Act	Declaration of Independence	U.S. Constitution written

1750 — 1760 — 1770 — 1780 — 1790

Apply Skills

✔ **TEST PREP** **Timeline Skill** Apply what you learned about making a timeline. Use this information about Pittsburgh's history to answer each question.

1754: French built Fort Duquesne
1761: British built Fort Pitt
1764: City of Pittsburgh planned around Fort Pitt
1787: University of Pittsburgh created

11. If you marked your timeline in 10-year periods, what period of time would you have to include?

   A. 1750 to 1760
   B. 1750 to 1850
   C. 1750 to 1790
   D. 1750 to 1780

12. Leaders signed the Declaration of Independence in 1776. Where would you place this entry on the timeline?

   A. to the left of 1750
   B. between 1770 and 1780
   C. between 1750 and 1770
   D. to the right of 1788

Critical Thinking

✔ **TEST PREP** Write a short paragraph to answer each question below.

13. **Cause and Effect** Describe what happened when the British tried to tax the colonists.

14. **Summarize** What led to growth in Pennsylvania's cities after the American Revolution?

Timeline

Use the Chapter Summary Timeline above to answer the question.

15. How many years after the Declaration of Independence was the U.S. Constitution written?

Activities

Math Activity Use an almanac or the Internet to find the number of people who lived in Philadelphia and Erie counties in 1800. Discuss possible reasons for the difference.

Writing Activity Write a short story describing how Pennsylvania colonists may have felt when they gained freedom from Britain.

Technology
Writing Process Tips
Get help with your story at
www.eduplace.com/kids/hmss/

Growth and Expansion

Technology

e • **glossary**
e • **word games**
www.eduplace.com/kids/hmss/

Vocabulary Preview

territory

The U.S. government bought the Louisiana **Territory** from France in 1803. This area of land doubled the size of the United States. **page 73**

transportation

Changes in **transportation** affected Pennsylvania. Steamboats and passenger wagons created new ways to carry people and goods. **page 78**

Chapter Timeline

1776	1794	1812
Three counties become Delaware	Lancaster Turnpike built	War of 1812

1775   1800   1825

Reading Strategy

Question As you read the lessons in this chapter, ask yourself questions about important ideas.

Quick Tip Stop and ask yourself questions. Do you need to go back and reread for the answers?

canal

In the early 1800s, workers built waterways such as the Main Line **Canal** to connect Pennsylvania rivers. These waterways helped make travel easier. **page 79**

textile

Textile means cloth or fabric. Pennsylvania's **textile** factories made goods that could be sold in other states and countries. **page 82**

1859
First oil well in Pennsylvania

1850   1875

Keystone State

1750   1800   1850   1900

1773–1834

VOCABULARY

territory
raid
surrender
negotiate

Vocabulary Strategy

surrender

Look at the prefix **sur-** in **surrender.** This means "over" or "up." To surrender means to hand over or give up.

READING SKILL

Cause and Effect As you read, make notes about the causes and effects of political changes in Pennsylvania during the late 1700s and early 1800s.

Cause   Effect

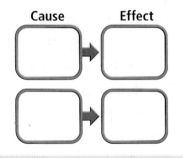

Build on What You Know Has a new family moved into your community? People have different reasons for moving. In the 1800s, jobs brought people to Pennsylvania.

The Second State

Main Idea Pennsylvania's people and politics changed after the Revolutionary War.

In 1704, the people in three counties in southern Pennsylvania decided they wanted their own government. These counties were originally given to William Penn by the King of England in 1682. In 1776, these lower three counties formed Delaware, which became the first state. Pennsylvania became the second state in 1787.

Pennsylvania would later become known as the Keystone State. A keystone is the center stone in an arch. It is the piece that holds the arch together. Pennsylvania was given this nickname because it was located in the center of the 13 original American colonies.

keystone

National Memorial Arch
This arch, located in Valley Forge, was dedicated in 1917 to honor the leaders of the American Revolution.

Schoolhouse Buildings like this one, built in Venango County in 1828, were used as schools for many Pennsylvania children.

Changes in Early Statehood

Pennsylvania experienced many changes after it became a state. One important change was the location of Pennsylvania's state capital.

Philadelphia was the first capital of Pennsylvania. As more people moved west of Philadelphia, however, state leaders thought the capital should also move west. In 1799, Lancaster became the capital city. In 1811, the capital was moved even farther west to Harrisburg. Harrisburg remains the state capital today.

Education in the state also changed. In 1834, state leaders passed the Free School Act. This law created free public schools for all children in the state. It also required Pennsylvania children to go to school. By 1840, about 3,000 elementary schools had opened across the state.

In 1838, state leaders wrote a new constitution. The new constitution gave the state's people more power in their government.

The Nation Grows

The young United States was also changing. In the early 1800s, France controlled a large area of land west of the Mississippi River called the Louisiana Territory. A **territory** is land that belongs to a country but has no representation in that country.

In 1803, President **Thomas Jefferson** bought the territory from France's ruler, **Napoleon Bonaparte.** This became known as the Louisiana Purchase. The region was so large that it doubled the size of the United States.

REVIEW Which three cities have been Pennsylvania's state capital?

The War of 1812

Main Idea The War of 1812 showed that the United States had become a powerful nation.

Although the United States won its independence from Great Britain, the two countries continued to have conflicts. The United States believed Britain was helping American Indian groups that fought settlers. The United States and Britain also both wanted land in Canada.

In the early 1800s, British sailors led raids on U.S. ships at sea. A **raid** is a surprise attack. British sailors captured U.S. sailors in these raids and forced them to work on British ships.

In 1812, the two countries went to war. Most of the fighting took place on the Atlantic Ocean and the Great Lakes.

The Battle on Lake Erie

The United States did not have a large navy before the war. It needed war ships. Pennsylvania's shipbuilders came to the city of Erie because it is located near the Great Lakes. They built a fleet of ships that could be used for battle.

One of these battles occurred on Lake Erie. On September 10, 1813, Captain **Oliver Hazard Perry** led his fleet of nine ships to meet the British fleet of six ships. The British were forced to surrender to the United States. To **surrender** means to give up.

The victory gave the United States confidence. People believed they could win the war. Captain Perry wrote a letter to a U.S. general saying, "We have met the enemy and they are ours." It was his way of saying that the United States had fought Britain and won.

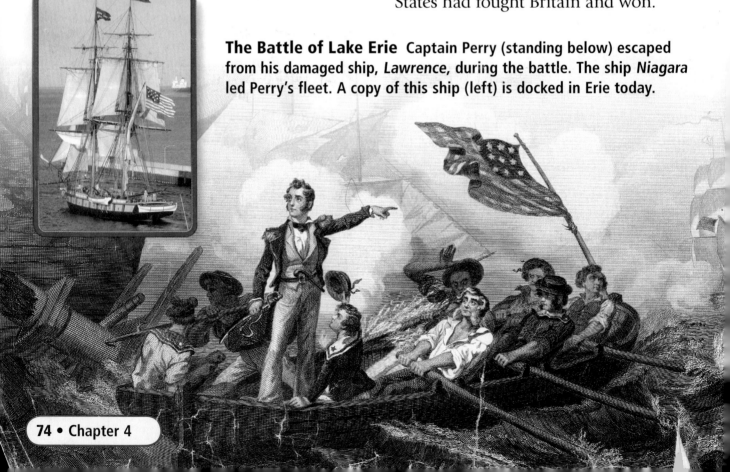

The Battle of Lake Erie Captain Perry (standing below) escaped from his damaged ship, *Lawrence*, during the battle. The ship *Niagara* led Perry's fleet. A copy of this ship (left) is docked in Erie today.

Ending the War

In 1814, Britain and the United States signed the Treaty of Ghent to end the war. Pennsylvanian **Albert Gallatin** helped to negotiate this agreement. To **negotiate** means to work together to come to an agreement.

The war changed people's ideas about the United States. Many were convinced that the country could now stand as an independent nation.

REVIEW What happened at the Battle of Lake Erie?

Lesson Summary

- Pennsylvania became known as the Keystone State.
- Pennsylvania's state capital changed three times. The state created a new constitution.
- The War of 1812 resulted in a victory for the United States.

Why It Matters . . .

The War of 1812 led people in the nation and the rest of the world to believe that the United States could survive as an independent nation.

Albert Gallatin Before negotiating the Treaty of Ghent, he was the Secretary of the Treasury.

Lesson Review

| 1803 | 1814 | 1834 |
| Louisiana Purchase | Treaty of Ghent | Free School Act |

1770   1785   1800   1815   1830   1845

❶ **VOCABULARY** Use the words **surrender** and **negotiate** to explain the end of the War of 1812.

❷ **READING SKILL** What **effect** did the Free School Act of 1834 have on children in Pennsylvania?

❸ **MAIN IDEA: Geography** Explain the changes in the Pennsylvania colony that created Delaware.

❹ **MAIN IDEA: Technology** In what way did Pennsylvanians contribute to the War of 1812?

❺ **TIMELINE SKILL** When was the Treaty of Ghent signed?

❻ **CRITICAL THINKING: Cause and Effect** In what way did buying the Louisiana Territory affect the United States?

HANDS ON **GEOGRAPHY ACTIVITY** Use library media to learn about other battles of the War of 1812. Show both land and sea battles on a world map.

Skillbuilder

Distinguishing Fact from Opinion

A writer may express opinions about a topic. An opinion is a belief or feeling that cannot be proved true or false. A writer tries to support an opinion with facts. A fact is information that can be proven true. It can be helpful to practice this skill when reading a newspaper or listening to a news report. Consider the facts and opinions before making a judgment or forming your own opinion about a topic.

Learn the Skill

Step 1: Read what the writer wrote.

Step 2: Find words that signal an opinion. Examples include *I think, I believe,* and *We should.* Other examples are words that suggest feelings or beliefs, such as *terrible, wonderful, proud, worst,* and *best.*

Step 3: Decide what the writer's opinion about the topic seems to be.

Step 4: Find facts, such as names or dates, that the writer has used. Think about the way you could check each fact.

Dear Commander,

It is my belief that the American navy is ready to battle the British. I think the British have abused their power and we should enter battle to stop them. They have raided our ships, taken our sailors, and prevented us from carrying out our business on the seas. The best plan to defeat the British is to be prepared. I think we should gather a group of shipbuilders near Lake Erie and challenge them to build a modern fleet of ships. Under my leadership, I believe that the United States can defeat the British Navy.

Respectfully yours,

Captain Davis

Practice the Skill

Read the letter on this page. Then answer these questions.

1. Who wrote the letter? When do you think the letter was written?

2. What words does the writer use to tell you an opinion?

3. What does the writer want the commander to agree with?

4. What are two facts that support the writer's opinion? How could you check the facts?

Apply the Skill

Write a statement of opinion about the Battle of Lake Erie or the War of 1812. Use information in Lesson 1 to write facts that support your opinion.

Transportation and Trade

1750   1800   1850   1900

1787–1846

Build on What You Know How long did it take you to get from home to school this morning? Did you ride in a car or bus? In the early 1800s, travel in Pennsylvania was much slower than it is today.

Transportation Improves

Main Idea New inventions and ideas improved transportation in Pennsylvania in the late 1700s.

As Pennsylvania grew, people needed new kinds of transportation. **Transportation** is the way people and goods are moved from one place to another.

In the late 1700s, travel in Pennsylvania was slow. People traveled from place to place on horseback or in older vehicles, like the Conestoga wagon. These vehicles could only carry a few people at a time. Dirt covered streets and rough roads made travel difficult. Pennsylvanians began working to find better kinds of transportation.

VOCABULARY

transportation
canal
toll
commerce

Vocabulary Strategy

canal

Canal comes from a word meaning "passageway." Canals allow boats to pass from one body of water to another.

READING SKILL
Problem and Solution
Chart transportation problems and how Pennsylvanians solved them.

Problem	Solution

Travel The first wagons used to carry passengers were called stage wagons.

The *Clermont* Pennsylvanian Robert Fulton designed the *Clermont*, which was the first steamboat to carry passengers.

Water Travel

Pennsylvania has three main river systems and many smaller waterways. By the late 1700s, several major cities had grown along the rivers.

Some people used boats to travel from city to city on the rivers. They pushed their boats along with oars or poles. This kind of travel was slow. People had to work very hard to keep the boats moving.

In 1787, a Pennsylvanian named **John Fitch** invented a boat that made water travel much easier. It was called a steamboat. Steam from boiling water powered the boat. Another Pennsylvanian named **Robert Fulton** improved the steamboat a few years later.

Water travel still was not easy. Rivers only flowed through certain parts of the state. Pennsylvanians wanted a way to travel by water across the entire state. In the early 1800s, workers began to build canals that connected rivers and waterways across the state. A **canal** is a human-made waterway.

Canals improved transportation but many of the waterways froze during the winter. During those times, the canals could not be used.

Canals were also difficult to build. Land in Pennsylvania was not level, so canal workers had to find a way to link rivers at different elevations. Workers risked their lives as they dug the canals. They could fall and be badly hurt.

REVIEW Why did travel along canals stop during winter months?

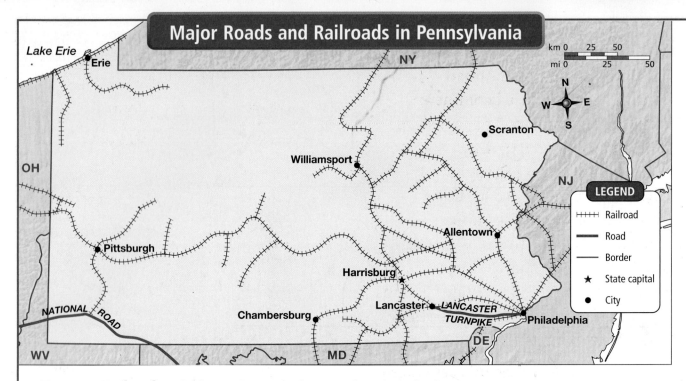

Major Roads and Railroads in Pennsylvania

LEGEND
├┼┼┼┤ Railroad
━━━ Road
─── Border
★ State capital
● City

Transporation in 1860 By the mid-1800s, railroads linked many of Pennsylvania's cities. **SKILL** Could a person travel from Erie to Williamsport by train during this time?

Roads and Railroads

Main Idea The construction of roads and railroads increased trade and economic activity.

In 1794, Pennsylvanians built a new kind of road. The road was lined with crushed stone instead of dirt. This made travel easier. It ran from Philadelphia to Lancaster and was called the Lancaster Turnpike. Travelers had to pay a toll to use the road. A **toll** is money people pay to use something. The toll helped pay the cost of building the road.

Pennsylvanian **Albert Gallatin** was the United States Secretary of Treasury. He encouraged the United States government to help build roads across the entire country.

In 1811, the government began to build the National Road. It was finished by 1818. The National Road ran through several states, including Pennsylvania.

Railroads changed transportation in the state. Railroads connected cities and allowed people to travel and transport goods quickly. Workers began to build the Pennsylvania Railroad in 1846. It linked the cities of Philadelphia and Pittsburgh.

Railroads also changed the state's economy. Many workers found jobs building railroads. Trains were able to transport resources like lumber and coal from Pennsylvania farms, mines, and mills to be sold across the nation. Railroads also brought new people to Pennsylvania cities.

Trade Increases

Canal, road, and railroad construction increased commerce. **Commerce** is the buying and selling of a large amount of goods.

Many goods being sold to other countries were shipped through Philadelphia ports. Steamboats transported goods from Pittsburgh along the Ohio River to the Mississippi River to be sold in other states. Goods also traveled on Pennsylvania's many miles of railroad tracks.

REVIEW In what way did railroads increase Pennsylvania commerce?

Lesson Summary

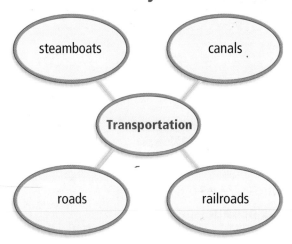

Why It Matters . . .

The improvement of transportation in the state helped Pennsylvania's economy grow.

Lesson Review

1787 **Steamboat invented** | 1794 **Lancaster Turnpike opens** | 1818 **National Road finished** | 1846 **Pennsylvania Railroad**

1775 | 1800 | 1825 | 1850

① **VOCABULARY** Write a sentence that explains how a **toll** is related to **transportation.**

② **READING SKILL** Identify a **solution** to the transportation problems of the late 1700s.

③ **MAIN IDEA: Technology** Describe an idea or invention that improved water travel in Pennsylvania in the 1700s or 1800s.

④ **MAIN IDEA: History** In what way did Pennsylvania's roads change in the late 1700s?

⑤ **TIMELINE SKILL** How many years passed between the invention of the steamboat and the construction of the National Road?

⑥ **CRITICAL THINKING: Draw Conclusions** Why do you think Albert Gallatin supported the idea of building the National Road?

WRITING ACTIVITY Write an announcement for the grand opening of a Pennsylvania canal, turnpike, or railroad. Include the date, time, main event, purpose of the event, and people involved.

Industry Changes

1750	1800	1850	1900

1793–1865

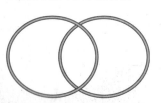
Build on What You Know Do you have a chore at home, such as setting the table? How would your life change if a machine could do the job faster? During the Industrial Revolution, new machines changed the way people worked.

The Industrial Revolution

Main Idea The Industrial Revolution changed the way people lived and worked.

In the 1700s, most Pennsylvanians made cloth, tools, and furniture by hand. In the early 1800s, factories began to make textiles. A **textile** is fabric or cloth. In textile factories, a spinning machine wove materials such as cotton and wool into cloth. The machines worked much faster than people could. Similar changes took place in other industries. New factories began to open in Pennsylvania and across the country. These changes became known as the Industrial Revolution.

Textile Mills By 1800, Philadelphia produced more textiles than any other state.

Pennsylvania Coal and Oil

Pennsylvania had a large supply of coal. People burned coal for fuel during the Industrial Revolution. Pennsylvania's coal powered the engines on trains and steamboats.

Pennsylvanians also used coal to make iron. Iron was a valued good. People used iron to make things such as railroad tracks.

Pennsylvania also had large supplies of oil. In the 1840s, **Samuel Kier,** from Pittsburgh, began to refine oil. To **refine** means to make a better or more pure form of something. Kier made the refined oil into fuel for lamps. The new lamp oil was called kerosene. In 1859, **Edwin Drake** drilled the first oil well in Titusville, Pennsylvania. Soon, oil wells were located throughout western Pennsylvania. Ships and railroad cars transported Pennsylvania's coal, iron, kerosene, and oil to other parts of the state, the country, and the world

Titusville Oil After Edwin Drake (center) drilled this well, other people drilled oil wells in nearby areas of western Pennsylvania. The state produced much of the world's oil during the late 1800s.

Mass Production

By the 1850s, factories in the United States made products using a new system of manufacturing called mass production. In **mass production,** workers use machines to make many goods in a short period of time. Mass production helped factories produce goods much faster than before.

The machines made many copies of the same parts, which were exactly the same in size and shape. Machines helped people put the pieces together to make a finished product.

REVIEW What is mass production?

Working for Change

Main Idea Pennsylvanians began to demand more equal rights.

New factories opened near transportation routes and Pennsylvania's natural resources. These factories needed workers. Some of the workers were people who left their farms to find new jobs. Others were immigrants.

Some of the immigrants who came to Pennsylvania in the 1840s were from Ireland. A disease in Ireland had destroyed the potato crop and left many people without food. Immigrants from Germany also came to Pennsylvania to find work. Immigrants, as well as children, usually worked in factories for low wages.

Workers during this time often worked long hours under difficult conditions, yet anyone who complained could be fired. Workers began to demand better working conditions. During the 1840s, Pittsburgh's cotton mill workers and iron mill workers held strikes. A **strike** happens when workers refuse to work until their demands for better working conditions are met.

The Women's Movement

Laborers were not the only Pennsylvanians who wanted to make their lives better. In the 1800s, many Pennsylvania women also began to demand changes. At the time, most women did not work outside the home. They did not have the right to vote or own property.

In 1848, a Pittsburgh woman named **Jane Grey Swisshelm** started a newspaper. It contained news stories about women's rights. Her news stories helped persuade the state legislature to pass a law in which married women gained the right to own property.

Lucretia Mott, a Philadelphia Quaker, was also a leader in the women's rights movement. She worked with a woman from New York named **Elizabeth Cady Stanton.** Together, they organized a large meeting in 1848 to talk about women's rights. Leaders at the meeting called on women to seek new rights, such as the right to vote.

Leaders of the Women's Rights Movement Stanton (left) and Mott (right) both worked to end slavery. They met at a large anti-slavery meeting in 1840, which gave them the idea to create a meeting for women's rights.

It took many years for women to gain the right to vote. The work that women such as Swisshelm, Mott, and Stanton did helped create a nationwide movement for equality for women.

REVIEW Who was Lucretia Mott?

Lesson Summary

In the 1800s, industries changed. People used machines to make goods more quickly. Workers and women demanded more equality.

Why It Matters . . .

The Industrial Revolution led to changes in Pennsylvania's commerce. At the same time, people in Pennsylvania and the nation worked for more equal rights.

Women's Rights This postage stamp was issued in 1948 to honor Pennsylvanian Lucretia Mott, as well as Carrie Chapman Catt and Elizabeth Stanton. They all worked to gain rights for women in the 1800s.

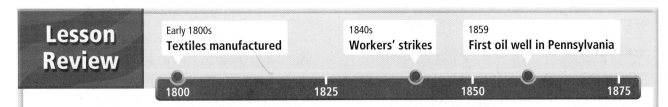

Lesson Review

Early 1800s — Textiles manufactured

1840s — Workers' strikes

1859 — First oil well in Pennsylvania

1800 — 1825 — 1850 — 1875

① **VOCABULARY** Choose the correct word to complete the sentence.

textile strike mass production

During the Industrial Revolution, a spinning machine wove a _____ such as cotton into cloth.

② **READING SKILL Compare and contrast** the work that Pennsylvanians did before and after the Industrial Revolution.

③ **MAIN IDEA: Economics** What kinds of new products did Pennsylvania begin to produce around the time of the Industrial Revolution?

④ **MAIN IDEA: History** What rights did women begin working for in the 1800s?

⑤ **TIMELINE SKILL** About how many years after workers began to hold strikes was the first oil well drilled in Pennsylvania?

⑥ **CRITICAL THINKING: Synthesize** Why did Pennsylvania's cities grow during the Industrial Revolution?

WRITING ACTIVITY Write an article for Jane Grey Swisshelm's newspaper explaining why women should have equal rights.

Chapter 4 — Review and Test Prep

Visual Summary

1 – 3. ✏️ Write a description of each item named below.

Pennsylvania Develops

Canals	
Railroads	
Industrial Revolution	

Facts and Main Ideas

☑ **TEST PREP** Answer each question below.

4. **History** Who was Albert Gallatin?

5. **Economy** Why were canals built in Pennsylvania during the late 1700s and early 1800s?

6. **History** Why is Pennsylvania known as the Keystone State?

7. **Economy** How did mass production change the way things were made?

Vocabulary

☑ **TEST PREP** Choose the correct word from the list below to complete each sentence.

territory, p. 73
transportation, p. 78
strike, p. 84

8. The goal of a _____ is to improve working conditions.

9. The United States bought a _____ from France in 1803.

10. Canals, roads, and railroads improved Pennsylvania's _____.

CHAPTER SUMMARY TIMELINE

1787	1811	1813	1834
Steamboat invented	Harrisburg becomes capital	Battle of Lake Erie	Free School Act

1780   1800   1820   1840

Apply Skills

✔ **TEST PREP** **Fact and Opinion** Read the paragraph below. Use what you have learned about fact and opinion to answer each question.

> Everyone should visit the Railroad Museum of Pennsylvania. It is located in Strasburg, Pennsylvania, in the southeastern part of the state. It is the best museum Pennsylvania has to offer. You can see old photographs of railroads in the state. The best part of the museum is the railroad cars. Some are 150 years old.

11. Which sentence is an opinion?

   A. Everyone should visit the Railroad Museum of Pennsylvania.

   B. It is located in Strasburg, Pennsylvania, in the southeastern part of the state.

   C. You can see old photographs of railroads in the state.

   D. Some are 150 years old.

12. Which sentence is a fact?

   A. It is the best museum Pennsylvania has to offer.

   B. The best part of the museum is the railroad cars.

   C. Some are 150 years old.

   D. Everyone should visit the Railroad Museum of Pennsylvania.

Critical Thinking

✔ **TEST PREP** Write a short paragraph to answer each question below.

13. **Draw Conclusions** Why do you think Pennsylvanians wanted children to go to school?

14. **Evaluate** What did Oliver Hazard Perry mean when he wrote, "We have met the enemy and they are ours"?

Timeline

Use the Chapter Summary Timeline above to answer the question.

15. Did the state capital move to Harrisburg before or after the Free School Act?

Activities

SPEAKING ACTIVITY Do you think *Industrial Revolution* is a good name for changes that happened in the 1800s? Prepare a short speech explaining your answer.

WRITING ACTIVITY Write a scene for a play in which factory workers are discussing changes in the workplace in the mid-1800s.

Technology
Writing Process Tips
Get help with your writing activity at
www.eduplace.com/kids/hmss/

Vocabulary and Main Ideas

✔ **TEST PREP** Write a sentence to answer each item below.

1. Why did the **Proclamation** of 1763 anger many colonists?

2. What did **Thomas Paine** do to support colonial **independence?**

3. Name two Pennsylvanians who were important in the American **Revolution.**

4. Who had to **surrender** at the Battle of Lake Erie?

5. Why did travelers on the Lancaster Turnpike have to pay a **toll?**

6. What led factory workers to go on **strike** in the mid-1800s?

Critical Thinking

✔ **TEST PREP** Write a short paragraph to answer each question. Use details to support your answer.

7. **Write to Explain** Explain in writing why the United States replaced the Articles of Confederation with the Constitution.

8. **Cause and Effect** Explain why many people in Pennsylvania were Patriots during the Revolution.

Apply Skills

✔ **TEST PREP** Use what you have learned about making a timeline to answer each question.

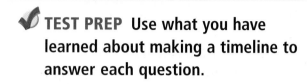

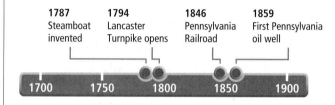

9. In 1818, the National Road opened. Where does this entry belong on the timeline?

   A. Between 1787 and 1794
   B. To the right of 1859
   C. To the left of 1787
   D. Between 1794 and 1846

10. Which of the following events would be placed between 1800 and 1850 on the timeline?

    A. The French and Indian War began in 1754
    B. The Declaration of Independence was signed in 1776
    C. The Free School Act of 1834
    D. Pennsylvania became a state in 1787

Unit Activity

Make a "Before-and-After" Mural

- Think about the way that railroads changed Pennsylvania in the late 1800s, such as increasing commerce.

- Make a sketch that shows Pennsylvania before the railroads were built. Make another sketch to show the late 1800s.

- Plan a mural that will combine your two sketches.

At the Library

You may find these books at your school or public library.

Meet the Webbers of Philadelphia (Early American Family) by John J. Loeper
Follows a free African American family in Pennsylvania through the 1800s and 1900s.

An American Plague: The True and Terrifying Story of the Yellow Fever Epidemic of 1793 (Newbery Honor Book) by Jim Murphy
An epidemic causes crisis in Philadelphia.

CURRENT EVENTS
WEEKLY (WR) READER

Connect to Today

Plan a trip to a place you would like to see.

- Find information about a place you find interesting.

- Locate the place on a map. Think about how to get there. Would you travel by car, train, boat, or plane?

Technology

Weekly Reader online offers social studies articles. Go to: **www.eduplace.com/kids/hmss/**

Growth and Change

The Big Idea

In what ways do people resolve conflict?

In 1865, President Abraham Lincoln said,

66 *With malice toward none, with charity for all . . .* 99

General George McClellan
1826–1885

McClellan became a leader in the Union army during the Civil War. The army grew strong under his command. **page 101**

History Makers

Henry John Heinz
1844–1919

Heinz created a company that sold jarred horseradish. His company eventually became the nation's largest producer of ketchup. **page 116**

Liliane Stevens Howard
1872–1967

Howard was determined to gain equal rights for women. She worked for women's organizations in Philadelphia. **page 126**

The Civil War

Technology

e • **glossary**
e • **word games**
www.eduplace.com/kids/hmss/

Vocabulary Preview

abolitionist

Pennsylvanian Julius LeMoyne became an **abolitionist** during the Civil War. He and other abolitionists helped enslaved people escape the South. **page 94**

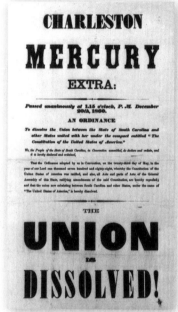

secede

Some southern states chose to **secede** from the United States in the 1860s and form a separate country. Newspapers announced this change. **page 97**

Chapter Timeline

1856
Buchanan elected President

1860
Lincoln elected President

1855

1860

Reading Strategy

Predict and Infer Use this strategy before you read this chapter.

Quick Tip Look at the pictures in a lesson to predict what it will be about. What do you think will happen?

enlist

Many Pennsylvanians decided to **enlist** when the Civil War began. These citizens became members of the army and often took part in battle. **page 101**

emancipate

Abraham Lincoln wanted to **emancipate** people from slavery. He wrote a document freeing all enslaved people in the Confederate states. **page 101**

1861	1863	1865
Civil War begins	Battle of Gettysburg	Civil War ends

1865

Divided States

1750   1800   1850   1900

1775–1861

VOCABULARY

abolitionist
fugitive
compromise
secede

Vocabulary Strategy

secede

The prefix **se-** in **secede** means "apart." To secede means to separate, or go apart from, the rest of a group.

READING SKILL

Main Idea and Details Provide details that support the idea that the United States was divided over the issue of slavery.

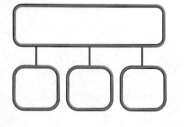

Slavery in Pennsylvania Within 75 years, people in Pennsylvania successfully ended slavery in the state.

Build on What You Know Have you ever disagreed with a friend or a neighbor about something important? The northern and southern states disagreed about slavery.

Pennsylvanians Against Slavery

Main Idea In the early and mid-1800s, the United States was divided over the issue of slavery.

People in the United States had different beliefs about slavery. Farmers in southern states often owned enslaved people, but most people in northern states did not.

Many Pennsylvanians believed slavery was wrong. In 1775, a group of Pennsylvanians met to talk about how to free enslaved persons. This group became the Pennsylvania Abolition Society. An **abolitionist** is someone who works to end slavery. Pennsylvania passed several laws to free enslaved people. One law did not allow ships carrying slaves to land in or set sail from Philadelphia's port. By 1850, there were no enslaved people in Pennsylvania.

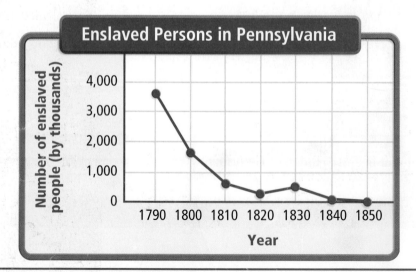

Enslaved Persons in Pennsylvania

Number of enslaved people (by thousands)

4,000
3,000
2,000
1,000
0

1790 1800 1810 1820 1830 1840 1850

Year

Dr. Francis Julius LeMoyne

In 1850, the United States Congress passed the Fugitive Slave Act. A **fugitive** is a person who is running away from something. This law said that people who helped fugitive slaves could be sent to prison. Some Pennsylvanians broke this law and continued to help escaping slaves.

REVIEW Why did Pennsylvania's location make it important to the Underground Railroad?

Safe Places The owner of this Gettysburg home created sliding shelves to hide a crawl space. Fugitive slaves hid here to avoid capture.

The Underground Railroad

Some Pennsylvanians were part of the Underground Railroad. The Underground Railroad was a series of escape routes and hiding places. Abolitionists used the Underground Railroad to bring enslaved people out of the South. Some Pennsylvania abolitionists, such as Washington resident **Dr. Francis Julius LeMoyne,** offered their homes as hiding places. Escaping slaves traveled these routes to avoid capture.

Pennsylvania was a very important part of the Underground Railroad. The state was located along the Mason-Dixon Line. This boundary divided slave states in the South from free states in the North. Enslaved people knew they had reached the North when they made it to the Pennsylvania border.

Buchanan Becomes President

Main Idea Pennsylvanian James Buchanan tried to find a way to unite the states.

Support for abolition grew in the northern states in the 1850s. The southern states continued to support slavery. Many southerners forced enslaved people to work on huge farms where crops such as cotton and tobacco were grown.

In 1856, James Buchanan was elected President of the United States. Although Buchanan was born and educated in Pennsylvania, he was not an abolitionist.

Buchanan thought slavery was morally wrong, but he also believed the Constitution protected people's right to own slaves. He believed that each state should be allowed to decide whether slavery would be legal there.

Buchanan wanted to solve the issue of slavery through a compromise. A **compromise** is a plan on which everyone agrees.

Buchanan worked for a compromise between northern and southern states, but was unable to find one. Northern abolitionists did not want to find a compromise. They believed that Buchanan should be against slavery.

James Buchanan Thousands of people attended the ceremony in Washington, D.C., on March 4, 1857, where Buchanan (right) began his presidency. This was the first photograph of a ceremony at the Capitol, which was still being built.

Southern States Rebel

James Buchanan chose not to run for a second term as President. A man from Illinois named Abraham Lincoln was elected President in 1860. Lincoln promised that new United States territories would be free states like those in the North.

After Lincoln's election, leaders in South Carolina decided to secede from the Union. The Union was a term used to refer to the United States. To **secede** means to separate from a group or an organization. Southern leaders were afraid that Lincoln would not support them if they wanted to continue to enslave people. Other southern states soon followed South Carolina.

REVIEW Why did southern states secede after Abraham Lincoln was elected President?

States Secede
Newspapers announced the split of the Union.

Lesson Summary

- Many Pennsylvanians wanted to end slavery.

- James Buchanan could not find a compromise to unite the country.

- When Abraham Lincoln was elected President, southern states seceded.

Why It Matters . . .

Disagreements over slavery would lead to a war between the states.

Lesson Review

1775 Pennsylvania Abolition Society	1856 Buchanan elected President	1860 Lincoln elected President

1750　　　　　　　1800　　　　　　　1850　　　　　　　1900

1 VOCABULARY Write a sentence about the Underground Railroad using the words **abolitionist** and **fugitive.**

2 READING SKILL Name a **detail** that explains how Pennsylvanians were working against slavery.

3 MAIN IDEA: History Why did fugitive slaves want to reach Pennsylvania?

4 MAIN IDEA: History What were President Buchanan's beliefs about slavery?

5 TIMELINE SKILL Who first served as President of the United States—James Buchanan or Abraham Lincoln?

6 CRITICAL THINKING: Draw Conclusions Why were the North and South unable to find a compromise on the issue of slavery?

WRITING ACTIVITY Write a news story about the southern states seceding from the Union. Be sure to include information about Abraham Lincoln's election.

Skillbuilder

Understand Point of View

VOCABULARY
point of view

People in the United States disagreed about whether to secede from the Union. In order to understand people's ideas, it is important to understand their points of view. A **point of view** is the way a person thinks about an issue, an event, or a person. Understanding a person's point of view can help you understand why people make certain choices or act in certain ways.

Learn the Skill

Step 1: Identify the author's point of view. Look for words such as "I" and "our." These words help show how the author feels about a subject.

Step 2: Think about the person who is writing. What experiences may have influenced the author's point of view?

Step 3: Describe the author's point of view in your own words.

It is our sincere desire to separate from the States of the North in peace, and leave them to develop their own civilization to their own sense of duty and of interest. But if, . . . , they decide otherwise, then be it so.

Governor Francis Wilkinson Pickens
Inaugural Message to the House of Representatives
December 18, 1860
South Carolina

All of you know that I am opposed to secession . . . To secede from the Union and set up another government would cause war. I advise you to remain in the Union. If you go to war with the United States, you will never conquer her, as she has the money and the men.

Sam Houston
State Conference of Secession
January 28, 1861
Texas

Practice the Skill

Read the passages above about seceding from the Union. Then answer the questions that follow.

1 What is Sam Houston's point of view?

2 What words tell you Sam Houston's point of view?

3 What is Governor Pickens' point of view?

Apply the Skill

Read the "Letters to the Editor" section of a daily newspaper. Choose one letter and describe the writer's point of view in a short paragraph.

Civil War

1750   1800   1850   1900

1861–1863

Build on What You Know Think about what it would be like if all of the men in your community left. During the Civil War, many Pennsylvania men had to leave their families to join the army.

The War Begins

Main Idea Eleven southern states seceded from the Union, which led to a war between the states.

After South Carolina seceded from the Union, other southern states followed. People in these states believed they should be allowed to own enslaved persons. They did not want a compromise. By July 1861, 11 states had seceded and formed a confederacy. A **confederacy** is a union of groups or states that join together for a common purpose. Their alliance was called the Confederate States of America.

In 1861, Confederate troops attacked Union soldiers at Fort Sumter in South Carolina. This battle began the Civil War.

VOCABULARY

confederacy
enlist
emancipate

Vocabulary Strategy

emancipate

Emancipate and enslave are antonyms. To emancipate means to free from ownership.

READING SKILL

Compare and Contrast Fill in this diagram by noting the ways in which the North and the South were alike and different.

North   South

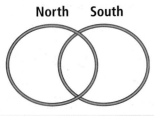

Civil War Uniforms Union and Confederate soldiers wore different uniforms.

Confederate

Union

African American Soldiers These soldiers served with the Union army in 1865.

Pennsylvanians Join the Fight

Pennsylvania entered the Civil War just days after Confederates attacked Fort Sumter. President Lincoln asked for soldiers to protect Washington, D.C. Pennsylvania quickly sent five units of soldiers. Their speedy arrival gave them the nickname "First Defenders."

More than 330,000 Pennsylvanians served in the Union army. Many trained at Harrisburg's Camp Curtin, which became the Union's largest military camp.

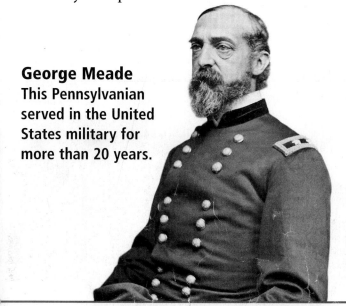

George Meade
This Pennsylvanian served in the United States military for more than 20 years.

Pennsylvania also provided many officers. Generals **George B. McClellan** and **George G. Meade** led Union soldiers in the war.

More than 8,600 free African Americans from Pennsylvania also enlisted. To **enlist** means to sign up to serve in the military. African American soldiers trained at Camp William Penn, north of Philadelphia.

The war first came to Pennsylvania in October 1862. Confederate soldiers attacked Chambersburg, stealing horses and supplies. This city would be attacked again two years later. In 1863, Confederate forces attacked Carlisle.

On January 1, 1863, Abraham Lincoln delivered the Emancipation Proclamation. To **emancipate** means to free someone from slavery. In the proclamation, Lincoln said that all southern slaves were free. The proclamation did not end the Civil War.

REVIEW In what ways did Pennsylvanians support the Union during the Civil War?

The Battle of Gettysburg

Main Idea The Battle of Gettysburg was an important Union victory.

In the summer of 1863, one of the most important battles of the Civil War took place in Gettysburg, Pennsylvania. The Confederate states were determined to defeat Union forces and invade the North. By doing this, the Confederate soldiers hoped they could weaken the Union states and win the war.

Confederate General **Robert E. Lee** ordered about 75,000 Confederate troops north into Pennsylvania. On July 1, Lee met 85,000 Union troops in Gettysburg. The Confederate and Union soldiers fought for three long days.

On July 3, Confederate General **George Pickett** ordered 12,000 troops to attack the Union soldiers. This attack was called Pickett's charge. Confederate soldiers failed, and the battle ended quickly.

About one of every four soldiers who took part in the Battle of Gettysburg lost his life. Still, the battle was an important victory for the North.

Gettysburg This statue (left) is one of hundred of monuments scattered throughout Gettysburg. Some of these memorials honor those who lost their lives in Pickett's charge (below).

The Gettysburg Address

In November 1863, President Lincoln made a speech at Gettysburg. There, he dedicated a national cemetery to the soldiers who lost their lives in the Battle of Gettysburg.

Lincoln's speech was called the Gettysburg Address. He promised that those who died there would not be forgotten. His speech lasted only two minutes. Yet it is remembered as one of the greatest speeches in U.S. history.

REVIEW What did Lincoln promise in the Gettysburg Address?

Lesson Summary

The Confederate army's attack on Fort Sumter marked the start of the Civil War. After this battle, many Pennsylvanians took part in the war effort. One of the most important battles of the war took place in 1863 at Gettysburg, Pennsylvania.

Why It Matters . . .

The Civil War divided the nation. It was the only time in history that people in the United States declared war against one another.

Gettysburg Address
Lincoln's speech said that the United States is "dedicated to the proposition [idea] that all men are created equal."

Four score and seven years ago our fathers brought forth, upon this continent, a new nation, conceived in Liberty, and dedicated to the proposition that all men are c...

Lesson Review

1861	1862	1863
Fort Sumter attacked	Chambersburg attacked	Battle of Gettysburg

1860   1861   1862   1863

① **VOCABULARY** Match each vocabulary word with its meaning.

confederacy   **emancipate**   **enlist**

a. free   b. union of states   c. sign up

② **READING SKILL: Contrast** Write a short paragraph **contrasting** the Union and the Confederacy.

③ **MAIN IDEA: History** Which state was the first to secede from the Union?

④ **MAIN IDEA: History** What did the Confederate states hope to accomplish in the Battle of Gettysburg?

⑤ **TIMELINE SKILL:** How many years passed between the attack on Fort Sumter and the attack on Chambersburg?

⑥ **CRITICAL THINKING: Evaluate** What effect do you think the Gettysburg Address had on the people who gathered at Gettysburg?

WRITING ACTIVITY Use library or Internet resources to learn more about Lincoln's Gettysburg Address. Then, write an introduction for President Lincoln's speech.

Skillbuilder

Identify Primary and Secondary Sources

VOCABULARY
primary source
secondary source

A primary source is a firsthand account of an event. It is written by a person who was there. Diaries, speeches, and letters are primary sources.

A secondary source is written by someone who was not present at an event. History books, encyclopedias, and museum Web sites are secondary sources. They often include information that someone at the scene would not have been able to include. The sources below tell about the Battle of Gettysburg.

One of the two major battles of the American Civil War was fought at the crossroads town of Gettysburg, Pennsylvania, from July 1 to 3, 1863. The defeat of the Southern forces at Gettysburg and their surrender of Vicksburg the next day foreshadowed General Robert E. Lee's eventual surrender at Appomattox Court House.

Lee's Army of Northern Virginia had crossed the Potomac River and marched into Pennsylvania. It threatened Harrisburg, the state capital, as well as Philadelphia and Baltimore, Maryland. Government leaders were even fearful that Washington itself might be taken.

—From *Britannica Student Encyclopedia,* 2005 from Encyclopedia Britannica Online

It is believed that the enemy suffered severely in these operations, but our own loss has not been light. General Barksdale is killed. Generals Garnett and Armistead are missing, and it is feared that the former is killed and the latter wounded and a prisoner. Generals Pender and Trimble are wounded in the leg. General Hood in the arm, and General Heth slightly in the head. General Kemper, it is feared, is mortally wounded. Our losses embrace many other valuable officers and men. General Wade Hampton was severely wounded in a different action in which the cavalry was engaged yesterday.

—*General Lee in a letter to Confederate President Jefferson Davis, July 4, 1863*

Learn the Skill

Step 1: Identify the subject of both sources.

Step 2: Read both passages. Look for clue words such as *I*, *my*, and *me*. These words are often used in primary sources.

Step 3: Identify each passage as a primary or secondary source. To help you figure this out, ask yourself questions such as these: *Who wrote the passage? Was the writer at the event?*

Practice the Skill

Answer these questions about the primary and secondary sources on page 104.

1 Which passage is a primary source?

2 Which passage is a secondary source?

3 What pieces of information are in both sources?

4 What is a difference between the secondary source and the primary source?

Apply the Skill

Using a newspaper, find one example of a primary source and one example of a secondary source. Write a paragraph explaining how the two sources are similar and how they are different.

The War and Pennsylvania

1750   1800   1850   1900

1861–1877

Build on What You Know Have you ever helped someone feel better? During the Civil War, women nurses helped the many wounded soldiers.

Life During the War

Main Idea The Civil War changed life in Pennsylvania as many people worked to support the Union and its soldiers.

Pennsylvanians supported the Union soldiers during the Civil War. The soldiers needed goods and services to help defeat the Confederate army. Pennsylvanians supplied the Union army with food, weapons, uniforms, healthcare, and more.

Pennsylvania Contributes A newspaper in Bucks County printed the advertisement (right) asking people in the state to provide goods, such as the blanket below, for the Union army.

BLANKETS NEEDED
A PATRIOTIC
APPEAL

As it is impossible for the United States to supply Blankets to the RINGGOLD REGIMENT, now going into Camp at Doylestown, an appeal is made to the patriotic citizens of Bucks County

TO FURNISH
BLANKETS.

Each family can at least supply the soldier of the Republic with this necessary article.

IF SENT TO QUARTER MASTER HENDRIE, DOYLESTOWN, they will be properly taken care of. The names of contributors with the number they furnish will be recorded in a book kept for that purpose. As the men will be in Camp

In a Day or Two,
And the weather is cool, it is necessary that the soldiers should have blankets. We hope this appeal will not be overlooked.

W. W. H. DAVIS,
COMMANDING RINGGOLD REGIMENT.
September 12, 1861.

Printed at the "Democrat" Office, Doylestown, Bucks County, Pa.

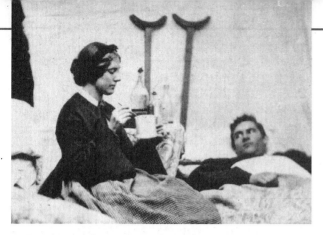

Civil War Nurses In this photo, a Civil War nurse prepares medicine for a wounded soldier.

Women Support the Union

As men left Pennsylvania to serve as Union soldiers, women took over jobs that men had performed. Women worked in factories and for the government. Some worked on family farms. They supplied food to the troops. Women also served as nurses for wounded soldiers.

Women sewed uniforms, gathered shipments of food, and made bandages for the troops. They also joined organizations that helped the military in a variety of ways.

Industries Provide for Troops

Pennsylvania's industries provided many goods to Union soldiers. The state supplied coal, iron, textiles, meat, and flour. Pennsylvania made about 80 percent of the nation's iron during the Civil War.

Pennsylvanians also produced weapons in foundries. A **foundry** is a building or factory where metals are shaped into goods. Foundries in Greencastle, Erie, and other cities made cannons, rifles, and bullets used in weapons. Pennsylvania factories built locomotives for the army. Shipbuilders in the state constructed gunboats for the navy.

The growth of these industries supported the Union army. The industries also created more jobs for Pennsylvanians.

REVIEW How did Pennsylvania's industries support the Union war effort?

Civil War Gunboats The Philadelphia Navy Yard manufactured large iron gunboats like this one.

Lee Surrenders General Lee (center) surrendered at Appomattox Court House in Virginia.

The War Ends

Main Idea When the Civil War ended, people worked to rebuild the country.

After Gettysburg, the Union began to win more battles in the Civil War. The Union had advantages over the Confederate states. It had more people and more industries. Northern states also had better railroads.

Fewer people lived in the South. The South had fewer industries because most southerners worked as farmers. The region's seaports were closed, so southern states could not ship goods to be sold in other places.

General Robert E. Lee, the leader of the Confederate army, surrendered to Union forces on April 9, 1865. The war officially came to an end on June 2, 1865.

After the war, a period called the Reconstruction Era began. Reconstruction was the government's plan to rebuild the South. The government passed several amendments to the U.S. Constitution during this time. One of these, the Thirteenth Amendment, ended slavery.

Chambersburg Pennsylvanians worked to rebuild this city, which was damaged by fires during an 1864 attack.

Pennsylvania After the War

Soldiers returned home after the war to find many new factories and improvements in manufacturing. The work Pennsylvania's industries did during the Civil War made the state's economy strong. It remained strong for many years afterward.

Pennsylvania soldiers who fought in the Civil War formed veterans' organizations. A **veteran** is a person who has served in the military. Veterans' organizations such as the Grand Army of the Republic, which formed in 1866, existed until the 1950s. In addition, Pennsylvania locations such as Gettysburg became historical sites.

REVIEW What kinds of changes did Pennsylvania experience when the Civil War ended?

Lesson Summary

> Pennsylvania's people and industries worked hard to support Union troops.

> After the Union won the Civil War, slavery ended and Reconstruction began.

> Pennsylvania industries remained important after the war.

Why It Matters . . .

President Lincoln's speech at Gettysburg is famous because he said that democracy must always include equality and freedom.

Lesson Review

1861
Civil War begins

1865
Reconstruction begins

1860 — 1865 — 1870

① **VOCABULARY** Write a sentence for the following two vocabulary terms that explains how each is related to the Civil War: **Reconstruction, veteran.**

② **READING SKILL** Name one **outcome** the end of the Civil War had on Pennsylvania.

③ **MAIN IDEA: Citizenship** In what ways did Pennsylvania women contribute to the Civil War?

④ **CRITICAL THINKING: Economics** How did Pennsylvania industries support the Union army?

⑤ **TIMELINE SKILL** How many years after the Civil War began did Reconstruction begin?

⑥ **CRITICAL THINKING: Analyze** What was the importance of the 13th Amendment?

WRITING ACTIVITY Think of a way in which fourth-grade students could have helped the Union soldiers. Then write a speech encouraging fourth graders in the early 1860s to help the Union army.

Review and Test Prep

Visual Summary

1 – 4. Write a description of each item or event shown below.

Southern States Secede	The Civil War	Pennsylvania and the War	Reconstruction

_____	_____	_____	_____
_____	_____	_____	_____
_____	_____	_____	_____
_____	_____	_____	_____

Facts and Main Ideas

TEST PREP Answer each question below.

5. **Culture** What effect did abolitionists have on slavery?

6. **History** What was the purpose of the Underground Railroad?

7. **Citizenship** About how many Pennsylvanians fought for the Union in the Civil War?

8. **Government** In what way did the U.S. Constitution change after the Civil War?

Vocabulary

TEST PREP Choose the correct word from the list below to complete each sentence.

abolitionist, p. 94
enlist, p. 101
Reconstruction, p. 108

9. The government passed the Thirteenth Amendment during the _____ Era.

10. Julius LeMoyne was a Pennsylvania _____ who helped slaves escape the South along the Underground Railroad.

11. During the Civil War, many free African Americans were able to _____ in the Union army.

CHAPTER SUMMARY TIMELINE

1860 Lincoln elected President	1861 Civil War begins	1863 Battle of Gettysburg	1865 Reconstruction begins

| 1860 | 1861 | 1862 | 1863 | 1864 | 1865 |

Apply Skills

☑ **TEST PREP Identify Primary and Secondary Sources** Use the passage below and what you have learned about primary and secondary sources to answer each question.

> One of the two major battles of the American Civil War was fought at the crossroads town of Gettysburg, Pennsylvania, from July 1 to 3, 1863. The defeat of the Southern forces at Gettysburg and their surrender of Vicksburg the next day foreshadowed [suggested] General Robert E. Lee's eventual surrender at Appomattox Court House.

12. What kind of source is this passage?

A. a secondary source

B. a primary source

C. a report

D. a dictionary entry

13. Which of the following is a secondary source?

A. a treaty

B. a letter

C. a museum Web site

D. an original map

Critical Thinking

☑ **TEST PREP** Write a short paragraph to answer each question below.

14. Synthesize Why was the Battle of Gettysburg important?

15. Summarize Why did other southern states join South Carolina in the Confederacy?

Timeline

Use the Chapter Summary Timeline above to answer the question.

16. How many years after Lincoln was elected did Reconstruction begin?

Activities

Research Activity Use library or Internet resources to learn more about the Battle of Gettysburg. Write a report on what you have learned.

Writing Activity Suppose that you were in charge of Reconstruction in the United States after the Civil War. Write a paragraph describing what you would do first.

Technology
Writing Process Tips
Get help with your essay at
www.eduplace.com/kids/hmss/

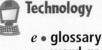

Technology

e • **glossary**
e • **word games**
www.eduplace.com/kids/hmss/

Vocabulary Preview

industry

Railroad construction was one **industry** that grew in Pennsylvania after the Civil War. Employees in this business built trains and railroad tracks. **page 114**

philanthropy

Andrew Carnegie spent much of his fortune on **philanthropy.** He gave money to build libraries and schools, such as Carnegie Mellon University. **page 121**

Chapter Timeline

1875
First Carnegie steel plant opened

1889
Johnstown Flood

1905
Hershey factory built

1850   1875   1900

Reading Strategy

Question To check your understanding of the text, use this strategy as you read.

Quick Tip Ask yourself whether you understand what you have just read. What do you need to know more about?

labor union

A **labor union** works to gain better pay and working conditions for its members. Pennsylvania coal miners joined the United Mine Workers of America. **page 124**

depression

In the 1930s, Pennsylvania entered the Great **Depression.** During this time period, prices fell and many people lost their jobs. **page 130**

1914
World War I begins

1939
World War II begins

1925

1950

Manufacturing and Business

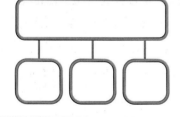

1850   1900   1950   2000

1862–1905

Build on What You Know Have you ever had a new idea that helped make a job easier? In the late 1800s and early 1900s, new ideas in Pennsylvania helped change manufacturing and business in the state.

Manufacturing Growth

Main Idea Pennsylvania's natural resources helped the state become a center of manufacturing after the Civil War.

After the Civil War, new industries began to grow in many parts of the United States. An **industry** is a business that makes a product or offers a service that can be sold to people. Pennsylvania had large amounts of natural resources such as coal, oil, natural gas, and lumber. New industries in the state needed these resources for fuel. Pennsylvania's growing railroad system made transporting goods easy and cheap.

Pennsylvania's Railroads
Trains also delivered coal and other resources from Pennsylvania to industries in other parts of the United States.

Pennsylvania's Natural Resources This photograph shows how a company used the Susquehanna River to transport lumber.

Industry and Natural Resources

Agriculture, the business of farming, was important in Pennsylvania. In the late 1800s and early 1900s, agriculture improved in the state. New farming equipment, such as the mechanical mower and steam tractor, made farm work easier. Farmers also started agricultural groups around this time. These groups shared information about new farming methods and equipment.

In 1862, the Agricultural College of Pennsylvania formed. It worked to improve production on farms. This college later became Pennsylvania State University.

In the late 1800s, large coal deposits were found around the city of Pittsburgh in the western Appalachian Mountains. Coal is a dependable fuel source that burns slowly. People used it to fuel trains.

Pennsylvania's new industries also used wood from the state's forests for fuel. In addition, wood was a valuable building material.

Pennsylvania became a leader in railroad manufacturing during this time. The Pennsylvania Railroad built many railroad engines in Altoona. Philadelphia's Baldwin Locomotive Works became the nation's largest producer of railroad engines.

REVIEW Which natural resources were important to Pennsylvania in the late 1800s and early 1900s?

New Ideas Bring Growth

Main Idea New ideas in Pennsylvania led to the development and growth of new industries.

Innovations helped the state's businesses and industries grow. An **innovation** is a new item, idea, or way of doing things. **George Westinghouse** set up a generator in Pittsburgh to power electric lighting systems. **Elihu Thomson**, from Philadelphia, also developed innovations in electricity.

Two Pennsylvanians created innovations in food processing, a system in which food is preserved for future use. Pittsburgh's **Henry J. Heinz** bottled food. By 1905, his company was the largest producer of pickles and ketchup in the United States. **Milton Hershey,** from Derry Church, created a candy company. Today, it is the largest chocolate manufacturer in the country.

Retail Grows

In the late 1800s, a number of Pennsylvanians became successful in retail. **Retail** is an industry in which goods are sold directly to consumers. Philadelphian **John Wanamaker** established one of the nation's first department stores. Wanamaker's was one large store that sold many different goods in a single location.

In 1879, **F.W. Woolworth** opened a store in Lancaster, Pennsylvania. He discovered that he could make money selling many items at low prices. Most of his items cost only five or ten cents. Eventually, Woolworth opened more than 1,000 five-and-dime stores throughout the country.

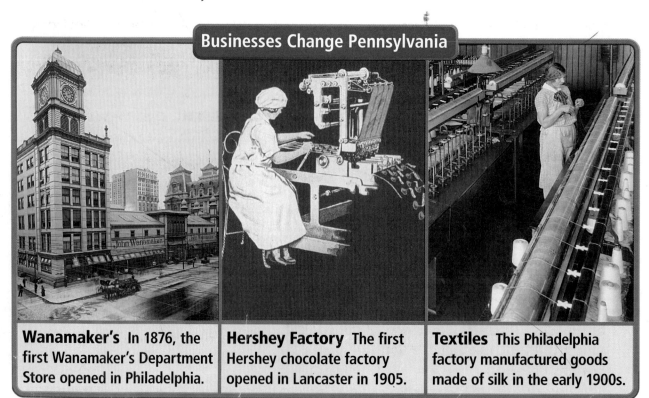

Businesses Change Pennsylvania

Wanamaker's In 1876, the first Wanamaker's Department Store opened in Philadelphia.

Hershey Factory The first Hershey chocolate factory opened in Lancaster in 1905.

Textiles This Philadelphia factory manufactured goods made of silk in the early 1900s.

Other Industries

Pennsylvania's textile industry also grew during the mid- to late 1800s. A textile is cloth or fabric. Cities such as Clifton Heights and Philadelphia manufactured textiles. Pennsylvania produced more cloth than any other state during this time period. The coal industry grew in southwestern Pennsylvania. The iron industry also grew in cities such as Pittsburgh, Homestead, and McKeesport.

Factories in the state manufactured many items, including saws, machines, carpets, and umbrellas. About 25 percent of all Pennsylvanians worked in manufacturing jobs in the late 1800s.

REVIEW What did John Wanamaker and F.W. Woolworth have in common?

Lesson Summary

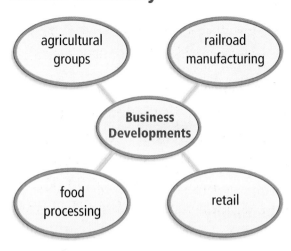

Why It Matters . . .

Innovations and growth in industry made Pennsylvania's economy strong.

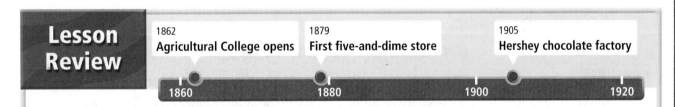

Lesson Review

1862	1879	1905
Agricultural College opens	First five-and-dime store	Hershey chocolate factory

1860   1880   1900   1920

❶ **VOCABULARY** Use each of the following words in a sentence about Pennsylvania: **industry, innovation, retail.**

❷ **READING SKILL** What effect did Pennsylvania's railroad system have on industries?

❸ **MAIN IDEA: Economics** How did Pennsylvania's natural resources encourage industries to come to the state?

❹ **MAIN IDEA: History** What kind of industry did H.J. Heinz and Milton Hershey develop?

❺ **TIMELINE SKILL** Did F.W. Woolworth open his first five-and-dime store before or after the Agricultural College of Pennsylvania opened?

❻ **CRITICAL THINKING: Fact and Opinion** Write one fact about Pennsylvania's industries. Then write an opinion based on that fact.

WRITING ACTIVITY Write a news article announcing the opening of one of the businesses about which you have just read.

Making Steel

1850   1900   1950   2000

1875–1900

Build on What You Know You use products every day that are made of steel. You may have come to school in a car or on a bus made of steel. Pennsylvania began to produce many steel products in the 19th century.

The Steel Industry

Main Idea In the late 1800s, Pennsylvania made much of the nation's steel.

Steel is a material that is much stronger and more flexible than iron. People have been making steel for many years, but for much of history it could only be made in small amounts by skilled workers. Steel was very expensive. Most people could not afford to buy it. In 1855, a British engineer named **Henry Bessemer** developed a way to make steel that was easier and less expensive than early methods. People could afford to make and buy more steel because of this process.

Bessemer converter

Molten iron poured in to make steel

Opening

U.S. Steel and Pennsylvania

Andrew Carnegie played a very important role in the steel industry in Pennsylvania. Carnegie was a Scottish immigrant whose family settled in Pittsburgh. He began working in a factory at the age of 12.

After the Civil War, Carnegie realized that soon the nation would need to replace its wooden bridges with strong, long-lasting iron bridges. He started Keystone Bridge Works. This company built the first iron bridge across the Ohio River.

Carnegie's interest in iron led to an interest in steel, especially after he learned about the Bessemer process. In 1875, he opened his first steel plant near Pittsburgh. By 1900, Carnegie Steel made more steel each year than did all of Great Britain. Carnegie had created one of the world's largest steel companies.

Andrew Carnegie

Carnegie worked to find cheaper, more efficient ways to make steel. This helped his company become profitable. A **profitable** company is one that makes money after its expenses have been paid.

In 1901, Carnegie sold his company to **John Pierpont Morgan**, a banker. Morgan decided to merge Carnegie Steel with his other steel companies. To **merge** means to combine. Morgan's merged companies became the U.S. Steel Corporation. This Pittsburgh company was one important reason Pennsylvania became a leader in steel production. In the early 1900s, the state produced more than 50 percent of the nation's steel. It also continued to produce more iron than any other state.

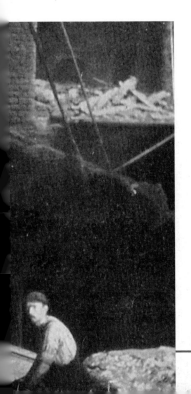

Bessemer Process
Henry Bessemer's process was 10 times faster than previous methods of making steel.

REVIEW What effect did Andrew Carnegie have on the steel industry?

Pittsburgh In the late 1800s, Pittsburgh became known as Steel City. The steel industry built houses next to the factories and rented them to workers.

Changes in Pennsylvania

Main Idea The steel industry's success brought many changes to Pennsylvania.

Railroads affected the growth of Pennsylvania's steel industry. By 1880, about three-fourths of all of the steel that Pennsylvania produced was made into steel rails. These rails were used as new railroad lines. They replaced the old iron rails on which many railroads had run. Within 10 years, steel was being used to make other railroad parts as well.

People also used steel to build other things. By the early 1900s, tall, steel-supported buildings changed city skylines. In addition, most machinery was made of steel.

Pittsburgh Grows

In 1872, workers in Pittsburgh discovered how to use steel cans to store food and other items. Railroad cars could carry large loads, so steel could easily be shipped to other parts of the country.

The steel industry created new jobs in Pennsylvania. This brought many people to Pennsylvania cities, especially Pittsburgh. Immigrants from Italy, Poland, Hungary, and other European countries traveled to Pittsburgh to find work in the city's factories. Pittsburgh's population grew quickly. In 1860, about 78,000 people lived in Pittsburgh. Forty years later, in 1900, there were more than 450,000 people living in Pittsburgh.

Philanthropy

Some of the people who became wealthy through their work in Pennsylvania industries practiced philanthropy. **Philanthropy** is the effort to help people improve their lives.

Andrew Carnegie believed in philanthropy. He believed he had a responsibility to help make life better for others. He gave away much of the money he made in the steel industry. He built almost 3,000 public libraries across the United States.

Another Pennsylvania steel industry leader, **Charles Schwab**, also practiced philanthropy. He gave money to Pennsylvania State University to build a performing arts center.

REVIEW In what way was Pittsburgh affected by the steel industry?

Lesson Summary

Steel brought money, jobs, and people to Pennsylvania. Scottish immigrant Andrew Carnegie was important to the growth of Pennsylvania's steel industry.

Why It Matters . . .

The steel industry made Pennsylvania's economy strong for many years.

Carnegie Mellon University Andrew Carnegie founded this Pittsburgh school in 1900.

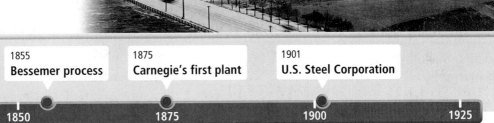

Lesson Review

1855 Bessemer process	1875 Carnegie's first plant	1901 U.S. Steel Corporation

1850   1875   1900   1925

❶ **VOCABULARY** Match each vocabulary word with its meaning.
profitable   **merge**   **philanthropy**
a. combine   b. makes money
c. helping others

❷ **READING SKILL** What **details** support the main idea that Pennsylvania made much of the nation's steel?

❸ **MAIN IDEA: History** Why did steel become a popular metal in the mid-1800s?

❹ **MAIN IDEA: Economy** What effect did railroads have on the steel industry?

❺ **TIMELINE SKILL** When did companies merge to create the U.S. Steel Corporation?

❻ **CRITICAL THINKING: Draw Conclusions** In what way might a new industry affect the lives of people in the region where the industry operates?

WRITING ACTIVITY Write a paragraph comparing the first part of Andrew Carnegie's life with the second part.

Immigration and Reform

1850　　　　1900　　　　1950　　　　2000

1879–1900

Build on What You Know Televisions, computers, and videos may have changed your classroom. In the same way, technology in the workplace changed the kinds of jobs that were available.

Immigration to Pennsylvania

Main Idea In the late 1800s and early 1900s, Pennsylvania's population grew very quickly.

In the late 1800s and early 1900s, many immigrants came to Pennsylvania seeking jobs in the state's coal, steel, and textile industries. They came from Italy, Poland, Russia, Ireland, Wales, and England.

Immigrants Enter the State Immigrants who entered the United States through Philadelphia's port came to this railroad station to purchase train tickets.

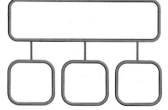

After the Flood In this photo, workers clean up the damage in Johnstown's downtown area, which was destroyed by the 1889 flood.

Changes in Population

Most immigrants entered the country through Ellis Island in the New York Harbor. Some entered the country through Philadelphia's port. Pennsylvania's railroads transported immigrants to cities throughout the state. Many settled in urban areas such as Pittsburgh and Philadelphia. In the late 1800s, immigrants made up about 25 to 30 percent of the population in Philadelphia.

Around 1910, a growing number of African Americans began leaving the South for jobs in northern cities. Many of them moved to Pennsylvania during this time. Some wanted to escape the unfair treatment they faced in the South. They also hoped to find jobs in Pennsylvania's industries. Jobs in the North paid more than the jobs that were available to African Americans in the South. This movement of people became known as the Great Migration.

The Johnstown Flood

Large numbers of people moving into an area in a short period of time can sometimes lead to problems. The growing city of Johnstown in southern Pennsylvania was a railroad center. It also had new steel and coal industries. Heavy rainfalls sometimes caused flooding in the city.

In the 1840s, engineers began to build a dam in the mountains above Johnstown. The lake created by the dam was to be part of a new canal system for the growing city. Work on the canal project stopped, and the dam was never finished.

On May 31, 1889, after a huge rainfall, the Johnstown dam collapsed. Lake waters swept through the city. More than 2,200 people lost their lives in the Johnstown Flood. It was one of the worst natural disasters in the United States.

REVIEW Why did immigrants settle in Pennsylvania's urban areas?

Changes for the Better

Main Idea In the late 1800s, Pennsylvanians tried to improve working conditions.

In the late 1800s, most employees received little pay for the long hours that they worked. Some workers believed that they might be able to improve their working conditions if they joined together. They began to form labor unions. A **labor union** is an organization that tries to improve pay and working conditions for its members. One of the earliest labor unions in Pennsylvania, the Knights of Labor, formed in Philadelphia in 1869.

Labor unions worked to reform the steel and iron industries. To **reform** is to change something for the better. When employers refused to make changes that unions demanded, union workers went on strike.

Child Labor Laws

In the mid- to late 1800s, many children worked in Pennsylvania's mining and manufacturing industries. Sometimes, children worked 11 or 12 hours a day for very little pay.

Child labor was not unusual in the 1800s. Children in rural areas often helped out on family farms. Working in the fields was very different from working in the mines, however. Working in mines meant working underground in darkness. It was hard work carrying heavy loads of coal and ore. It was also very dangerous.

Pennsylvanians worked to change rules about child labor. In 1879, Pennsylvania passed its first law aimed at protecting children. More laws on child labor were passed later. Some children still worked, but laws made their jobs safer.

Child Labor These children worked for the Pennsylvania Coal Company in Scranton.

Rights for Women

Pennsylvania women also worked for reform. In the late 1800s, **Florence Kelley,** from Philadelphia, worked for new laws to protect employees. Later, Kelley worked for women's suffrage. **Suffrage** means the right to vote. Philadelphian **Liliane Stevens Howard** also worked to help women gain the right to vote.

Both Kelley and Howard were members of the National American Woman Suffrage Association (NAWSA), which formed in 1890. Women gained the right to vote nationwide in 1920.

REVIEW What did Florence Kelley and Liliane Stevens Howard have in common?

Lesson Summary

- Immigration helped Pennsylvania's population grow in the late 1800s and early 1900s.

- Many people tried to improve the lives of Pennsylvania's workers, children, and women.

Why It Matters . . .

The rights and reforms gained during the years after the Civil War still affect the lives of Pennsylvanians.

Florence Kelley In addition to women's rights, Kelley also worked to reform child labor laws.

Lesson Review

	1869 Knights of Labor	1879 Child labor law	1890 NAWSA formed
1860	1870	1880	1890

❶ **VOCABULARY** Write a sentence or two explaining how **labor unions** worked to **reform** working conditions in Pennsylvania.

❷ **READING SKILL** Choose one reform and write a summary of what **effect** it had on Pennsylvanians.

❸ **MAIN IDEA: History** Why did people immigrate to Pennsylvania in the late 1800s and early 1900s?

❹ **MAIN IDEA: Government** During the 1800s, how did Pennsylvania leaders help protect Pennsylvania's children?

❺ **TIMELINE SKILL** How many years passed between the forming of the Knights of Labor and child labor laws?

❻ **CRITICAL THINKING: Draw Conclusions** Why would someone working for women's rights also be interested in workers' rights?

WRITING ACTIVITY Write a letter to a state legislator explaining your support for better child labor laws in the late 1800s.

Citizenship Skills

Skillbuilder

Make a Decision

You make decisions every day. A decision involves choosing what to do or what to say in a situation. Some decisions can be easy—like choosing what to wear or what to eat. Other decisions may require more thought. In this case, you must carefully consider the consequence of each choice. A consequence is something that happens because of a decision or action.

Learn the Skill

Step 1: Identify the decision you must make.

Step 2: List all of your choices.

Step 3: Consider the consequence of each choice, both good and bad.

Step 4: Make your decision. Choose the option with the best possible outcome.

Decision to Be Made:
How to raise money for a student trip

Option 1:
Have a car wash

Option 2:
Sell wrapping paper

Consequence:
• It's fun, and we would keep all of the money we earn
• We will earn nothing if it rains

Consequence:
• We would only earn half of what we sell
• Last year's class earned $500

Final Decision: Sell wrapping paper

Practice the Skill

Suppose there is farmland near your school that local leaders will be making a decision about. School officials would like the farmland to be used to build a new gymnasium for the school. Some leaders in the state would like to use the land to build a large park with walking trails. What would you choose? Use a chart like the one on page 126 to decide the best use of the land.

Apply the Skill

Choose an issue in your school that requires a decision. Use the steps you have learned to think about your choices. Use a chart like the one on page 126 to help you determine your choices and the consequences of each choice. Then write a paragraph about your decision and why you made it.

Changing Times

1850　　　　1900　　　　1950　　　　2000

1907–1965

Build on What You Know As you grow older, you may have to make hard decisions. As the United States grew larger and more powerful, it also made new and difficult decisions.

World War I

Main Idea The early 1900s brought new challenges to the state of Pennsylvania.

In 1914, a terrible war began on the continent of Europe. On one side were France, Britain, and their allies, called the Allied Powers. Allies are people or groups that join together to reach a goal. On the other side were Germany and its allies, called the Central Powers. This war became known as World War I.

At first, the United States remained neutral, which means it did not take sides in the conflict. In 1917, Germans sank three U.S. ships. Because of this, President **Woodrow Wilson** declared war on Germany. The United States joined the Allied Powers.

VOCABULARY

armistice
depression
dictator
segregation

Vocabulary Strategy

segregation

The prefix **se-** means "apart." Segregation means keeping different groups apart, or separate, from one another.

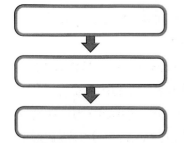

READING SKILL
Sequence Use the organizer to note the order of some of the major events that occurred in the United States in the 1900s.

The 28th Division
Members of this group of Pennsylvania soldiers served in Europe during World War I.

World War I Powers

LEGEND

- Central Powers
- Allied Powers
- Neutral countries

Taking Sides The United States fought with the Allied Powers in World War I. **SKILL** **Map Skill** What countries did not join either side in the war?

Pennsylvania and the War

Pennsylvania helped the United States and its allies during World War I. More than 300,000 soldiers in the U.S. forces were Pennsylvanians. A group of Pennsylvania National Guard soldiers won several important battles during the war.

Some Pennsylvanians supported the war by buying savings bonds, called Liberty or Victory bonds. The money from the bonds helped the government pay for the war. Bonds benefited the government by supplying needed money. People buying the bonds were later paid back more money than they loaned the government.

Pennsylvania's industries also supported the war. The state's shipyards, mills, and factories produced many of the materials that the nation would use in the war such as ammunition and other steel products.

World War I ended in 1918 when Germany agreed to an armistice. An **armistice** is an agreement to end fighting. The Allied Powers had won.

After the war ended, the United States made and sold many goods to other countries. Most people were able to find jobs. The successful economy lasted for several years.

REVIEW When did the United States enter World War I?

The 1930s and 1940s in Pennsylvania

Main Idea The Great Depression brought difficult times to many Pennsylvanians.

The economy in the United States grew strong after World War I. Many citizens had enough money to buy stocks. A stock is a small share of ownership in a company.

In October 1929, most stocks lost their value at once. Thousands of people lost money. This was the start of an economic depression. A **depression** is a period when businesses fail, prices drop, and jobs are hard to find. This depression was so long and difficult that it is remembered as the Great Depression.

Unemployment, or lack of jobs, was a serious problem during the Great Depression. By 1933, nearly 40 percent of Pennsylvanians were unemployed. People lost their homes. Many did not have enough money to buy food.

Governor **Gifford Pinchot** started new programs to try to help Pennsylvanians through the Depression. Pinchot proposed building 20,000 miles of roads in Pennsylvania. The roads were built with as little machinery as possible. This allowed more people to work on them.

More help came from President **Franklin D. Roosevelt's** "New Deal." These programs put many people back to work building roads, public buildings, and parks.

Working in the 1930s and 1940s

The Great Depression Thousands of Pennsylvanians did not have jobs during the Depression.

The New Deal Pennsylvanians do road work in Mifflin County in 1933. Their jobs were created by one of Roosevelt's New Deal programs.

World War II

During the 1930s, a dictator named **Adolf Hitler** ruled Germany. A dictator is a leader who has complete control of a country's government. Hitler wanted Germany to get back the power it had before World War I. Italy and Japan joined Germany because they hoped to conquer other countries and become world powers. Great Britain, France, the Soviet Union, China, and the United States wanted to stop this from happening. This led to World War II, which officially began in 1939.

Many people in the U.S. did not want to go to war. That changed on December 7, 1941, when Japan bombed Hawaii's Pearl Harbor. The next day, the United States declared war on Japan. Germany and Italy joined Japan in declaring war on the United States.

About 1.25 million Pennsylvanians served in World War II. This was one out of every eight people in the state. Pennsylvanians made up more than 10 percent of all of the U.S. soldiers in the war.

One Pennsylvanian, **George Marshall** of Uniontown, became Army Chief of Staff during the war. Chief of Staff is the top military officer in the Army. Later, he served as U.S. Secretary of State.

The country needed new workers to fill the jobs left by people serving in the military. Many women and African Americans filled these jobs in Pennsylvania industries.

In 1945, Germany and Japan surrendered. The United States and its allies had won the war.

REVIEW What effects did the Great Depression have on Pennsylvania?

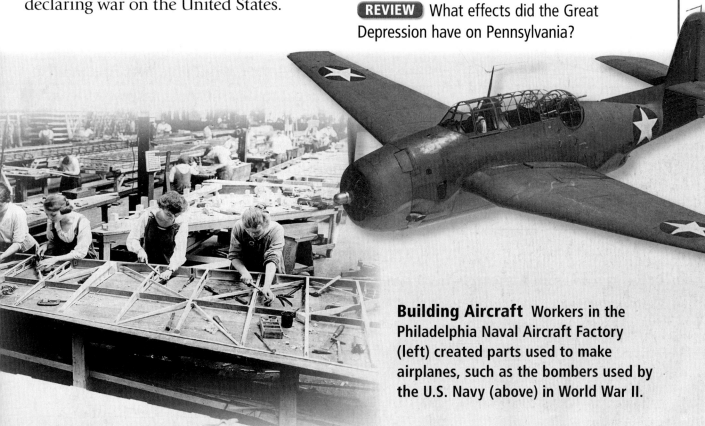

Building Aircraft Workers in the Philadelphia Naval Aircraft Factory (left) created parts used to make airplanes, such as the bombers used by the U.S. Navy (above) in World War II.

131

Struggle for Equal Rights Civil rights leaders such as Pennsylvanian Bayard Rustin (above) encouraged African Americans to organize demonstrations.

Civil Rights

Main Idea In the mid-1900s, African Americans worked to gain equal rights.

In the early 1950s, segregation was legal in many places in the United States. **Segregation** is the separation of people on the basis of their race. African Americans could not use the same restaurants and schools as whites. Many jobs were also closed to African Americans. Segregation was often based on stereotypes. A stereotype is an unfair idea about an individual or a group.

Segregation took away important civil rights from African Americans. Civil rights are the rights that the government guarantees its citizens. As a result of unfair treatment, African Americans began to work hard for change after World War II.

In 1954, the United States Supreme Court ruled that public schools could not separate students by race. Later, it ruled that Philadelphia's Girard College, a private school, had to accept students of all races.

In 1964, President Lyndon Johnson signed the Civil Rights Act. This made it illegal to discriminate against African Americans. To discriminate means to treat particular groups of people unfairly. The Civil Rights Act ended segregation in public places.

African American leaders worked to make sure that all Americans were given the same rights. One of these leaders, **Martin Luther King Jr.,** attended the University of Pennsylvania as a young man. He encouraged people to fight injustice peacefully. **Bayard Rustin,** who was born in West Chester, worked closely with King to support equal rights.

Progress and Change

In the second half of the 1900s, Pennsylvania grew and attracted people from all over the world. Thousands of jobs became available in new fields, such as electronics and pharmaceuticals. The pharmaceutical industry makes drugs and medications.

REVIEW Why did African Americans seek equal rights in the mid-1900s?

Lesson Summary

The United States and its allies, with strong support from Pennsylvania, won both World Wars. Between the wars, the nation survived the Great Depression. In the mid-1900s, African Americans worked for equal rights.

Why It Matters . . .

Pennsylvanians helped the United States win its wars and begin solving the problem of racial discrimination.

New Industries Today, computer specialists such as this Pennsylvania worker perform jobs in new industries.

Lesson Review

1918	1929	1945	1964
World War I ends	Great Depression begins	World War II ends	Civil Rights Act

1900 — 1925 — 1950 — 1975

1. **VOCABULARY** Explain what the terms **armistice** and **dictator** have to do with World Wars I and II.

2. **READING SKILL** Describe the **sequence** of major events in World War II.

3. **MAIN IDEA: History** Why did the United States not remain neutral during World War I?

4. **MAIN IDEA: History** Who was Bayard Rustin?

5. **TIMELINE SKILL** What occurred between the two World Wars?

6. **CRITICAL THINKING: Infer** In what way did the Supreme Court's ruling about Girard College affect African Americans?

WRITING ACTIVITY Write a letter to a friend describing life in Pennsylvania during one of the World Wars or during the Great Depression.

133

Skillbuilder

Identify Cause and Effect

Historians often want to know why events happened. They look at causes and effects of events. A **cause** is an event that makes another event happen. An **effect** is what happens as a result of a cause. Sometimes a cause can have more than one effect. Sometimes an effect can have more than one cause.

VOCABULARY

cause

effect

Cause	Effect
Fighting in Europe led to German attacks on U.S. ships.	As a result, President Woodrow Wilson declared war on Germany.

Learn the Skill

Step 1: Look for clue words that tell whether an event is a cause or an effect.

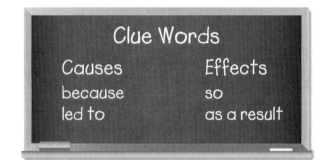

Clue Words

Causes	Effects
because	so
led to	as a result

Step 2: Identify the cause of an event. Check to see whether there is more than one cause.

Step 3: Identify the effect. Check to see whether there is more than one effect.

Practice the Skill

Reread page 131 of Lesson 4 about World War II. Then answer the following questions and fill out a diagram like the one below.

Cause	Effect

1 What caused the United States to declare war on Japan?

2 What was the effect when the United States declared war on Japan?

3 What helped you figure out what the causes and effects were?

Apply the Skill

Reread page 132 about the civil rights movement. Then make a chart to show causes and effects. Name some of the clue words that helped you figure out the causes and effects.

Visual Summary

1 – 4. Write a description of each item named below.

Great Depression

_____
_____
_____
_____

Labor Unions

_____
_____
_____
_____

Pennsylvanians in World War I

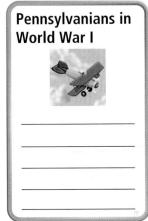

_____
_____
_____
_____

Civil Rights Act

_____
_____
_____
_____

Facts and Main Ideas

✔ **TEST PREP** Answer each question below.

5. **Geography** What natural resources in Pennsylvania were good sources of fuel for industries?

6. **Economics** In what way did Henry Bessemer's innovation affect the steel industry?

7. **Economics** In what way did railroads affect the production of steel?

8. **Culture** What did Andrew Carnegie do to help others?

9. **History** Who was Liliane Stevens Howard?

Vocabulary

✔ **TEST PREP** Choose the correct word from the list below to complete each sentence.

> **innovation,** p. 116
> **profitable,** p. 119
> **depression,** p. 130

10. Between the World Wars, the nation experienced a(n) _____.

11. New technologies helped Pennsylvania's steel industry become more _____.

12. A generator to power electric lighting systems was a(n) _____ developed by George Westinghouse.

Apply Skills

✔ **TEST PREP** **Make Decisions** Read the passage below. Then use the passage and what you have learned about making decisions to answer each question.

> Livia is looking for a place to live. She works in Allentown, Pennsylvania. Her family lives outside the city. If she moves near her family, she will have to drive many miles to work every day. If she lives in the city, she will be far from her family. Livia decides that she will live in the city and visit her family on the weekends.

13. What decision does Livia face?

  A. where to live

  B. where to work

  C. whether she should buy a car

  D. whether she should quit her job

14. What will be a consequence of her decision?

  A. She will have to find a job outside the city.

  B. She will have to drive many miles to see her family.

  C. She will not have a job.

  D. She will have to drive many miles to work.

Critical Thinking

✔ **TEST PREP** Write a short paragraph to answer the questions below. Use details from the chapter to support your responses.

15. **Cause and Effect** What did Governor Pinchot do to help Pennsylvanians during the Depression?

16. **Analyze** Could the Johnstown Flood have been avoided? Explain your answer.

Timeline

Use the Chapter Summary Timeline above to answer the question.

17. What events happened between 1900 and 1950?

Activities

 Art Activity Research some of the many uses of steel. Then cut out newspaper or magazine pictures of things made of steel. Use the pictures to create a collage titled "Steel."

 Writing Activity Write a letter that a steel industry leader in the late 1800s could have written to encourage people to move to Pennsylvania.

 Technology **Writing Process Tips** Get help with your essay at www.eduplace.com/kids/hmss/

UNIT 3 Review and Test Prep

Vocabulary and Main Ideas

✔ **TEST PREP** Write a sentence to answer each item below.

1. What did **abolitionists** in Pennsylvania do to end slavery?

2. What event was meant to **emancipate** enslaved persons in the South?

3. What was the **Reconstruction** Era?

4. Name a Pennsylvanian who contributed an **innovation** in the mid-1800s. Note what the new idea was.

5. In what way did Liliane Stevens Howard support **suffrage?**

6. What effect did the Great **Depression** have on Pennsylvania?

Critical Thinking

✔ **TEST PREP** Write a short paragraph to answer each question. Use details to support your answers.

7. **Write to Describe** Describe some of the contributions women made during the Civil War.

8. **Summarize** Describe how Pennsylvania played an important role in the rise of steel production in the United States.

Apply Skills

✔ **TEST PREP** Use what you have learned about cause and effect to answer these questions.

9. Which of the following was one cause of the Civil War?

   A. The northern states and southern states disagreed over whether slavery should be allowed.
   B. James Buchanan was elected President.
   C. Abraham Lincoln issued the Emancipation Proclamation.
   D. The Gradual Abolition of Slavery Act was passed.

10. What effect did the steel industry have on Pittsburgh in the late 1800s?

   A. The population grew.
   B. People left the city to find jobs in Philadelphia.
   C. The Johnstown dam collapsed.
   D. President Roosevelt created the New Deal.

Unit Activity

Design a cover for "Changing Pennsylvania" Magazine

- Look back at Unit 3. Choose a Pennsylvanian who helped change the state.

- Do research to find facts about how the person changed Pennsylvania.

- Design a magazine cover to feature the person you chose. Find ways to combine words and pictures on the cover.

At the Library

You may find these books at your school or public library.

The Long Road to Gettysburg by Jim Murphy
The battle of Gettysburg is described.

Johnstown Flood: The Day the Dam Burst by Mary Gow
The day of the Johnstown Flood is relived.

Connect to Today

- Create a bulletin board about different jobs and how they help people.

- Find information about an interesting job.

- Write a paragraph that tells why the job is important. Explain how doing the job helps others.

- Draw a picture of someone doing the job.

- Post your paragraph and picture.

 Technology
Weekly Reader online offers social studies articles. Go to:
www.eduplace.com/kids/hmss/

UNIT 4

Pennsylvania Today

The Big Idea

What part will you play in Pennsylvania's future?

66 *We have the opportunity to build a Pennsylvania that does justice to the tremendous spirit and pride of its people.* 99

Edward G. Rendell, Governor of Pennsylvania, 2003

Robert Nelson Cornelius Nix Sr.
1898–1987

Nix was the first African American from Pennsylvania to be elected to the House of Representatives. **page 147**

History Makers

Rachel Carson
1907–1964

Carson shared her love of nature in her writing. Her books taught readers the importance of taking care of the environment. **page 157**

Marian Anderson
1897–1993

Anderson was one of the greatest opera singers of the 20th century. She was the first African American singer to perform with the New York Metropolitan Opera. **page 165**

Chapter 7

Government in Pennsylvania

Technology

e • **glossary**
e • **word games**
www.eduplace.com/kids/hmss/

Vocabulary Preview

citizen

A **citizen** of a country has special rights as well as special responsibilities. These children act as good citizens by volunteering at a food bank. **page 144**

democracy

Democracy is government by the people. The U.S. government is a democracy in which citizens choose government leaders. **page 145**

Reading Strategy

Summarize Use this strategy to better understand information in the text.

Quick Tip A summary includes only the most important information. Use the main ideas to help you.

preamble

The U.S. and Pennsylvania constitutions both contain a **preamble.** These statements introduce the reasons and ideas behind government. **page 148**

jury

Many Americans will be asked to serve on a **jury** at some point in their lives. A jury is a group of citizens who watch a trial and decide what its outcome will be. **page 156**

United States Government

READING SKILL
Problem and Solution
Identify and describe the problems that government is supposed to solve.

Problem	Solution

Build on What You Know An American flag probably hangs in your classroom. Schools in all 50 states have the same national flag. We are all part of the same nation, even when we live many miles apart.

Government by the People

Main Idea The government is made by the people, of the people, and for the people of the United States.

The United States has many regions. The land and the ways in which people live differ from place to place. Yet all of these people and places are part of the same nation.

The United States government is "by the people." This means that the people create the government. The government is also "of the people" because each American citizen has a say in what the government does. A **citizen** is someone who is born in a country or who promises to be loyal to the country. The United States government is supposed to protect people's rights and serve the common good. The **common good** means the good of the whole population. That is why we say the United States government is "for the people."

Becoming Citizens People take an oath to become American citizens.

United States Congress Once a year, all members of Congress meet in the House of Representatives to hear the President speak about the country.

How the People Rule

The United States is a democracy. A **democracy** is a system in which the people hold the power of government. The people decide who will lead them and what the government will do.

Democracy can take several forms. In many small towns, every person votes on every rule and decision. This does not work well, however, for a huge nation. Think about what might happen if millions of citizens had to vote on every law. It would take far too long to make a decision.

Instead, the government of the United States is a representative democracy. Citizens choose people who will make decisions for them.

These representatives make day-to-day decisions in government. They represent the voters. That is what makes this country a democracy.

Citizens decide who will represent them through elections. An **election** is the way voters choose people to serve in government. On election day, citizens cast their votes for the people they want to represent them. Whoever gets the most votes usually wins the election. Voting is the responsibility of citizens in a democratic system.

REVIEW What is the job of representatives in our democratic system?

Liberty, Equality, and Justice for All

United States citizens generally agree on some basic ideas. They agree on the value of liberty. This is the freedom from control by others. They agree on the idea of justice and the rule of law. This means that laws should apply to everyone in the same way.

Before 1776, the states were colonies controlled by Great Britain. Many colonists wanted more liberty. They wrote the Declaration of Independence. It states that all people are equal and that the people have a right to "life, liberty, and the pursuit of happiness." Colonists fought the British to win these rights and establish the United States.

The Constitution

Main Idea The United States Constitution limits the power of the government and divides the government into three branches.

United States leaders wrote a constitution in 1787. The Constitution tries to ensure liberty, equality, and justice for all. It sets limits on the power of government. The Constitution also sets up three branches, or sections, of national government. This helps prevent any one part of the government from becoming too powerful.

Bill of Rights The Bill of Rights says that all Americans have certain rights and freedoms.

SKILL **Reading Charts** What does the freedom of assembly allow Americans to do?

Some Freedoms Protected by the Bill of Rights

Freedom to Practice Religious Beliefs

Freedom of Speech

Freedom of the Press

Freedom of Assembly

The Three Branches of Government

The legislative branch is the U.S. Congress. It makes the nation's laws. Congress has two parts, the House of Representatives and the Senate. Voters elect senators and members of the House. Some senators are elected many times. **Robert Nelson Cornelius Nix Sr.** served in Congress for more than 20 years. He was the first African American from Pennsylvania to be elected as a member of the House. Both the House and the Senate meet in the Capitol building.

The executive branch carries out the nation's laws. It is headed by the President, who is elected. The President lives and works at the White House.

The judicial branch includes the federal courts. It decides questions about the nation's laws. The Supreme Court is the country's highest court. It has the power to decide which laws are allowed by the Constitution. Judges and justices are not elected. They are chosen by the President and approved by the Senate.

REVIEW Why are there three branches of government?

Lesson Summary

- The many people of the United States are united under one government.
- The United States government is based on the values of liberty, equality, and justice.
- The Constitution limits the power of the branches of government.

Why It Matters ...

The United States government unites Americans through shared values of liberty and justice.

Lesson Review

1 **VOCABULARY** Write a paragraph about the United States government that uses the terms **election** and **citizen.**

2 **READING SKILL** How does the Constitution solve the **problem** of the government's becoming too powerful?

3 **MAIN IDEA: Citizenship** What is a representative democracy?

4 **MAIN IDEA: Government** What are the three branches of government?

5 **FACTS TO KNOW** What was the purpose of the Declaration of Independence?

6 **CRITICAL THINKING: Infer** Why do you think judges and justices in the national government are not elected?

WRITING ACTIVITY Write a "Declaration of Unity" for the United States. Describe how the government brings people together. Explain why it is important for the country to stay united.

State Government

VOCABULARY

preamble
checks and balances
governor

Vocabulary Strategy

preamble

Preamble contains the prefix *pre-*, which means "before." A **preamble** is an introduction. It comes before the rest of the text in the document.

READING SKILL

Compare and Contrast
As you read the lesson, compare the responsibilities of the three branches of government.

Build on What You Know What are the rules of your classroom? As a member of your class, you follow these rules. Citizens of Pennsylvania also follow certain rules.

Pennsylvania Government

Main Idea Pennsylvania's state government has three branches that carry out the state's laws.

Pennsylvania's government is located in Harrisburg, the state capital. The state constitution outlines the plan for state government in 11 parts known as articles. The U.S. Constitution and the state constitution begin with a preamble. A **preamble** is the introduction of a document. The first article in Pennsylvania's state constitution is the Declaration of Rights. It lists Pennsylvanians' rights. The constitution also describes the three branches of state government.

Pennsylvania's Capitol State government leaders work in the capitol building in Harrisburg.

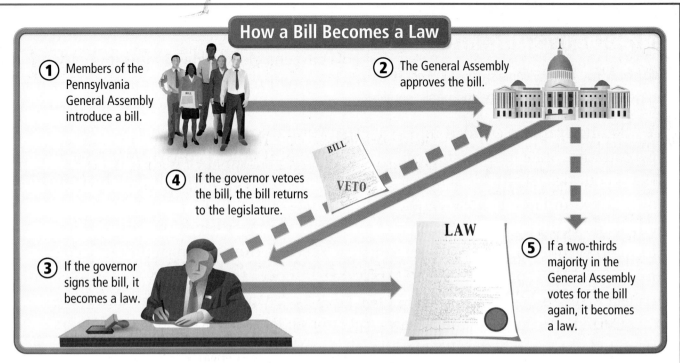

How a Bill Becomes a Law

1. Members of the Pennsylvania General Assembly introduce a bill.

2. The General Assembly approves the bill.

4. If the governor vetoes the bill, the bill returns to the legislature.

BILL VETO

LAW

3. If the governor signs the bill, it becomes a law.

5. If a two-thirds majority in the General Assembly votes for the bill again, it becomes a law.

Bills Become Laws A bill is a proposal to create or change a law.

SKILL **Reading Charts** Who approves bills in order to make them laws in Pennsylvania?

Branches of Government

The three branches of Pennsylvania's state government are legislative, executive, and judicial. The branches work together through a system of checks and balances. **Checks and balances** give each branch of government different responsibilities. No one branch has too much power.

The legislative branch makes state laws. The General Assembly leads this branch. It is made up of 203 representatives in the House of Representatives and 50 senators in the Senate. These lawmakers are elected by Pennsylvanians. Each new law begins in the General Assembly as a bill, or a proposed law.

The executive branch carries out the laws. The governor leads this branch. The **governor** is the chief executive of the state. He or she has the power to veto a bill. Citizens elect a governor every four years.

The judicial branch is responsible for settling disagreements about laws. The state supreme court heads the judicial branch. Citizens elect state supreme court justices. There are other courts, too, such as county courts. Judges decide whether someone has broken a law. Judges also decide whether a law is fair and is allowed by the constitution. The state government works with the federal government and local governments.

REVIEW Who leads the legislative branch?

Local Government

Main Idea Pennsylvania's cities and counties have their own governments and public services.

Pennsylvania is divided into 67 counties. State leaders created these counties to provide services and carry out laws. Pennsylvania cities and counties have their own local governments. Local governments make local laws, provide services, and collect taxes.

Citizens elect people to represent them in local governments. People who are elected usually belong to one of two major politcal parties, which are the Democratic and Republican parties. In some cities, such as Pittsburgh, people elect a mayor and a city council. The mayor is the head of city government. A city council is a group of elected officials who decide how to run the city. The council works with the mayor to pass laws.

In other cities, such as Bradford, citizens elect a mayor and four city council members. The mayor and the city council members have an equal voice in city government.

Still other Pennsylvania towns, such as Johnstown, elect a city council. The council hires a city manager. A city manager keeps the city and its services running smoothly.

Local governments are responsible for protecting people and enforcing laws. Police officers and firefighters work for local governments. Local governments maintain hospitals, take care of parks, and support libraries. Local governments may also provide public goods. Public goods are services or items that may be used and enjoyed by everyone, such as street signs, traffic lights, and fireworks displays.

Philadelphia's Government The Central Library and the Family Court Building (below) provide services to the people of Philadelphia. Mayor John Street (right) was elected in 1999 to lead Philadelphia's government.

Taxes

State and local governments must pay for the services they provide. Governments collect tax money. They use the money to pay for services.

Pennsylvanians pay sales tax and a state income tax. A sales tax is a tax that people pay when they buy certain products. Sales tax is a percentage of the cost of an item. An income tax is a part of a person's yearly earnings. The taxes pay for services, such as education and roads.

REVIEW Why did state leaders divide Pennsylvania into counties?

Lesson Summary

Governments work together → Federal Government

Governments work together → State Government

Governments work together → Local Government

Why It Matters . . .

Pennsylvania's state constitution is the basis for Pennsylvania's government. The government protects citizens and provides services.

Sales Tax In Pennsylvania, people pay a sales tax of six cents on every dollar they spend.

Lesson Review

1 **VOCABULARY** Write a few sentences describing Pennsylvania's state government. Use the terms **checks and balances** and **governor.**

2 🕐 **READING SKILL** Contrast the responsibilities of the judicial branch and the legislative branch of state government.

3 **MAIN IDEA: Government** Explain the importance of checks and balances in Pennsylvania's state government.

4 **MAIN IDEA: Government** Which public services do local governments provide?

5 **CRITICAL THINKING: Evaluate** Why is it important for states to have their own governments?

HANDS ON **DRAMA ACTIVITY** Pennsylvania's constitution was written before the U.S. Constitution. With a small group, learn more about the people who wrote the first state constitution. Then plan a scene from a play. In the scene, actors hold a meeting to discuss key ideas that should be included in the new state constitution.

Skillbuilder

Resolve Conflicts

Conflicts occur when people want different things. Conflicts can occur in society and in government. People should listen to one another to resolve a conflict. To **resolve** means to find a way to settle a problem. To resolve a conflict, people usually figure out a compromise that works for everyone. Use the steps below to help resolve conflicts.

▶ **VOCABULARY**
resolve

Learn the Skill

Step 1: Identify the conflict.

> **Conflict:** The softball team and the school band want to use the auditorium after school on Tuesdays.

Step 2: Understand the reasons for the conflict. Have the people involved in the conflict state their goals.

> **Goal:** The softball team wants to hold meetings on Tuesdays.

> **Goal:** The school band wants to rehearse on Tuesdays.

Step 3: Think of all the possible ways to resolve the conflict.

> **Possible Solution:** The softball team offers to hold meetings every other Tuesday.

> **Possible Solution:** The school band offers to practice at a later time.

Step 4: Choose the plan or compromise that is most acceptable to everyone involved. Each side may need to compromise on its goals.

> **Solution:** The softball team will hold meetings every other Tuesday. The band will practice in the evening on the days that the softball team has meetings.

Read the paragraph below. Then answer the questions.

> In the late 1800s, people who worked in the timber industry wanted to cut down many of the trees in Pennsylvania's forests. They could make money by selling the wood from the trees. People could use the wood to build houses. Some people, such as Governor Gifford Pinchot, thought the timber industry harmed the environment by cutting down too many trees. Trees help keep the air clean and support different plant and animal species.

1 Identify the conflict. What differences of opinion did people have about Pennsylvania's forests?

2 What are the goals of the people involved in the conflict?

3 Brainstorm ways that the two groups can work together to solve this conflict.

Apply the Skill

Find out about a conflict that exists in your community. Learn about ways that people have tried to compromise in order to find a solution.

Rights and Responsibilities

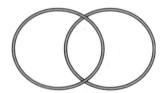

READING SKILL
Classify As you read, think about the difference between rights and responsibilities.

Build on What You Know You have the right to go to school and get an education. You also have the responsibility to attend school and do your schoolwork. Your rights as a citizen come with responsibilities.

Government and Citizens

Main Idea People in the United States have rights that are protected by the government.

People in the United States sometimes say they live in a free country. By this, they mean that U.S. citizens have rights. The government has the responsibility to protect the rights of its citizens. The country's early leaders wrote the Bill of Rights to protect people's freedoms. Pennsylvania's state constitution protects people's rights as well.

The governments of Pennsylvania and of the United States have the responsibility to work for the common good. This means that the governments are responsible for providing services and making laws that do the most good for everyone. For example, traffic laws are meant to keep all citizens safe. Such laws benefit the common good.

Bill of Rights The Bill of Rights was added to the Constitution of the United States on December 15, 1791.

Elections Citizens take part in making laws by voting for leaders who share their ideas.

Citizens' Rights

Pennsylvania citizens enjoy rights protected by the federal and state constitutions. Pennsylvanians have the right to work and earn money in a safe environment. This was not always true. Workers in cities such as Homestead held strikes and organized unions to persuade the government to protect workers' rights. The government then created laws to keep employees safe.

Laws today also prevent discrimination. All citizens have the right to be treated fairly. Laws are meant to protect this right so that people of different races, genders, ages, and cultures are treated equally.

Citizens have the right to voice their opinions, even if they disagree with something the government has done. Citizens have the right to practice any religion they choose and to live anywhere they want. Citizens also have the right to privacy.

Both the state and federal governments are based on the idea of popular sovereignty (SAHV uhr ihn tee). **Popular sovereignty** happens when citizens create the government and have the power to vote and influence laws.

Citizens have the right to vote for the leaders they believe will represent their views in government. Voting is an important right. Voting helps make sure that a democracy succeeds.

REVIEW What is an example of a law that is meant to protect a right?

Citizens' Responsibilities

Main Idea Citizens have responsibilities to society.

Citizens have responsibilities as well as rights. Citizens have the responsibility to obey local and federal laws. Judges and juries have the responsibility to decide the consequences for people who do not obey the law. A **jury** is a group of citizens who decide a case in court.

Citizens have the responsibility to participate in government. One way to do this is by serving on a jury. A juror is a person who is part of a jury. Jurors have a responsibility to remember the rights of people accused of crimes. People have the right to a fair trial. They also have the right to have a lawyer and to be thought of as innocent until proven guilty.

Another way to participate in government is by voting. Voters have the responsibility to learn about candidates. A **candidate** is a person who runs for election to a political office. Citizens aged 18 and older have the responsibility to vote in elections. They also have the responsibility to agree to be governed by the winning candidate, even if they voted for someone else.

Citizens have the responsibility to pay taxes so that governments can provide services. Another responsibility of citizens is to respect the rights of others. This means that when people disagree, they have the responsibility to respect one another's beliefs.

Citizenship is the term used to describe the rights and responsibilities of citizens. Serving on a jury, voting, and paying taxes are all part of good citizenship.

Jurors A citizen is usually asked to serve as a member of a jury at some point in his or her life.

Good citizens help make their community a better place. For example, they pick up trash around their neighborhood because they want to make it cleaner and more beautiful.

There are many ways to show good citizenship. One way is to stand when the national anthem, "The Star-Spangled Banner," is sung. Another way is to recite the "Pledge of Allegiance."

Rachel Carson, who was born in Springdale, practiced good citizenship. As a scientist, she learned about pollution. She worked to show people and government leaders how to protect nature.

REVIEW What responsibility do jurors have?

Volunteering Giving your time to help others is one way to be a good citizen.

Lesson Summary

Citizens in the United States have rights and responsibilities. Voting is one of a citizen's most important rights. It is also every citizen's responsibility in a democracy.

Why It Matters . . .

Pennsylvania's government depends on the participation of its citizens.

Lesson Review

❶ **VOCABULARY** Complete the sentences with the words **citizenship** and **candidate.**

Voting is an important part of good _____. Before voting, a good citizen learns about a _____.

❷ **READING SKILL** Explain how you can **classify** voting as both a right and a responsibility.

❸ **MAIN IDEA: Government** Name three rights of Pennsylvania citizens.

❹ **MAIN IDEA: Citizenship** Describe some of the responsibilities of Pennsylvania citizens. In what way do these responsibilities show good citizenship?

❺ **CRITICAL THINKING: Analyze** Why is it important for governments to protect the common good?

WRITING ACTIVITY Think about someone you know who is a good citizen. Write a list of the characteristics that he or she has. What makes this person a good citizen?

Visual Summary

1 – 3. ✏️ Write a description of each item named below.

Government	
Constitution of the United States	
Three branches of state government	
Cities and counties	

Facts and Main Ideas

✔️ **TEST PREP** Answer each question below.

4. Government What is the purpose of government?

5. Citizenship How can citizens take part in government?

6. Government What are the responsibilities of a city government?

7. Government Who is responsible for deciding the consequences for citizens who do not obey laws?

8. Government How does the government protect the rights of citizens accused of a crime?

Vocabulary

✔️ **TEST PREP** Choose the correct word from the list below to complete each sentence.

democracy, p. 145
popular sovereignty, p. 155
candidate, p. 156

9. Citizens vote for the _____ who shares their goals and ideas.

10. _____ means that citizens have the ability to influence laws.

11. The United States government is a _____ in which people hold the power of government.

✔️ **TEST PREP** **Resolve Conflicts** Read the paragraph below. Then use what you have learned about resolving conflicts to answer each question.

> In the early 1900s, Pennsylvania's environment was in trouble. The air and streams were polluted. Much of this was caused by the coal industry. Citizens wanted a cleaner environment. Pennsylvania's coal industry did not want to spend money cleaning up the industry. The government resolved the conflict with a compromise. The government helped pay the clean-up costs. It also made laws that required industries to reduce pollution.

12. What did the coal industry want in this conflict?

    A. to reduce pollution
    B. to prove that pollution was not a problem
    C. to continue doing business without making changes
    D. to pass new pollution laws

13. How was the conflict resolved?

    A. Citizens said that pollution was not a problem.
    B. Laws required the coal industry to change.
    C. The coal industry shut down.
    D. The government did not take any action.

✔️ **TEST PREP** Write a short paragraph to answer each question below.

14. **Synthesize** Why is the United States government said to be "for the people," "of the people," and "by the people"? Is Pennsylvania's government the same? Explain your answer.

15. **Draw Conclusions** What are the costs and benefits of paying taxes?

Activities

Math Activity Suppose 6¢ of every $1 you spend is tax. Figure out how much tax would be collected if you bought 10 notebooks that cost a total of $3.

Research Activity Use reference materials to learn about local government leaders. Plan a display showing their work and political party.

Technology
Writing Process Tips
Get help with your description at
www.eduplace.com/kids/hmss/

Chapter 8

People and the Economy

Vocabulary Preview

Technology

e • **glossary**
e • **word games**
www.eduplace.com/kids/hmss/

population

Pennsylvania's **population** is made up of people from all over the world. People of many different backgrounds and traditions live in the state. **page 162**

metropolitan area

Many people live in the **metropolitan area** of Pittsburgh. This area includes the city of Pittsburgh and the communities that surround it. **page 163**

Reading Strategy

Question As you read the lessons in this chapter, ask yourself questions about important ideas.

Quick Tip Ask yourself what you want to know more about. Write your question and go back to it after you finish reading.

tourism

Pennsylvania's Hershey Park is an important part of the **tourism** industry. This industry provides services to people who are on vacation. **page 169**

specialization

Some Pennsylvania companies practice **specialization.** They make just one product rather than many different products. **page 173**

People of Pennsylvania

VOCABULARY

population
metropolitan area
multicultural
ethnic group

Vocabulary Strategy

population

The word **populate** is a verb that means "to live in an area or region." **Population** means all of the different people living in one area.

READING SKILL

Draw Conclusions Note facts about where people live in Pennsylvania and why they live there. Write your conclusions.

Facts	Conclusions

Build on What You Know Do you know anyone who has just moved to or from your community? Pennsylvania changes all the time as people move into and out of the state's communities.

Pennsylvania's Population

Main Idea Pennsylvania has a large and changing population.

Every 10 years, the United States government takes a census. A census is a count of the people living in the country. The government uses a census to learn about the population of the United States. Population means all of the people who live in a certain area.

In a census, Pennsylvanians answer questions about ages, their jobs, and where they live. This provides information about the state's population. The 2000 census showed that more than 12 million people live in Pennsylvania.

Population Pennsylvania has the sixth largest population of all of the states in the country.

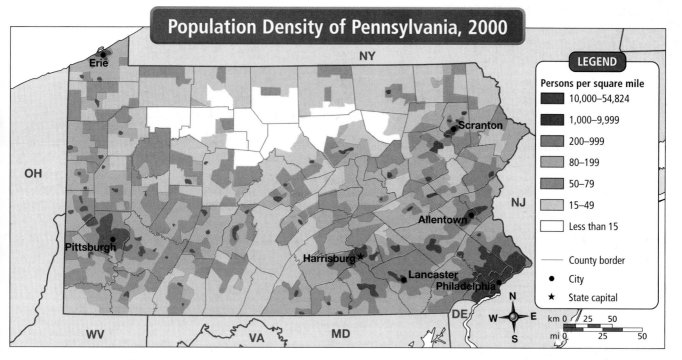

Population Density of Pennsylvania, 2000

LEGEND

Persons per square mile
- 10,000–54,824
- 1,000–9,999
- 200–999
- 80–199
- 50–79
- 15–49
- Less than 15

County border
● City
★ State capital

Pennsylvania's population Southeastern Pennsylvania is one of the state's most heavily populated areas. **SKILL** Reading Maps In which part of Pennsylvania do the least amount of people live?

Urban and Rural Living

About seven out of every ten Pennsylvanians live in urban areas. Philadelphia and Pittsburgh are the state's largest metropolitan areas. A **metropolitan area** is a city and the communities that surround it. More than five million people live in Philadelphia's metropolitan area. More than two million people live in Pittsburgh's metropolitan area.

About three out of every ten Pennsylvanians live in rural areas. Counties such as Cameron, Forest, Sullivan, and Fulton are considered rural. These counties have populations of less than 20,000.

Changing Population

When people move into or out of an area, the population goes up or down. Some areas of Pennsylvania are increasing in population, and others are decreasing.

Pennsylvania's population changes as its industries change. When new businesses open, new people move into the area to work. When businesses close, employees lose their jobs. Sometimes they have to move to another city to find work.

REVIEW Do most people in Pennsylvania live in urban areas or rural areas?

Pennsylvania Cultures Different ethnic groups have brought their customs to Pennsylvania. The Pennsylvania Dutch (above) often use traditional farming methods. Laotians from the Asian country of Laos make works of art with cloth and silk (left).

Customs and Cultures

Main Idea People of different cultures live throughout Pennsylvania.

Pennsylvania is multicultural. A **multicultural** population is made up of people from many different countries and backgrounds. Pennsylvanians have a mix of languages and traditions.

Examples of this multicultural population can be seen all around. Buildings might look like those in Germany or Holland. Restaurants might serve food from countries like China, Mexico, or France. Even the names of places in Pennsylvania are multicultural. For example, Bellefonte means "beautiful fountain" in French.

The 12 million people who live in the state belong to different ethnic groups. An **ethnic group** is made up of people who share the same culture. When immigrants move to Pennsylvania, they often continue to practice their traditional customs. They may speak English as well as the language of their homeland. Language is one thing that can unite an ethnic group.

One ethnic group in the state is the Pennsylvania Dutch. This group is related to German farmers who settled in southeastern Pennsylvania in the early 1700s. Today, Pennsylvania Dutch farms are located in Northampton, Berks, Lancaster, and York counties. They share a common language, food, and style of art.

Celebrating Cultures

Pennsylvania holds festivals that celebrate different cultures and ethnic groups. The Ferio del Barrio is the largest Latino festival in the Philadelphia area. Harrisburg hosts the International Unity Festival, which celebrates Indian, Polish, Croatian (kro AY shun), Chinese, and Vietnamese cultures. Carbondale holds the Eisteddfod (Y stehth vahd), a Welsh festival.

Pennsylvania organizations and museums also celebrate diversity. For example, the African American Museum in Philadelphia has exhibits on African American culture. This museum sometimes provides information on people like Philadelphian **Marian Anderson.** Anderson was the first successful African American opera singer.

REVIEW Who are the Pennsylvania Dutch?

Traditions These Philadelphia children are performing a West African dance in honor of Kwaanza, a holiday celebrating African culture and values.

Lesson Summary

Pennsylvania's population is different in rural and urban areas. It is affected by industry as well as culture.

Why It Matters . . .

Pennsylvania's ethnic diversity comes from the different cultures and customs that people have brought to the state.

Lesson Review

① **VOCABULARY** Explain how **ethnic groups** make Pennsylvania a **multicultural** state.

② **READING SKILL** Name a **conclusion** you drew from the facts presented about where Pennsylvanians live.

③ **MAIN IDEA: Culture** Why does population change?

④ **MAIN IDEA: Culture** What examples of Pennsylvania's multicultural population can be seen throughout the state?

⑤ **CRITICAL THINKING: Analyze** Name some things in your community that show that Pennsylvania is multicultural.

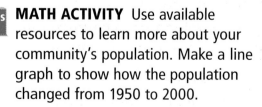

MATH ACTIVITY Use available resources to learn more about your community's population. Make a line graph to show how the population changed from 1950 to 2000.

Skillbuilder

Read a Circle Graph

A circle graph is a circle that is divided into sections to show how information is related. Circle graphs are sometimes called pie charts. Circle graphs can help you see how the whole of something is broken up into different parts. For example, a circle graph can show you how a state's population is made up of different groups. It also lets you see how these groups compare with each other.

Learn the Skill

Step 1: Read the title to find out what information the graph presents. This graph gives information about the people in Pennsylvania.

Pennsylvania Population by Age

Step 2: Read the labels for each section of the circle. Each section of this graph represents an age group.

20 to 34 years old

Step 3: Compare the sizes of the different sections. In this graph, a larger section means that more people of that age group live in the state. A smaller section means that fewer people of that age group live in the state.

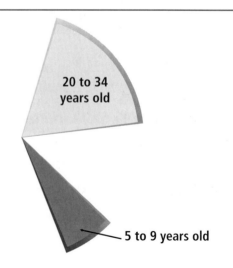

20 to 34 years old

5 to 9 years old

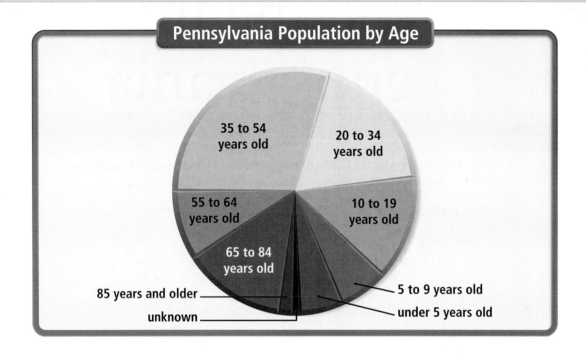

Pennsylvania Population by Age

- 35 to 54 years old
- 20 to 34 years old
- 55 to 64 years old
- 10 to 19 years old
- 65 to 84 years old
- 85 years and older
- 5 to 9 years old
- unknown
- under 5 years old

Practice the Skill

Use the circle graph to answer the questions.

1 Most people living in Pennsylvania belong to which age group represented in the circle graph?

2 How many groups are represented in the circle graph?

3 Which group has more people: people age 65 to 84 years, or children under 5 years old?

Apply the Skill

Create a circle graph to show how you spend your time during a typical school day. First, draw a circle that stands for the 24 hours in a whole day. Then divide it into sections to show all of your activities and the time you spend on them.

Working in Pennsylvania

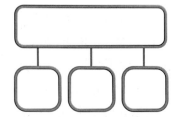

Build on What You Know What kind of work would you like to do someday? What kind of work do adults in your family or in your community do? Pennsylvanians have different jobs in the state's industries.

Pennsylvania's Economy

Main Idea Pennsylvania's economy is based on a wide variety of industries.

People say that the economy of an area is strong when businesses are profitable and produce many goods, and when most people have jobs. In Pennsylvania, the industries with the most employees are education, health and social services, manufacturing, and retail trade. Many of the employees in these industries work to produce goods and offer services. Consumers buy goods from the people who make or sell goods and services. A **consumer** is someone who buys or uses goods and services.

Buying and Selling
At farmer's markets, local farmers sell their crops to consumers.

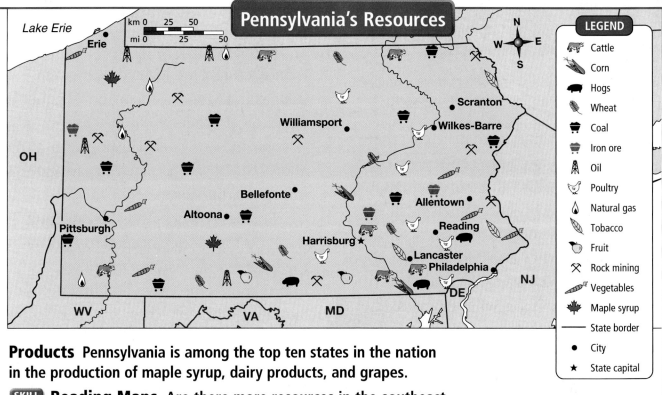

Pennsylvania's Resources

Lake Erie

Erie

km 0 25 50
mi 0 25 50

Scranton
Wilkes-Barre

Williamsport

OH

Bellefonte

Altoona

Pittsburgh

Harrisburg ★

Allentown

Reading

Lancaster
Philadelphia

NJ

DE

WV

VA

MD

LEGEND

Cattle
Corn
Hogs
Wheat
Coal
Iron ore
Oil
Poultry
Natural gas
Tobacco
Fruit
Rock mining
Vegetables
Maple syrup
— State border
• City
★ State capital

Products Pennsylvania is among the top ten states in the nation in the production of maple syrup, dairy products, and grapes.

SKILL **Reading Maps** Are there more resources in the southeast or the northeast?

Today's Job Market

Some Pennsylvania industries are located near natural resources. Southeastern Pennsylvania has fertile farmland. Agriculture is an important industry in the southeastern counties of Lancaster, York, and Chester. Mining provides jobs in Indiana and Armstrong counties.

Some industries are located in urban areas with better access to transportation, such as Pittsburgh. Access to transportation makes trade easier and strengthens the economy.

Tourism has become an important industry as transportation has improved. **Tourism** is the business of organizing travel for people. Pennsylvania's mountains, cities, and historic sites attract many visitors.

Today, most Pennsylvanians work in industries that provide services. These services include health care, banking, law, and entertainment.

Manufacturing is important to the economy. Workers in Erie and Philadelphia manufacture products like electronics and food. Steel production is still an important part of Pennsylvania's manufacturing industry. The textile industry is strong in Philadelphia and Schuylkill counties.

Some Pennsylvanians work in the retail and wholesale industries. The retail industry includes all businesses that sell goods in stores. Wholesale is the industry in which businesses sell large quantities of goods to these retail businesses.

REVIEW In what industry do most Pennsylvanians work?

Business Choices

Main Idea Business owners make choices to decide how to run profitable businesses.

Many Pennsylvanians create their own jobs by becoming entrepreneurs. An **entrepreneur** (ahn truh preh NOOR) is someone who starts a new business. When people decide to open new businesses, they must decide what goods and services they will produce, how the goods and services will be produced, and which consumers will be most likely to purchase their products.

Business owners also have to decide where they will locate their businesses. Some business owners open businesses in metropolitan areas where there are more people to fill jobs and purchase products.

Some Pennsylvania steel manufacturers are located near rivers such as the Monongahela and Allegheny rivers. Steel products can be easily transported on water. This location allows the business owner to save on transportation costs.

Business owners must decide how to spend the money needed to operate the business. A business might want to hire more employees and buy new factory equipment. There may not be enough money to do both. Choosing to hire more employees might mean giving up the opportunity to buy new factory equipment. The loss of new equipment is called an opportunity cost. An **opportunity cost** is the thing you give up when you decide to do or have something else.

Making Choices

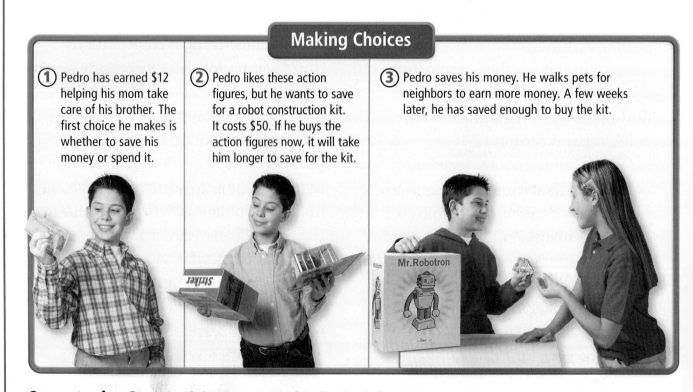

① Pedro has earned $12 helping his mom take care of his brother. The first choice he makes is whether to save his money or spend it.

② Pedro likes these action figures, but he wants to save for a robot construction kit. It costs $50. If he buys the action figures now, it will take him longer to save for the kit.

③ Pedro saves his money. He walks pets for neighbors to earn more money. A few weeks later, he has saved enough to buy the kit.

Opportunity Cost Both businesses and individuals have opportunity costs. **SKILL** What is the opportunity cost of Pedro's choice?

Personal Choices

Employees earn money for working. This is called income. People make choices about how to spend or save their income.

A consumer can decide to buy a less expensive kind of juice to save money. If the consumer buys an expensive orange juice, he or she will have less money to spend on something else.

Some people save part of their income in savings accounts at a bank. Some save money in a piggy bank. Some buy savings bonds. When people save money in a bank account, they sometimes earn interest. Interest is money that a bank pays a person to hold their money. This is one benefit of saving.

REVIEW How do employees use their income?

Comparing Prices Shopping around for the best price is one way consumers can save money.

Lesson Summary

- Pennsylvanians hold a variety of jobs.
- Business owners make choices about how to sell products.
- Pennsylvanians make choices about how to spend money.

Why It Matters . . .

Pennsylvanians depend on the state's industries in order to find jobs and to earn income to meet their needs.

Lesson Review

1. **VOCABULARY** Complete the sentence with the following words:

   opportunity cost   **consumer**

   A(n) _____ is what a(n) _____ gives up to gain something else.

2. **READING SKILL** List two details about Pennsylvania's industries.

3. **MAIN IDEA: Economics** Name two industries that are important to Pennsylvania's economy.

4. **MAIN IDEA: Economics** What kinds of questions must business owners attempt to answer?

5. **CRITICAL THINKING: Evaluate** Describe the way in which a new factory in your area might affect the economy.

WRITING ACTIVITY Write a paragraph that explains the opportunity cost of a personal choice you made. Tell the costs and benefits of your decision.

Connections to the World

VOCABULARY

scarcity
specialization
import
export

Vocabulary Strategy

import   export

To remember the difference between **import** and **export,** think of *into* and *exit.* **Imports** come *into* a country. **Exports** *exit,* or leave, a country.

READING SKILL
Cause and Effect List some of the effects of competition.

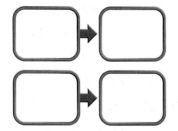

Build on What You Know You may have clothes or games that were made in another country. Pennsylvanians do not produce all of the goods that consumers in the state want and need. They depend on other states and countries to supply these products.

Price and Competition

Main Idea Prices are influenced by many factors.

Business owners set prices for their products. Some businesses offer lower prices to compete with other businesses. If two stores sell the same product, and one store is selling the product for less money, most people choose the lower cost. The store with the higher priced product would have to lower its price in order to compete. Competition means having two or more businesses offering the same item or service. Competition helps keep prices low. When only one business sells a product, the price can be higher.

Competition Businesses in Philadelphia's shopping district use advertising to attract more customers.

Pennsylvania Products

Agriculture The state's fertile farmland still produces important crops, including fruit, vegetables, and wheat.

Food Products Pennsylvania produces nearly 25 percent of the potato chips made in the United States.

Manufacturing Factories like this one in Philadelphia continue to produce steel products.

Buying and Selling

Taxes add to the cost of goods and services. Sales tax is added to the cost of many goods. This increases prices.

Supply and demand also influence price. Supply is the amount of a product made. Demand is the amount of a product consumers want to buy. Supply and demand affect each other.

Suppose that a company makes a new cereal. The company advertises to persuade people to buy the cereal and demand for the cereal is high. As demand rises, the price tends to rise.

As the price of the cereal rises, fewer people will want to buy it. The demand will lessen. The cereal company may lower the price.

Scarcity also affects price. **Scarcity** means a limited supply of something. When there is scarcity, the supply is low but the demand is high. The price of the product will probably be high.

Specialization

Many companies in Pennsylvania specialize. **Specialization** means that a business only makes a certain kind of product. Specialization happens when people decide to focus on making the goods they are best able to produce. In the Lehigh Valley in southeastern Pennsylvania, for example, many businesses specialize in making cement. This is because limestone is one of the most important materials needed for making cement. Limestone is found in this part of the state. Businesses also sometimes specialize so that they will have less competition.

Businesses can become skilled at producing one product when they specialize. More goods can be produced. Sometimes the product's cost can be lowered.

REVIEW Describe the effect of supply and demand on prices.

Trade

Main Idea Pennsylvania's economy is part of a world economy.

Pennsylvanians cannot provide every kind of good or service that citizens want or need. For this reason, Pennsylvanians sometimes buy imports. An **import** is a product brought in from another state or country. For example, Pennsylvania industries buy iron ore from Michigan and Minnesota. The iron ore is used to make steel.

In the same way, Pennsylvania products are exported to other places. An **export** is a product that is sold to another country or state. People throughout the world depend on Pennsylvania's steel and timber.

When countries trade with one another, it is called international trade. The United States trades its products for products made in other countries. Countries now depend on one another to supply products and services for their citizens. This is called interdependence.

Pennsylvania is linked to other states and countries through its transportation networks. These include roads, railways, waterways, and airways. These networks make trade easier.

Different countries use different forms of money, or currency. For example, the United States uses dollars. Mexico uses pesos (PAY sohs). When the United States and Mexico trade products, they need to know how many pesos equal one dollar. They use the exchange rate to find out. The exchange rate shows the way to make different currencies equal. The exchange rate makes international trade more fair.

Transportation Networks Interstate highways, railroads, waterways, and airways connect Pennsylvania to places around the world.

Trading Partners

Countries sometimes form trade alliances. An alliance is an agreement between two or more countries seeking a common goal. The North American Free Trade Agreement, or NAFTA, is an example of a trade alliance. NAFTA allows the United States, Canada, and Mexico to trade goods with one another, usually without paying taxes or fees. Pennsylvania exports to Canada and Mexico have almost doubled since NAFTA was created in 1994.

REVIEW What is NAFTA?

Lesson Summary

Prices are affected by factors such as competition and taxes.

↓

These prices affect the choices that business owners make.

↓

Prices, costs, and business choices are all part of the economy.

↓

Pennsylvania's economy is part of the world economy.

Why It Matters . . .

People in the United States and the world use and depend on products from Pennsylvania.

Increased Trade Trade alliances help countries increase the number of items they export, such as timber from Pennsylvania.

Lesson Review

❶ **VOCABULARY** Write a short paragraph that explains how **imports** and **exports** are part of international trade.

❷ 🕐 **READING SKILL** What **effect** can competition have on prices?

❸ **MAIN IDEA: Economics** Why do businesses in Lehigh Valley specialize in making cement?

❹ **MAIN IDEA: Economics** How does specialization affect trade between countries?

❺ **CRITICAL THINKING: Evaluate** Why would a business have less competition if it specializes in a certain product?

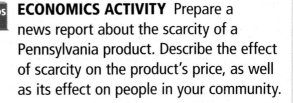

ECONOMICS ACTIVITY Prepare a news report about the scarcity of a Pennsylvania product. Describe the effect of scarcity on the product's price, as well as its effect on people in your community.

Visual Summary

1 – 3. Write a description of each item named below.

Pennsylvania's Diverse Population

_____
_____
_____
_____
_____

Jobs in Pennsylvania

_____
_____
_____
_____
_____

Pennsylvania Trade

_____
_____
_____
_____
_____

Facts and Main Ideas

TEST PREP Answer each question below.

4. **Geography** Why is the population of Pennsylvania decreasing in some areas while it is increasing in other areas?

5. **Culture** What are some ethnic groups found in Pennsylvania?

6. **Economics** How are Pennsylvanians involved in the production of goods and services?

7. **Geography** Name two industries in Pennsylvania that are located near natural resources.

8. **Government** Why do countries use an exchange rate during trade?

Vocabulary

TEST PREP Choose the correct word from the list below to complete each sentence.

population, p. 162
entrepreneur, p. 170
scarcity, p. 173

9. _____ occurs when there are not enough resources to produce all of a product that consumers want or need.

10. More than 12 million people live in Pennsylvania, giving it the sixth largest _____ of all of the states.

11. Andrew Carnegie was a(n) _____ who helped Pennsylvania's steel industry grow.

Apply Skills

TEST PREP **Read a Circle Graph** Read the circle graph below. Then use what you have learned about reading a circle graph to answer each question.

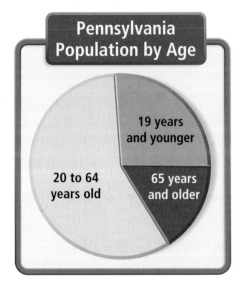

Pennsylvania Population by Age

- 19 years and younger
- 20 to 64 years old
- 65 years and older

12. Which age group has the least amount of people in Pennsylvania?

A. 19 years and younger
B. 20 to 64 years old
C. 65 years and older
D. none of the above

13. How many groups are represented in the circle graph?

A. 1
B. 2
C. 3
D. 4

Critical Thinking

TEST PREP Write a short paragraph to answer each question below.

14. Generalize How would you describe Pennsylvania's economy? Explain your answer.

15. Summarize What kinds of industries employ people in Pennsylvania?

16. Fact and Opinion Is competition good or bad for businesses? Explain your answer.

Activities

HANDS ON **Research Activity** Use the Internet and library resources to learn more about the different ways of saving income. Make a chart showing the benefits of each.

Writing Activity Write a persuasive essay giving reasons for a business to move to your community.

Technology
Writing Process Tips
Get help with your persuasive essay at
www.eduplace.com/kids/hmss/

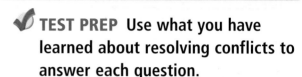

UNIT 4

Review and Test Prep

Vocabulary and Main Ideas

✔ **TEST PREP** Write a sentence to answer each item.

1. Why is it important for **citizens** to vote in an **election?**

2. What does a **governor** do?

3. What is the purpose of a **jury?**

4. Describe two of Pennsylvania's **metropolitan areas.**

5. Describe the way a **consumer** affects the economy.

6. Name an **opportunity cost** that **entrepreneurs** have.

Critical Thinking

✔ **TEST PREP** Write a short paragraph to answer each question.

7. **Summarize** Describe how citizens have both rights and responsibilities.

8. **Draw Conclusions** Why do some areas of Pennsylvania have a larger population than other areas?

Apply Skills

✔ **TEST PREP** Use what you have learned about resolving conflicts to answer each question.

Four friends are trying to decide what they want to do on Saturday. One wants to go to a movie. One wants to play video games. Two want to ride bikes in the park.

9. What describes the conflict?

   A. Friends want to see different movies.
   B. Friends want to go to different parks.
   C. Friends are bored on a weekend.
   D. Friends have different ideas about what to do.

10. What would help the friends reach a compromise?

   A. The friends find an activity most of them can agree on.
   B. Each friend makes a choice without discussion.
   C. All friends avoid talking about the conflict.
   D. One friend makes a choice for everyone.

Unit Activity

Draw an "I Am Pennsylvania's Future" Portrait

- Think of what you might do in the future to help Pennsylvania.

- Draw a picture that shows you working and living in Pennsylvania.

- Give your picture a caption that explains your role.

I will open a new business that will bring products and new jobs to the economy.

At the Library

Check your school or public library for books about Pennsylvania.

Pennsylvania Government for Kids!: The Cornerstone of Everyday Life in Our State! by Carole Marsh
Readers learn facts about the state government.

Pennsylvania by Gwenyth Swain
Readers learn about the state's people and industries.

Connect to Today

Make a poster that encourages people to fulfill their responsibility to take care of their environment.

- Look for information about caring for the environment or about preventing pollution.

- Think of a saying or slogan about the environment that will get people's attention.

- Design a poster with words and pictures to convince people to help take care of their environment.

Technology

Weekly Reader online offers social studies articles. Go to: **www.eduplace.com/kids/hmss/**

UNIT 5

The East

The Big Idea

What do you like most about the place where you live?

❝*The thing that struck me most all over the United States was the physical beauty of the country, and the great beauty of the cities.*❞

Gertrude Stein, writer, 1937
From *Everybody's Autobiography* from *America the Quotable,* by Mike Edelhart published by Facts on File Publications

Chapter 9

Exploring the East

Technology

e • **glossary**
e • **word games**
www.eduplace.com/kids/hmss/

Vocabulary Preview

coast

Many people enjoy beaches along the **coast.** The United States has a long east coast, a long west coast, and a southern coast along the Gulf of Mexico. **page 184**

market economy

The United States has a **market economy.** In this system, people have choices about what to make, how to make it, and for whom to make it. **page 190**

Reading Strategy

Summarize As you read, use the summarize strategy to focus on important ideas.

Review the main ideas to get started. Then look for important details that support the main idea.

human resources

Human resources are a very important part of any company. Workers provide needed skills that help the company produce goods and services. **page 192**

commuter

Many people in urban areas are **commuters.** They travel from home to work on a road or train running between a suburb and a city. **page 197**

Land and Climate

VOCABULARY

coast
coastal plain
cape
bay

Vocabulary Strategy

coastal plain

A **coast** is land next to an ocean. A **coastal plain** is a plain next to an ocean.

READING SKILL
Main Idea and Details
List details that describe the mountains of the East.

Mountains

Build on What You Know Think of a road that cuts through a mountain. You would see many layers of rock. Scientists can tell the age of mountains by looking at these layers. The Appalachian Mountains are hundreds of millions of years old.

Land and Water of the East

Main Idea The East has many landforms and bodies of water.

The region between the Atlantic Ocean and the Great Lakes is known as the East. Canada borders the region to the north. Our nation's capital, Washington, D.C., is at the southern tip.

The East includes six states in New England and five Mid-Atlantic states. Some of our nation's oldest cities are in the New England region. The nation's largest city, New York, is in the Mid-Atlantic region.

Nine states in the East are on the coast. A **coast** is land that borders an ocean. Coastal areas form a landform region called the coastal plain. A **coastal plain** is flat, level land along a coast.

Western New York The Genesee River flows between steep cliffs and thick forests. The cliffs show layers of rock.

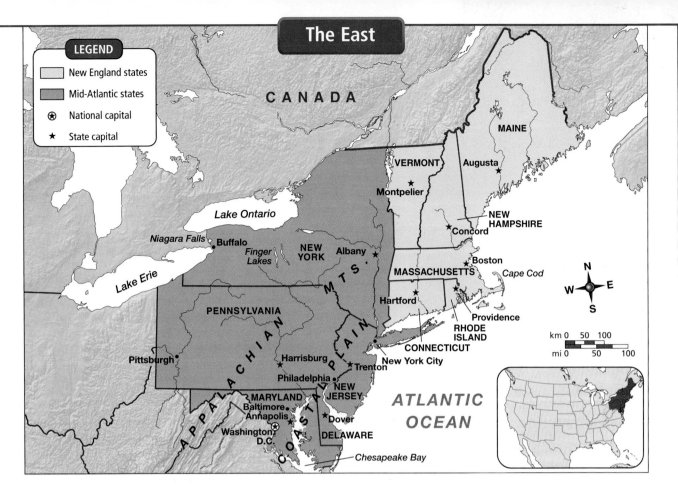

The East Two main landform regions are the Appalachian Mountains and the coastal plain.

Mountains and Plains

The Appalachian Mountains were formed by the movement of the earth. Over millions of years, two moving continents came together. The land between them slowly buckled and rose up. These huge piles of rocks became the Appalachians.

Wind, weather, and the water flowing in rivers slowly wore the Appalachians down. Glaciers also changed the mountains' shape. They carved out valleys or leveled the land with the rocks and dirt they left behind.

East of the Appalachians is the coastal plain. In northern New England, this plain lies mostly underwater.

It is wider from Massachusetts to Florida. Here, the plain has major cities, farms, and factories. Rock and sand left from glaciers formed islands with sandy beaches, such as Long Island. They also formed capes, such as Cape Cod. A **cape** is a point of land that sticks out into the water.

More people live on the coastal plain than in the mountains. The land is less rugged and closer to water routes. In the mountains, some people mine coal or cut down trees for timber. People also farm on the mountainsides and in the mountain valleys.

REVIEW Why are more cities built on the coastal plain than in the mountains?

Winter Nor'easter Waves pounded the Massachusetts coast in this March 2001 storm. Heavy snow forced many schools to close.

Bodies of Water

The East is a land of lakes, rivers, and ocean. As rivers flow from mountains down to the plain, great changes in elevation create waterfalls. Waterfalls made early travel on rivers difficult. However, people learned to use the water's force to power machines in mills and factories. The usefulness of water power led to the growth of major cities on these waterways.

People built settlements near the best harbors along the Atlantic coast. These settlements grew into cities. Ships carrying people and goods from other continents arrived in the harbors and bays. A **bay** is a body of water partly surrounded by land but open to the sea. The Chesapeake Bay, which reaches into Maryland, is important for shipping. It also supports thousands of plants and animals.

Climate and Its Effects

Main Idea The East has a temperate climate.

The East lies in the middle latitudes, about halfway between the North Pole and the equator. This location gives it four seasons and a temperate climate. Temperate means without extremes, such as the very cold weather in the Arctic or the very hot weather near the equator. Cool breezes blow from the Atlantic Ocean on hot days, and warm breezes blow on cold days. Winters in the East are cold and snowy, though, and summers are warm and humid.

The East sometimes has storms called "nor'easters." These storms bring strong winds from the northeast. Nor'easters also bring high ocean waves and heavy snow or rain. People need warm clothing and snow shovels to help them cope with winter conditions.

Plants and Animals

Climate affects the plants and animals that can live in a region. In the East, trees such as maple, birch, hickory, and oak drop their leaves before winter. This helps them survive the lack of water in the frozen soil.

Eastern animals must cope with both cold winters and changing food supplies. Squirrels bury nuts during the warmer months. In the winter, when food is hard to find, they can dig up the nuts and eat them. Other animals, such as black bears, hibernate during the winter. They use leaves and twigs to make a den in a cave or other shelter. Then they sleep for up to 100 days. Raccoons, skunks, and chipmunks also hibernate during the winter.

REVIEW In what ways does the climate of the East affect people, animals, and plants?

Lesson Summary

- The landforms of the East include mountains and plains.

- Rivers, harbors, and bays are important for development.

- The climate of the East is temperate, but winters are cold and snowy.

Why It Matters . . .

Water power, travel routes, and a temperate climate helped the East develop.

Black Bear Bears sleep through the coldest part of eastern winters.

Lesson Review

❶ **VOCABULARY** Write a paragraph about the eastern **coast.** Include **capes** and **bays** in your paragraph.

❷ 🔄 **READING SKILL** List two **details** that support this **main idea:** People learned to use bodies of water in the East.

❸ **MAIN IDEA: Geography** Describe two landforms and two waterways that a visitor to the East might see.

❹ **MAIN IDEA: Culture** Explain one effect of the climate on people's lives in the East.

❺ **CRITICAL THINKING: Fact and Opinion** Write one fact about New England. Then write an opinion based on that fact.

HANDS ON **SCIENCE ACTIVITY** Use a reference book, such as an encyclopedia, to find out why the leaves of certain trees change color in the fall. Draw a diagram to show the process.

Resources and Economy

READING SKILL

Classify Use a chart to list some natural resources of the East.

Natural Resources

Build on What You Know Suppose you want to sell lemonade in your neighborhood. What price will you charge? Every business owner must choose what to sell, where to sell it, and for how much.

Natural Resources of the East

Main Idea The natural resources of the East include forests, soil, and minerals.

The East has fewer of some natural resources than other regions. For example, western states have more minerals than eastern states. However, the East has rivers, forests, farmland, fish, and the ocean. People use these resources to make goods for themselves and to sell to other people.

The Appalachian Mountains contain coal. Workers mine coal in Pennsylvania. Power plants burn it to make electricity. In Maine and Vermont, workers dig out granite and marble. These kinds of stone are used in buildings and monuments.

Coal Mine Workers take coal from mine shafts dug deep into the ground.

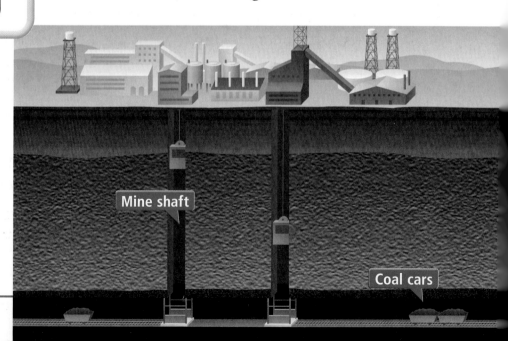

Mine shaft

Coal cars

Natural Resources of the East

Resource	Uses
Granite	Stones for building
Marble	Monuments, tombs, parts of buildings
Coal	Fuel to make electricity, steel, iron, glass, stone, paper
Forests/Wood	Building materials, furniture, paper, fuel, maple syrup
Soil	Fruits, vegetables, grain, dairy cows
Fish	Food, fertilizer
Rivers/Ocean	Moving goods or people, source of water and power, fish

SKILL **Reading Charts** Which resources are used for fuel or power?

Apple Picking In the fall, easterners can pick their own apples.

Using the East's Resources

In the East, many houses are made of wood. Forests provide wood for buildings, paper, furniture, and fuel. Wood can also be used to make chemicals for many other products, including plastics and textiles.

Do you like pancakes with syrup for breakfast? Maple syrup comes from sugar maple trees. Vermont produces more maple syrup than any other state. Maine, Massachusetts, New York, and New Hampshire also produce syrup.

The soil and climate of the East allow farmers to use their land in different ways. Blueberries grow well in the soil of Maine and New Hampshire. The soil of the Aroostook Valley in Maine is perfect for potatoes.

Massachusetts and New Jersey have sandy marshes where farmers can grow cranberries. The warm, rainy summers in New York and Vermont make grasses grow well. These conditions are good for dairy cows, which eat the grasses. Eastern farmers also grow vegetables such as tomatoes, corn, and beans. Some farmers raise fruit trees, including apple and peach trees.

The Atlantic Ocean is an important resource for the East. From Maine to Maryland, people catch lobsters, sardines, flounder, and bass. Maryland and Delaware produce many blue crabs.

REVIEW Why is the farmland of the East an important natural resource?

Working in the East

Main Idea In a market economy, people decide what to make, buy, and sell.

A nation's economy is the system in which it uses resources to meet its needs and wants. The United States has a market economy. In a **market economy,** people are free to decide what to make, how to make it, and for whom to make it. If the law allows it, they can run any business they want.

A market economy is different from a command economy. In a command economy, the government decides what to make, who will make it, and who will get it. The government also sets the prices for goods.

Business owners keep their profits in a market economy. Profit is the money left over after a business pays its expenses. Some businesses make profits by selling natural resources. Others make goods from resources. Then they sell the goods. Paper, maple syrup, and furniture are goods.

Some businesses sell services that people want. A service is any kind of work that one person does for another person as a job. Lawyers, plumbers, and engineers all provide services. In recent years, more and more people have worked in service businesses. Many of these service jobs involve computers, or information technology.

Market Economy In a market economy, people have many choices.

Trading Resources

Businesses use trade to get the resources they want. Trade begins when one person has what another wants. These people exchange resources or money for goods or services. In that way, both people get what they want. When people trade a lot, the economy grows.

Moving goods is important for trade. Imagine that a chemical factory in Delaware needs to buy raw materials from an owner in another region. The factory must pay a trucking company to bring the materials to the factory. Many businesses settle near big cities because the roads, waterways, and airports in these cities make trade easier.

Factories in the East make many kinds of goods. For example, New Jersey businesses make chemicals, medicines, machinery, and clothing. In Connecticut, factory workers make weapons, sewing machines, jet engines, and clocks.

Many eastern businesses provide services. For example, banks offer a safe place for people to keep their money. Banks also lend money to people. Many banks started in eastern cities. Today, Philadelphia and New York City are important banking centers. In banks, people can work as bank tellers, loan officers, and even computer programmers.

REVIEW How is making goods different from performing services?

Service Businesses in the East

Banking	Insurance
Communication	Legal services
Education	Recreation
Engineering	Repairs
Health care	Restaurants
Hotels	Tourism

Services Restaurants perform a service. The chart shows other service businesses that provide jobs in the East.

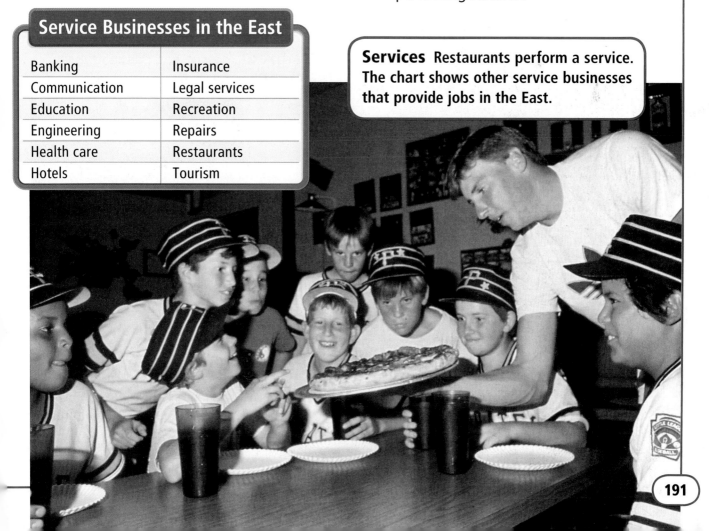

Elements of Business

Main Idea In a system of private ownership, individuals own the factors of production.

A business needs equipment, workers, and often some raw materials. These things are the factors of production. Factors of production are the people and materials needed to make goods or provide services. The four factors are labor, capital, land, and entrepreneurship (ahn truh pruh NUHR ship). Entrepreneurs are people who are willing to take the risk of starting a new business.

Factors of Production Skilled workers are needed to make sap into maple syrup.

SKILL **Reading Visuals** What capital resources do you see in the pictures below?

Some businesses use natural resources. All businesses use human resources and capital resources. **Human resources** are the services, knowledge, skills, and intelligence that workers provide. **Capital resources** are the tools, machines, buildings, and other equipment that a business uses to make goods or provide services.

The East has a long tradition of successful businesses. Settlers near York, Maine, built the nation's first sawmill in 1623. Philadelphia had the nation's first bank and its first daily newspaper in the 1780s. Some of the nation's oldest companies still operate in the East today.

Maple Syrup Production

Natural and capital resources + Human resource = Product

Entrepreneurs and Ownership

Entrepreneurs are people who use the factors of production to start new businesses. Entrepreneurs take risks when they start new businesses. They invest their time and money in their businesses. However, people might not want to buy their goods or services. Then, instead of making a profit, the entrepreneurs could lose money. Entrepreneurs must plan carefully and work hard to have the best chance of earning a profit.

Entrepreneurs own their own businesses. Private ownership is an important part of a market economy. Private ownership means that individual people, not the government, own the factors of production. Individuals also make their own business decisions, hoping to earn a profit.

REVIEW Why is private ownership important in a market economy?

Entrepreneurship A person who opens a new store is an entrepreneur.

Lesson Summary

- People use the natural resources of the East to make products and trade with businesses in other areas.

- Businesses make profits by selling resources, goods, and services.

- Entrepreneurship and resources—natural, human, and capital—are necessary in any business.

Why It Matters . . .

A market economy can give people more freedom to choose how they work and live.

Lesson Review

❶ **VOCABULARY** Explain how **human resources** and **capital resources** are used to make goods.

❷ **READING SKILL** List two things that can be **classified** as human resources and two that can be classified as capital resources.

❸ **MAIN IDEA: Geography** What are two natural resources of the East, and how are they used?

❹ **MAIN IDEA: Economics** In what way is a market economy different from a command economy?

❺ **CRITICAL THINKING: Analyze** Why might someone start a business near a city?

HANDS ON **INTERVIEW ACTIVITY** Interview several adults who work in different jobs. Ask each person if his or her job involves making a product or providing a service. Make a chart of these products and services.

Skillbuilder

Use Reference Materials

To find facts about a topic, you can use reference materials. Reference books include encyclopedias, atlases, almanacs, and dictionaries. Nonfiction books and the Internet are other sources of information.

▶ **VOCABULARY**
index
search engine

Learn the Skill

Step 1: Decide on the topic you want to explore. Then list words or ideas that are related to your topic. These key words will help you find information.

Topic: The East

agriculture in the East
East's economy
Eastern farms
Eastern U.S. crops
New England farming
Mid-Atlantic agriculture

Step 2: Choose reference sources that might have the information you need. Encyclopedias have basic facts on many people, places, things, and events. Atlases have maps and geographical information. Almanacs give up-to-date facts. The Internet offers a wide variety of information. Ask a librarian to help you find Web sites you can trust.

Step 3: Use your key words or ideas to look up information in your sources. Many reference sources organize information alphabetically. Other sources have indexes. An **index** is an alphabetical listing of the topics in a book. To find information on the Internet, type key words into a computer search engine. A **search engine** is a Web site that finds other Web sites related to your key words.

temperature, 395
United States
  East
  agriculture, 692
  industry, 694
  minerals, 697
  population, 700
  Midwest
  agriculture, 840

| New England farming | **Search** |

Search results for *New England farming*

Showing 1–10 of 433,657

1. **New England Farming**
State and county yearly reports. Fruit, vegeta
other crops, livestock, dairy. Total spending.
Total income. Exports …

2. **New England Farms**
Complete list of farms in New England. Lists
grown. Provides map of farm locations …

3. **New England Farmer's Association**
Support for farmers of New England. Non-pr
organization …

Practice the Skill

1 Which reference source do you think would be the most helpful in locating major cities in the East?

2 Suppose you want to find the populations of the largest cities in the United States. Which reference source do you think would be the most helpful?

3 Make a list of key words that would help you find information about the major industries of the East.

4 Which reference source would you use to find basic facts about a topic?

Apply the Skill

Write a short paragraph explaining the steps you would take to find information on mineral resources of the East.

The Mid-Atlantic

VOCABULARY

skyscraper
commuter

Vocabulary Strategy

commuter

Find the word **commute** in **commuter**. To commute means to travel to and from work.

READING SKILL

Compare and Contrast
List details that compare and contrast each area of the Mid-Atlantic region.

New York City	Suburbs	Rural Areas

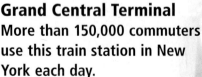

Grand Central Terminal
More than 150,000 commuters use this train station in New York each day.

Build on What You Know How tall is your school? If it were 100 stories tall, it would hold a lot of students! In large cities, many people work in buildings even taller than that.

Where People Live

Main Idea People in the Mid-Atlantic region live and work in big cities, suburbs, and rural areas.

The Mid-Atlantic region contains Delaware, Maryland, New Jersey, New York, Pennsylvania, and the nation's capital, Washington, D.C. It is the most thickly settled region in the nation. Many major cities are found in the Mid-Atlantic. One is New York City, the largest city in the United States.

New York's location at the mouth of the Hudson River led to its growth. European settlers used the river and New York's harbor to move goods from inland North America to Europe. Shipping led to the growth of trade. Today, New York is a world center for banking, publishing, advertising, and technology.

Living in New York City

New York City started on an island called Manhattan. As the city grew, people settled in four new neighborhoods—Queens, Staten Island, the Bronx, and Brooklyn. Today, skyscrapers fill Manhattan. A **skyscraper** is a very tall building.

New York is filled with people from around the world. More than eight million people live in the city. Millions of others visit each year. They come to shop, to go to museums, and to attend plays. Most people rely on subways, buses, or taxis to move around this crowded city.

Suburbs of the Mid-Atlantic

Suburbs surround the majo_ of the Mid-Atlantic region. A subu__ a community that grows outside of a larger city. People began to move from cities to the suburbs in the 1800s. They wanted to find less crowded places to live.

Some people are commuters. A **commuter** travels between work and home each day. People in suburbs also drive their cars to work, to schools, and to shopping malls.

REVIEW Why was New York's location important to its growth?

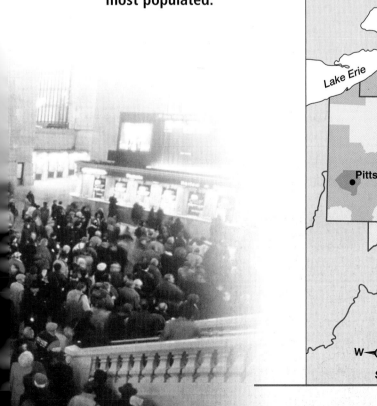

Mid-Atlantic Population
The coastal plain of the Mid-Atlantic region is the most populated.

Mid-Atlantic Population

LEGEND

People per square mile

- 99 or fewer
- 100 to 499
- 500 to 4,999
- 5,000 or more

CANADA

Lake Ontario

Rochester
Buffalo
NEW YORK
Albany
Lake Erie

PENNSYLVANIA
Newark
New York
Pittsburgh

Philadelphia
NEW JERSEY

MARYLAND
Baltimore
Washington, D.C.
DELAWARE

ATLANTIC OCEAN

km 0   50   100
mi 0   50   100

N
W   E
S

Rural Areas

Although urban and suburban areas cover much of the Mid-Atlantic, forest and farmland fill large areas, too. The soil here is much easier to farm than it is in New England. Mid-Atlantic farms produce flowers, chickens, and many dairy products. Mines in Pennsylvania rank fourth in producing the most coal in the United States.

The natural environment and historic landmarks draw millions of visitors to the Mid-Atlantic states. They enjoy winter sports in the mountains of New York and Pennsylvania. They sunbathe on Delaware and New Jersey beaches. They boat and fish in the Chesapeake Bay. Many visitors also tour our nation's capital.

State Governments

Main Idea State government is divided into three branches.

Each state has a capital city where the state government is located. Within the state capital is a state house or a building called the capitol. This is where lawmakers, or legislators, meet.

Each state has a constitution. The constitution divides state government into three parts, or branches. These are the legislative, executive, and judicial branches. The legislative branch makes laws. The executive branch puts the laws into action. The judicial branch interprets, or explains, the laws in the courts.

Suppose the legislative branch of the New Jersey government made a law that provided money for new parks. The governor would sign the law to put it into action. The governor is the official who leads the executive branch. If people disagreed about the law, the judicial branch would have to decide exactly what the law meant.

Annapolis, Maryland Maryland's capitol is the oldest still in use. It was built in 1772.

SKILL Reading Chart Which people in Maryland's government are not elected?

Maryland State Government

Executive	Legislative	Judicial
Governor • Elected by the voters • Serves a 4-year term	**Senators, Delegates** • Elected by the voters • Serve 4-year terms	**Judges** • Some elected by voters • Some appointed to 10-year terms

Public and Private Services

State governments are public institutions. That means they serve the state's people and communities. State services for the public include education, fire and police protection, and highways. States pay for public services by collecting taxes. A tax is a fee paid to the government. States may tax the money people earn, the property they own, and the things they buy.

State services are public. Services provided by a group or individual are private. For example, New Jersey builds public roads for everyone to use. However, private companies sell the cars and trucks that travel on the roads.

REVIEW What are the three branches of state government, and what do they do?

Lesson Summary

- The Mid-Atlantic has many large cities surrounded by suburbs.

- New York City, a financial and industrial center, is the biggest city in this region.

- Rural regions of the Mid-Atlantic support farming, mining, and tourism.

- State governments divide power among three branches.

Why It Matters . . .

Millions of people live and work in the Mid-Atlantic region. Workers in this region provide goods and services to the entire nation and the world.

Lesson Review

❶ **VOCABULARY** Match each vocabulary term with its description.

commuter **skyscraper**

(a) very tall building; (b) travels back and forth

❷ **READING SKILL** Compare and **contrast** public and private services.

❸ **MAIN IDEA: Culture** In what ways is living in a city different from living in a rural area?

❹ **MAIN IDEA: Geography** What is one difference between a capital city and other cities?

❺ **FACTS TO KNOW** Which branch of government does the governor lead?

❻ **CRITICAL THINKING: Infer** Why do you think people from so many countries live in New York City?

HANDS ON **CURRENT EVENTS ACTIVITY** Read about what is happening in one Mid-Atlantic state. What is one major issue the state's government is dealing with?

Visual Summary

1 – 3. Write a description of each item named below.

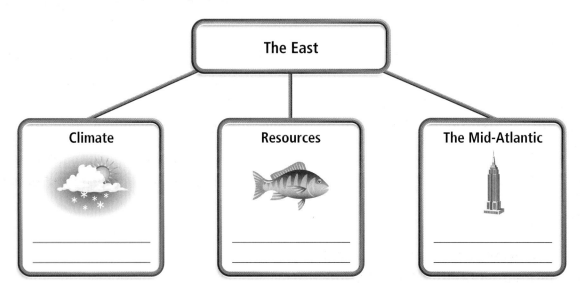

The East

Climate

Resources

The Mid-Atlantic

Facts and Main Ideas

✓ **TEST PREP** Answer each question below.

4. **Geography** In what ways have glaciers affected landforms in the East?

5. **Economics** In a market economy, what decisions must a business owner make?

6. **Economics** In what ways do businesses get resources?

7. **Geography** What is the most thickly settled region in the United States?

8. **Technology** Name some of the goods made in factories in the East.

Vocabulary

✓ **TEST PREP** Choose the correct word from the list below to complete each sentence.

cape, p. 185
human resources, p. 192
commuter, p. 197

9. Skills provided by workers in a factory are _____.

10. A point of land that sticks out into the water is a _____.

11. A _____ is someone who makes a daily trip from a home in the suburbs to a job in the city.

Apply Skills

✔ **TEST PREP** **Use Reference Materials** Use what you have learned about reference materials to answer each question.

12. Which source would be the most helpful in locating major rivers in the East?

    A. an atlas
    B. an encyclopedia
    C. an almanac
    D. the Internet

13. What would be the best way to find out whether a book titled *Animals of the Northeast* has information about black bears?

    A. Look up "black bear" in the index.
    B. Read the book cover.
    C. Skim all of the pages.
    D. Look at all the pictures.

14. Which key word or phrase would be most helpful in finding information about tourism in the Mid-Atlantic states?

    A. Chesapeake Bay
    B. tourism
    C. Mid-Atlantic historic landmarks
    D. winter sports

Critical Thinking

✔ **TEST PREP** Write a short paragraph to answer each question below.

15. Cause and Effect Why have many people in the East chosen to live on the coastal plain instead of in the mountains?

16. Infer Why might more people in the East choose to build houses out of wood instead of brick or stone?

Activities

 Art Activity Draw pictures of some of the natural resources of the East that show how people have used them.

 Writing Activity Write a personal essay describing what you think the East's most important resource is.

 Technology
Writing Process Tips
Get help with your essay at
www.eduplace.com/kids/hmss/

Review and Test Prep

Vocabulary and Main Ideas

✔ **TEST PREP** Write a sentence to answer each question.

1. What are some of the features of a **coastal plain** ?

2. Why would a group of people build a settlement near a harbor or a **bay** ?

3. What is the difference between a **market economy** and a command economy?

4. Explain how a **cape** is different from a **coast.**

5. How is a **skyscraper** different from other types of buildings?

6. Is an office building a **capital resource** or a **human resource** ?

Critical Thinking

✔ **TEST PREP** Write a short paragraph to answer each question.

7. Cause and Effect What are some natural resources of the East? How do they help determine the jobs that people do?

8. Evaluate Describe a suburb. Why do people choose to live in suburbs instead of cities?

Apply Skills

✔ **TEST PREP** Use what you have learned about reference materials to answer each question.

9. Explain how you might use a search engine to learn more about the history of banking in Philadelphia.

10. Make a list of key words that you think would help you find information about agriculture in New England.

11. Suppose you want to find the populations of the state capitals of each of the states in the Mid-Atlantic region. Write a short paragraph explaining the steps you would take to find this information.

Unit Activity

Make a State Government Poster

- Make a chart of the three branches of your state government. List the name of the governor and other top officials.

- Find out when and where the state legislature meets and what law they are planning to vote on. Add the information to your poster.

- Write a sentence stating how you think they should vote on the issue.

- Present your poster to the class.

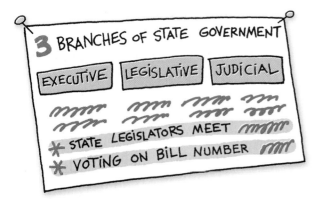

At the Library

You may find this book at your school or public library.

Capital by Lynn Curlee

This history of Washington, D.C., provides information on the National Mall.

WEEKLY (WR) READER

Current Events Project

Create a bulletin board about the freedoms that Americans have.

- Find information about the Constitution and the Bill of Rights.

- Pick one of the ten Amendments. Think about how it keeps Americans free today.

- Write a paragraph about your amendment. Include drawings of people using their freedom.

- Post your paragraph on a bulletin board.

Technology

Weekly Reader online offers social studies articles. Go to: **www.eduplace.com/kids/hmss/**

References

Citizenship Handbook

Pledge of Allegiance R2

Excerpts from Pennsylvania Constitution R3

Character Traits R4

Pennsylvania Governors R6

Pennsylvania Counties R8

Songs of Our Nation R12

History Makers—Biographical Dictionary R16

Resources

Geographic Terms R20

Atlas R22

Gazetteer R27

Glossary R31

Index R35

Acknowledgments R41

Pledge of Allegiance

I pledge allegiance to the flag of the United States of America and to the republic for which it stands, one Nation, under God, indivisible, with liberty and justice for all.

Spanish
Prometo lealtad a la bandera
de los Estados Unidos de América,
y a la república que representa,
una nación bajo Dios, indivisible,
con libertad y justicia para todos.

Pennsylvania Constitution Excerpts

The Constitution of the Commonwealth of Pennsylvania

ADOPTED 1776

Preamble

We, the people of the Commonwealth of Pennsylvania, grateful to Almighty God for the blessings of civil and religious liberty, and humbly invoking His guidance, do ordain and establish this Constitution.

Article 1
DECLARATION OF RIGHTS

SECTION 2

All power is inherent in the people, and all free governments are founded on their authority and instituted for their peace, safety, and happiness.

Article 3
PUBLIC SCHOOL SYSTEM

SECTION 14

The General Assembly shall provide for the maintenance and support of a thorough and efficient system of public education to serve the needs of the Commonwealth.

Article 1
ELECTIONS

SECTION 5

Elections shall be free and equal; and no power, civil, or military, shall at any time interfere to prevent the free exercise of the right of suffrage.

Article 4
DUTIES OF GOVERNOR

SECTION 2

The supreme executive power shall be vested in the Governor, who shall take care that the laws be faithfully executed; he shall be chosen on the day of the general election, by the qualified electors of the Commonwealth. . .

Character Traits

Character includes feelings, thoughts, and behaviors. A character trait is something people show by the way they act. To act bravely shows courage, and courage is one of several character traits.

Positive character traits, such as honesty, caring, and courage, lead to positive actions. Character traits are also called "life skills." Life skills can help you do your best, and doing your best leads to reaching your goals.

Edith Sampson

Responsibility Sampson worked hard to achieve her goals. She became a lawyer and a judge. She was also the first African American woman to serve as a delegate to the United Nations.

Gifford Pinchot

Civic virtue Pinchot cared deeply about Pennsylvania's land and people. As governor, he created programs that worked to protect the state's forests and provide jobs for citizens.

Courage means acting bravely. Doing what you believe to be good and right, and telling the truth, requires courage.

Patriotism means working for the goals of your country. When you show national pride, you are being patriotic.

Responsibility is taking care of work that needs to be done. Responsible people are reliable and trustworthy, which means they can be counted on.

Respect means paying attention to what other people want and believe. The "golden rule," or treating others as you would like to be treated, shows thoughtfulness and respect.

Fairness means working to make things fair for everyone. Often one needs to try again and again to achieve fairness. This is diligence, or not giving up.

Civic virtue is good citizenship. It means doing things, such as cooperating and solving problems, to help communities live and work well together.

Caring means noticing what others need and helping them get what they need. Feeling concern or compassion is another way to define caring.

Pennsylvania Governors

State Governors

Thomas Mifflin
Term: 1790–1799
Political Party: None
Lifespan: (1744–1800)
Birthplace: Philadelphia, Pennsylvania

Thomas McKean
Term: 1799–1808
Political Party: Jeffersonian
Lifespan: (1734–1817)
Birthplace: Chester County, Pennsylvania

Simon Snyder
Term: 1808–1817
Political Party: Jeffersonian Democrat
Lifespan: (1759–1819)
Birthplace: Lancaster, Pennsylvania

William Findlay
Term: 1817–1820
Political Party: Jeffersonian Democrat
Lifespan: (1768–1846)
Birthplace: Mercersburg, Pennsylvania

Joseph Heister
Term: 1820–1823
Political Party: Jeffersonian Democrat
Lifespan: (1752–1832)
Birthplace: Berks County, Pennsylvania

John A. Schulze
Term: 1823–1829
Political Party: Jeffersonian Democrat
Lifespan: (1774–1852)
Birthplace: Tulpehocken Township, Pennsylvania

George Wolf
Term: 1829–1835
Political Party: Jeffersonian Democrat
Lifespan: (1777–1840)
Birthplace: Northampton County, Pennsylvania

Joseph Ritner
Term: 1835–1839
Political Party: Anti-Masonic
Lifespan: (1780–1869)
Birthplace: Alsace Township, Pennsylvania

David R. Porter
Term: 1839–1845
Political Party: Jacksonian Democrat
Lifespan: (1788–1867)
Birthplace: Montgomery County, Pennsylvania

Francis R. Shunk
Term: 1845–1848
Political Party: Jacksonian Democrat
Lifespan: (1788–1848)
Birthplace: Trappe, Pennsylvania

William F. Johnston
Term: 1848–1852
Political Party: Whig
Lifespan: (1808–1872)
Birthplace: Greensburg, Pennsylvania

William Bigler
Term: 1852–1855
Political Party: Democratic
Lifespan: (1814–1880)
Birthplace: Cumberland County, Pennsylvania

James Pollock
Term: 1855–1858
Political Party: Whig and Republican
Lifespan: (1811–1890)
Birthplace: Milton, Pennsylvania

William F. Packer
Term: 1858–1861
Political Party: Democratic
Lifespan: (1807–1870)
Birthplace: Howard Township, Pennsylvania

Andrew G. Curtin
Term: 1861–1867
Political Party: Peoples Party
Lifespan: (1817–1894)
Birthplace: Bellefonte, Pennsylvania

John W. Geary
Term: 1867–1873
Political Party: Republican
Lifespan: (1819–1873)
Birthplace: Mount Pleasant, Pennsylvania

John F. Hartranft
Term: 1873–1879
Political Party: Republican
Lifespan: (1830–1889)
Birthplace: New Hanover Township, Pennsylvania

Henry M. Hoyt
Term: 1879–1883
Political Party: Republican
Lifespan: (1830–1892)
Birthplace: Kingston, Pennsylvania

Robert E. Pattison
Term: 1883–1887 and 1891–1895
Political Party: Democratic
Lifespan: (1850–1904)
Birthplace: Maryland

James A. Beaver
Term: 1887–1891
Political Party: Republican
Lifespan: (1837–1914)
Birthplace: Millerstown, Pennsylvania

Daniel H. Hastings
Term: 1895–1899
Political Party: Republican
Lifespan: (1849–1903)
Birthplace: Lamar Township, Pennsylvania

William A. Stone
Term: 1899–1903
Political Party: Republican
Lifespan: (1846–1920)
Birthplace: Delmar, Pennsylvania

Samuel W. Pennypacker
Term: 1903–1907
Political Party: Republican
Lifespan: (1843–1916)
Birthplace: Phoenixville, Pennsylvania

Edwin S. Stuart
Term: 1907–1911
Political Party: Republican
Lifespan: (1853–1937)
Birthplace: Philadelphia, Pennsylvania

State Governors (continued)

John K. Tener
Term: 1911–1915
Political Party: Republican
Lifespan: (1863–1946)
Birthplace: Ireland

Martin G. Brumbaugh
Term: 1915–1919
Political Party: Republican
Lifespan: (1862–1930)
Birthplace: Huntingdon County, Pennsylvania

William C. Sproul
Term: 1919–1923
Political Party: Republican and Washington
Lifespan: (1870–1928)
Birthplace: Colerain Township, Pennsylvania

Gifford Pinchot
Term: 1923–1927 and 1931–1935
Political Party: Republican
Lifespan: (1865–1946)
Birthplace: Connecticut

John S. Fisher
Term: 1927–1931
Political Party: Republican
Lifespan: (1867–1940)
Birthplace: South Mahoning Township, Pennsylvania

George H. Earle III
Term: 1935–1939
Political Party: Democratic
Lifespan: (1890–1974)
Birthplace: Devon, Pennsylvania

Arthur H. James
Term: 1939–1943
Political Party: Republican
Lifespan: (1883–1973)
Birthplace: Plymouth, Pennsylvania

Edward Martin
Term: 1943–1947
Political Party: Republican
Lifespan: (1879–1967)
Birthplace: Washington Township, Pennsylvania

John C. Bell Jr.
Term: January 2–21, 1947
Political Party: Republican
Lifespan: (1892–1974)
Birthplace: Philadelphia, Pennsylvania

James H. Duff
Term: 1947–1951
Political Party: Republican
Lifespan: (1883–1969)
Birthplace: Mansfield, Pennsylvania

John S. Fine
Term: 1951–1955
Political Party: Republican
Lifespan: (1893–1978)
Birthplace: Alden, Pennsylvania

George M. Leader
Term: 1955–1959
Political Party: Democratic
Lifespan: 1918–
Birthplace: York County, Pennsylvania

David L. Lawrence
Term: 1959–1963
Political Party: Democratic
Lifespan: (1889–1966)
Birthplace: Pittsburgh, Pennsylvania

William W. Scranton
Term: 1963–1967
Political Party: Republican
Lifespan: 1917–
Birthplace: Connecticut

Raymond P. Shafer
Term: 1967–1971
Political Party: Republican
Lifespan: 1917–
Birthplace: New Castle, Pennsylvania

Milton J. Shapp
Term: 1971–1979
Political Party: Democratic
Lifespan: (1912–1994)
Birthplace: Ohio

Dick Thornburgh
Term: 1979–1987
Political Party: Republican
Lifespan: 1932–
Birthplace: Pittsburgh, Pennsylvania

Robert P. Casey
Term: 1987–1995
Political Party: Democratic
Lifespan: (1932–2000)
Birthplace: New York

Tom Ridge
Term: 1995–2001
Political Party: Republican
Lifespan: 1945–
Birthplace: Munhall, Pennsylvania

Mark S. Schweiker
Term: 2001–2003
Political Party: Republican
Lifespan: 1953–
Birthplace: Levittown, Pennsylvania

Edward Rendell
Term: 2003–
Political Party: Democratic
Lifespan: 1944–
Birthplace: New York

Pennsylvania Counties

County	County Seat	Year Organized	Population	Origin of Name
Adams	Gettysburg	1800	96,456	for President John Adams
Allegheny	Pittsburgh	1788	1,261,303	for the Allegheny River
Armstrong	Kittanning	1800	71,659	For General John Armstrong, who served as Secretary of War under President James Madison
Beaver	Beaver	1800	178,697	for the Beaver River
Bedford	Bedford	1771	49,941	for the Duke of Bedford, a leader in British Parliament
Berks	Reading	1752	385,307	for Berkshire, England
Blair	Hollidaysburg	1846	127,175	for U.S. Supreme Court Justice John Blair
Bradford	Towanda	1810	62,643	for William Bradford, second U.S. Attorney General
Bucks	Doylestown	1682	613,110	for Buckinghamshire, England
Butler	Butler	1800	180,040	for General Richard Butler, an officer in the American Revolution
Cambria	Ebensburg	1804	149,453	for Cambria township in Somerset County
Cameron	Emporium	1860	5,777	for U.S. Senator Simon Cameron
Carbon	Jim Thorpe	1843	60,131	name alludes to deposits of coal
Centre	Bellefonte	1800	141,636	for its location at the center of the state
Chester	West Chester	1682	457,393	for Cheshire, England
Clarion	Clarion	1839	41,208	for the Clarion River
Clearfield	Clearfield	1804	82,874	for Clearfield Creek
Clinton	Lock Haven	1839	37,435	for Governor DeWitt Clinton of New York
Columbia	Bloomsburg	1813	64,605	for explorer Christopher Columbus

County	County Seat	Year Organized	Population	Origin of Name
Crawford	Meadville	1800	89,846	for Colonel William Crawford
Cumberland	Carlisle	1750	219,892	for Cumberland County, England
Dauphin	Harrisburg	1785	253,388	for a French title given to the eldest sons of kings
Delaware	Media	1789	554,432	for the Delaware River
Elk	Ridgway	1843	34,310	for the elk that roamed the county
Erie	Erie	1800	279,966	for Lake Erie
Fayette	Uniontown	1783	146,121	for the Marquis de la Fayette
Franklin	Chambersburg	1784	133,155	for Benjamin Franklin
Forest	Tionesta	1848	4,989	for its forests
Fulton	McConnellsburg	1851	14,534	for Robert Fulton, steamboat inventor
Greene	Waynesburg	1796	40,398	for American Revolution General Nathanael Greene
Huntingdon	Huntingdon	1787	45,865	for the county seat
Indiana	Indiana	1803	89,054	for Indiana Territory
Jefferson	Brookville	1804	45,945	for President Thomas Jefferson
Juniata	Mifflintown	1831	23,065	for the Juniata River
Lackawanna	Scranton	1878	210,458	for the Lackawanna River
Lancaster	Lancaster	1729	482,775	for Lancashire, England
Lawrence	New Castle	1849	93,408	for Oliver Perry's first ship, the U.S. Brig Lawrence
Lebanon	Lebanon	1813	122,652	from a Biblical word meaning "White Mountain"
Lehigh	Allentown	1812	320,517	for the Lehigh River
Luzerne	Wilkes-Barre	1786	313,528	for the Chevalier de la Luzerne, a French diplomat

County	County Seat	Year Organized	Population	Origin of Name
Lycoming	Williamsport	1795	118,438	for Lycoming Creek
McKean	Smethport	1804	45,236	for Governor Thomas McKean
Mercer	Mercer	1800	119,895	for General Hugh Mercer, a leader in the American Revolution
Mifflin	Lewistown	1789	46,335	for Governor Thomas Mifflin
Monroe	Stroudsburg	1836	154,495	for President James Monroe
Montgomery	Norristown	1784	770,747	for American Revolution General Richard Montgomery
Montour	Danville	1850	18,083	For Madame Montour, an Indian interpreter
Northampton	Easton	1752	278,169	For Northamptonshire, England
Northumber-land	Sunbury	1772	93,323	For Northumberland, England
Perry	Bloomfield	1820	44,188	for military leader Oliver Hazard Perry
Philadelphia	Philadelphia	1682	1,479,339	From a Greek word meaning "brotherly love"
Pike	Milford	1814	52,163	for explorer and military General Zebulon Pike
Potter	Coudersport	1804	18,141	for government and military leader James Potter
Schuylkill	Pottsville	1811	147,944	for the Schuylkill River
Snyder	Middleburg	1855	38,015	for Governor Simon Snyder
Somerset	Somerset	1795	79,365	for Somersetshire, England
Sullivan	Laporte	1847	6,427	for Senator Charles Sullivan
Susquehanna	Montrose	1810	41,812	for the Susquehanna River
Tioga	Wellsboro	1804	41,557	for the Tioga River
Union	Lewisburg	1813	42,552	for the Federal Union of states
Venango	Franklin	1800	56,600	from the American Indian name for French Creek

County	County Seat	Year Organized	Population	Origin of Name
Warren	Warren	1800	42,820	for General Joseph Warren, leader in American Revolution
Washington	Washington	1781	204,286	for George Washington
Wayne	Honesdale	1798	49,092	for General Anthony Wayne
Westmoreland	Greensburg	1773	368,224	for a county in England
Wyoming	Tunkhannock	1842	28,153	for the Wyoming Valley
York	York	1749	394,915	for James, Duke of York, who became King of England in 1685

Songs of Our Nation

Who wrote the patriotic songs we sing and why did they do it? There are as many reasons as there are songs.

Our national anthem, "The Star-Spangled Banner," was written by Francis Scott Key. In 1814, this American lawyer watched from a ship as the British attacked Fort McHenry near Baltimore, Maryland. The fight lasted all night. As the morning dawned, Key saw the American flag still flying proudly over the fort. The sight inspired him to write these verses.

"The Star-Spangled Banner"

by Francis Scott Key

O say, can you see, by the dawn's early light,
What so proudly we hailed at the twilight's last gleaming,
Whose broad stripes and bright stars, through the perilous fight,
O'er the ramparts we watched were so gallantly streaming?
And the rockets' red glare, the bombs bursting in air,
Gave proof through the night that our flag was still there
O say, does that Star-Spangled Banner yet wave
O'er the land of the free and the home of the brave?

On the shore, dimly seen through the mists of the deep.
Where the foe's haughty host in dread silence reposes,
What is that which the breeze, o'er the towering steep,
As it fitfully blows, half conceals, half discloses?
Now it catches the gleam of the morning's first beam,
In full glory reflected now shines on the stream;
'Tis the Star-Spangled Banner, O long may it wave
O'er the land of the free and the home of the brave!

O thus be it ever when free man shall stand
Between their loved homes and the war's desolation!
Blest with victory and peace, may the heaven-rescued land
Praise the Power that hath made and preserved us as a nation.
Then conquer we must, for our cause it is just,
And this be our motto: 'In God is our trust.'
And the Star-Spangled Banner in triumph shall wave
O'er the land of the free and the home of the brave.

Fort McHenry

Have you ever heard the tune to the British national anthem? When Samuel F. Smith heard it in 1832, he wrote words so that Americans could sing it. "America," or "My Country, 'Tis of Thee," quickly became a favorite of many people in the United States. It remains a favorite today.

"America"
("My Country, 'Tis of Thee")

by Samuel F. Smith

My country, 'tis of thee,
Sweet land of liberty,
  Of thee I sing;
Land where my fathers died,
Land of the Pilgrims' pride,
From every mountain-side
  Let freedom ring.

My native country, thee,
Land of the noble free,
  Thy name I love;
I love thy rocks and rills,
Thy woods and templed hills;
My heart with rapture thrills
  Like that above.

In 1893, a teacher from the east named Katharine Lee Bates took a trip west. She loved the beauty of the United States, its mountains, plains, and open skies. Bates's poem became the words for the song "America the Beautiful."

"America the Beautiful"

by Katharine Lee Bates

Oh beautiful for spacious skies,
    For amber waves of grain
For purple mountain majesties
    Above the fruited plain.
America! America!
    God shed His grace on thee
And crown thy good with brotherhood
    From sea to shining sea.

O beautiful for patriot dream
    That sees beyond the years
Thine alabaster cities gleam
    Undimmed by human tears.
America! America!
    God shed His grace on thee
And crown thy good with brotherhood
    From sea to shining sea.

Biographical Dictionary

The page number after each entry refers to the place where the person is first mentioned. For more complete references to people, see the Index.

A

Allen, Richard 1760–1831, Leader who helped African American Pennsylvanians create their own schools, churches, and communities (page 65).

Anderson, Marian 1897–1993, Pennsylvanian who became the first successful African American opera singer (page 165).

B

Bartram, John 1699–1777, Scientist from Pennsylvania who is remembered as "the father of American botany" (page 38).

Bessemer, Henry 1813–1898, British engineer who developed a way to make steel that was easier and less expensive than early methods (page 118).

Bonaparte, Napoleon 1769–1821, French ruler who agreed to the Louisiana Purchase (page 73).

Buchanan, James 1791–1868, Pennsylvanian who became the 15th President of the United States, 1857–1861 (page 96).

C

Carnegie, Andrew 1835–1919, Scottish immigrant to Pennsylvania who went on to become the most successful steel company in the United States (page 119).

Carson, Rachel 1907–1964, Pennsylvania biologist who tried to help solve the problem of pollution (page 157).

Charles II 1630–1685, English king who signed the Charter of 1681 granting land in North America to William Penn (page 26).

D

Dickinson, John 1732–1808, Pennsylvania lawyer who wrote series of essays called *Letters From a Farmer in Pennsylvania* protesting British taxes (page 53).

Drake, Edwin 1819–1880, drilled the first oil well in Titusville, Pennsylvania (page 83).

F

Fitch, John 1743–1798, inventor of the steamboat (page 79).

Franklin, Benjamin 1706–1790, Colonial Pennsylvania leader who was a noted inventor and statesman (page 38).

Fulton, Robert 1765–1815, Pennsylvanian who made improvements on the steamboat (page 79).

G

Gallatin, Albert 1761–1849, Pennsylvanian who helped negotiate the Treaty of Ghent, which ended the War of 1812 (page 75).

H

Heinz, Henry J. 1844–1919, Pennsylvanian who developed new innovations for bottling and preserving food, and founded a company that became the largest producer of ketchup in the United States (page 116).

Hendrickson, Cornelius Unknown, Early Dutch explorer to the Delaware Bay area, set up a trading post in the Schuylkill River area (page 23).

Hershey, Milton 1857–1945, Pennsylvanian who founded the Hershey chocolate company (page 116).

Hitler, Adolph 1889–1945, German dictator in the 1930s who led his country into World War II (page 131).

Howard, Liliane Stevens 1872–1967, Pennsylvanian who worked for women's right to vote (page 125).

Hudson, Henry 1575?–1611, English explorer; first European to travel to the Delaware Bay area (page 23).

Jefferson, Thomas 1743–1826, 3rd President of the United States, 1801–1809 (page 73).

Johnson, Lyndon B. 1908–1973, 36th President of the United States; signed the Civil Rights Act of 1964, 1963–1969 (page 132).

Jones, Absalom 1746–1818, Pastor who helped build a community for free blacks in Philadelphia (page 65).

K

Kelley, Florence 1859–1932, Pennsylvanian who worked for the rights of women and workers in the late 1800s (page 125).

Kier, Samuel 1831–1892, Pennsylvanian who refined oil to use for lamp fuel (page 83).

King, Martin Luther, Jr., 1929–1968, Civil Rights leader (page 132).

Lappawinsoe, Chief Unknown, Lenni Lenape leader who signed the Walking Purchase (page 35).

Lee, Robert E. 1807–1870, Civil War general; led the Confederate troops in the Battle of Gettysburg (page 102).

LeMoyne, Dr. F. Julius 1798–1879, Pennsylvania abolitionist before the Civil War (page 95).

Lincoln, Abraham 1809–1865, 16th President of the United States; served as president during the Civil War, and issued the Emancipation Proclamation, 1861–1865 (page 97).

M

Marshall, George 1880–1959, native of Uniontown, Pennsylvania, who became Army Chief of Staff during World War II (page 131).

Masters, Sybilla ?–1720, Pennsylvania woman who invented a machine that ground corn into cornmeal; remembered as the first woman inventor in North America (page 38).

McClellan, George B. 1826–1885, Pennsylvania general during the Civil War (page 101).

Meade, George G. 1815–1872, Pennsylvania general during the Civil War (page 101).

Morgan, John Pierpont 1837–1913, a banker who bought Carnegie Steel from Andrew Carnegie in 1901, and then merged it with other companies to create steel giant U.S. Steel (page 119).

Morris, Robert 1734–1806, Philadelphia banker who gave money to support the Continental Army in the American Revolution (page 56).

Mott, Lucretia 1793–1880, leader of the women's movement who helped start the Philadelphia Female Anti-Slavery Society as well as the first women's rights convention (page 84).

Muhlenberg, John 1746–1807, Pennsylvania general who led troops during the American Revolution (page 59).

N

Nix, Robert Nelson Cornelius, Sr. 1898–1987, Pennsylvanian who served in U.S. Congress from 1958 to 1979; the first African American from Pennsylvania to serve in the U.S. House of Representatives (page 147).

P

Paine, Thomas 1737–1809, Philadelphian who published a booklet called *Common Sense* calling for colonists to declare independence from Britain (page 55).

Penn, Hannah Callowhill 1671–1726, second wife of colonial leader William Penn and important leader in the Pennsylvania colony (page 29).

Penn, William 1644–1718, Englishman who established the Pennsylvania colony (page 26).

Perry, Oliver Hazard 1785–1819, American naval captain who defeated British fleet on Lake Erie during War of 1812 (page 74).

Pickett, George 1825–1875, Confederate military general who took part in the Battle of Gettysburg (page 102).

Pinchot, Gifford 1865–1946, the 30th governor of Pennsylvania, who developed programs to try to help Pennsylvanians during the Depression (page 130).

Pontiac ?–1769, Ottawa chief; united several American Indian nations (page 50).

Printz, Armegott 1627–1676, Swedish immigrant to North America who helped her father, Johan Printz, secure Tinicum Island for the capital of New Sweden (page 24).

Printz, Johan 1592–1663, Swedish military leader; set up boundaries for the colony of New Sweden and the capital of New Sweden at Tinicum Island (page 24).

R

Roosevelt, Franklin D. 1882–1945, 32nd President of the United States who developed a work program during the Depression called the New Deal, 1933–1945 (page 130).

Ross, Elizabeth "Betsy" 1752–1836, used her Philadelphia business to make flags for the Pennsylvania Navy (page 56).

Rustin, Bayard 1910–1987, Pennsylvania Civil Rights leader (page 132).

S

Schwab, Charles 1862–1939, Pennsylvania steel industry leader who practiced philanthropy (page 121).

Smith, John 1580–1631, one of the first explorers to come to present-day Pennsylvania, explored the Chesapeake Bay and the Susquehanna River (page 23).

Stanton, Elizabeth Cady 1815–1902, Women's rights leader who helped to organize the first women's convention (page 84).

Steuben, Frederick von 1730–1794, German military leader who helped train the Continental troops during the American Revolution (page 58).

Stuyvesant, Peter 1610–1672, Dutch leader who encouraged settlers in New Amsterdam to take over Swedish land (page 25).

Swisshelm, Jane Grey 1815–1884, Pittsburgh leader of the women's movement who started a newspaper containing news stories about women's rights (page 84).

 T

Thomson, Elihu 1853–1937 Pennsylvanian who developed a lighting system and eventually founded a company that would become General Electric (page 116).

Wanamaker, John 1838–1922, Philadelphian who established one of the nation's first department stores (page 116).

Washington, George 1732–1799, Military leader in the French and Indian War who became the first president of the United States, 1789–1797 (page 48).

Wayne, Anthony 1745–1796, Pennsylvania military leader during the American Revolution (page 57).

Westinghouse, George 1846–1914, Pennsylvanian who developed a generator to power electric lighting systems (page 116).

Wilson, Woodrow 1856–1924, 28th President of the United States who led the country into World War I, 1913–1921 (page 128).

Woolworth, F.W. 1852–1919, opened the nation's first five-and-dime store in Lancaster, Pennsylvania (page 116).

Geographic Terms

basin
a round area of land surrounded by higher land

bay
part of a lake or ocean that is partially enclosed by land

canyon
a valley with steep cliffs shaped by erosion

cape
a piece of land that points out into a body of water

coast
the land next to a sea or ocean

coastal plain
a flat area of land near an ocean

delta
land that is formed by soil deposited near the mouth of a river

desert
a dry region with little vegetation

fault
a break or crack in the earth's surface

▲ **glacier**
a large ice mass that pushes soil and rocks as it moves

hill
a raised area of land

island
an area of land surrounded by water

isthmus
a narrow piece of land connecting two larger land areas

lake
a large body of water surrounded by land

mountain
a raised mass of land with steep slopes

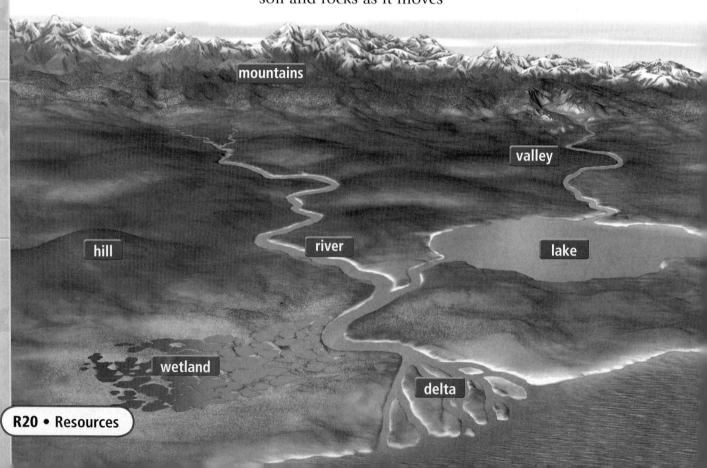

mountains

valley

hill

river

lake

wetland

delta

ocean
a large body of salt water that covers much of Earth's surface

peninsula
a strip of land surrounded by water on three sides

plain
a large area of flat land

plateau
a high, flat area of land

port
a sheltered part of a lake or ocean where ships can dock

prairie
a flat area of grassland with few trees

rain forest
a thick forest that receives heavy rainfall throughout the year

river
a body of water that flows from a high area to a lower area

river basin
an area that is drained by a river

tectonic plate
a huge slab of rock in Earth's crust that can cause earthquakes and volcanoes when it moves

tributary
a river or stream that flows into another river

valley
a low area of land between hills or mountains

▲ **volcano**
an opening in Earth's surface through which melted rock and gases escape

wetland
an area that is soaked with water, such as a marsh or a swamp

plateau

cape

bay

plain

peninsula

coastal plain

Atlas

The World: Political

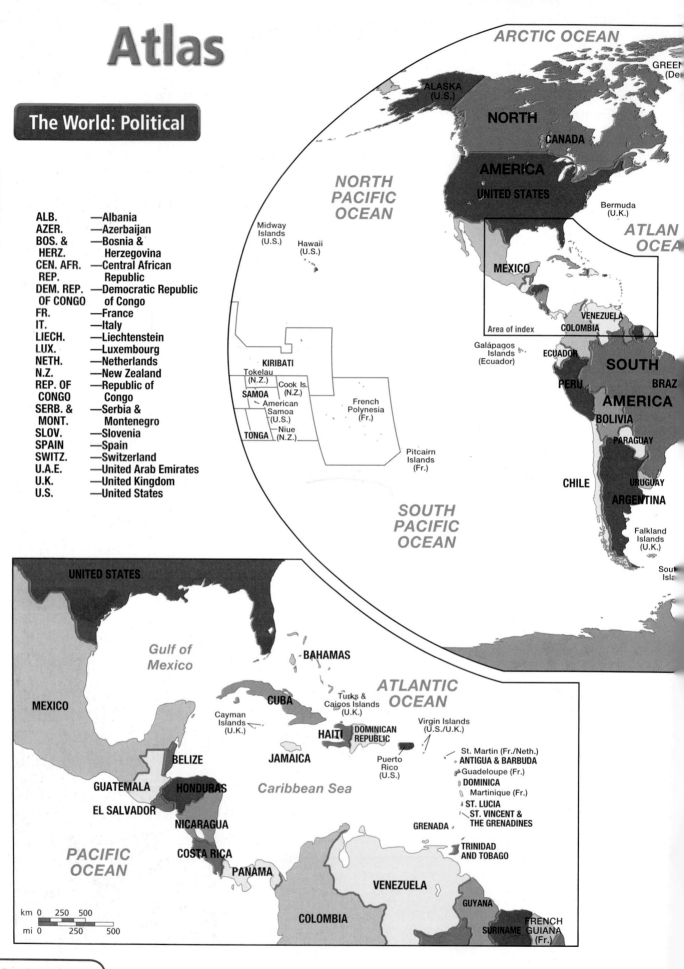

ALB. —Albania
AZER. —Azerbaijan
BOS. & —Bosnia &
HERZ.   Herzegovina
CEN. AFR. —Central African
REP.   Republic
DEM. REP. —Democratic Republic
OF CONGO   of Congo
FR. —France
IT. —Italy
LIECH. —Liechtenstein
LUX. —Luxembourg
NETH. —Netherlands
N.Z. —New Zealand
REP. OF —Republic of
CONGO   Congo
SERB. & —Serbia &
MONT.   Montenegro
SLOV. —Slovenia
SPAIN —Spain
SWITZ. —Switzerland
U.A.E. —United Arab Emirates
U.K. —United Kingdom
U.S. —United States

ARCTIC OCEAN

GREEN
(De

ALASKA
(U.S.)

NORTH

CANADA

NORTH
PACIFIC
OCEAN

AMERICA

UNITED STATES

Bermuda
(U.K.)

ATLAN
OCEA

Midway
Islands
(U.S.)

Hawaii
(U.S.)

MEXICO

Area of index

VENEZUELA
COLOMBIA

Galápagos
Islands
(Ecuador)

ECUADOR

SOUTH

KIRIBATI

Tokelau
(N.Z.)

Cook Is.
(N.Z.)

SAMOA

American
Samoa
(U.S.)

French
Polynesia
(Fr.)

PERU

BRAZ

AMERICA

BOLIVIA

TONGA

Niue
(N.Z.)

PARAGUAY

Pitcairn
Islands
(Fr.)

CHILE

URUGUAY

ARGENTINA

SOUTH
PACIFIC
OCEAN

Falkland
Islands
(U.K.)

Sout
Isla

UNITED STATES

Gulf of
Mexico

BAHAMAS

ATLANTIC
OCEAN

MEXICO

CUBA

Cayman
Islands
(U.K.)

Turks &
Caicos Islands
(U.K.)

Virgin Islands
(U.S./U.K.)

HAITI

DOMINICAN
REPUBLIC

St. Martin (Fr./Neth.)

ANTIGUA & BARBUDA

BELIZE

JAMAICA

Puerto
Rico
(U.S.)

Guadeloupe (Fr.)

DOMINICA

Martinique (Fr.)

GUATEMALA

HONDURAS

Caribbean Sea

ST. LUCIA

ST. VINCENT &
THE GRENADINES

EL SALVADOR

NICARAGUA

GRENADA

TRINIDAD
AND TOBAGO

PACIFIC
OCEAN

COSTA RICA

PANAMA

VENEZUELA

GUYANA

COLOMBIA

FRENCH
GUIANA
(Fr.)

SURINAME

km 0   250   500
mi 0   250   500

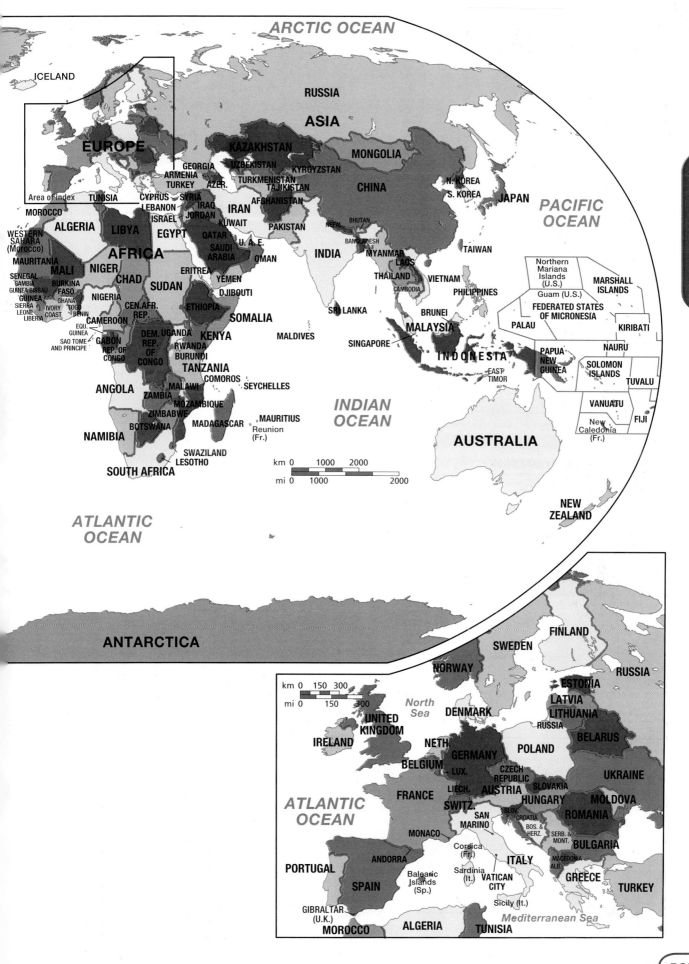

ARCTIC OCEAN

ICELAND

RUSSIA

ASIA

EUROPE

KAZAKHSTAN

MONGOLIA

GEORGIA
ARMENIA
TURKEY
AZER.

UZBEKISTAN

KYRGYZSTAN

CHINA

N. KOREA
S. KOREA

JAPAN

PACIFIC
OCEAN

Area of index

TUNISIA

CYPRUS
LEBANON

SYRIA
IRAQ
JORDAN

TURKMENISTAN
TAJIKISTAN
AFGHANISTAN

Atlas

MOROCCO

ISRAEL

IRAN

KUWAIT

PAKISTAN

NEPAL

BHUTAN

TAIWAN

WESTERN
SAHARA
(Morocco)

ALGERIA

LIBYA

EGYPT

QATAR

U. A. E.

SAUDI
ARABIA

INDIA

BANGLADESH
MYANMAR

LAOS

Northern
Mariana
Islands
(U.S.)

MARSHALL
ISLANDS

AFRICA

OMAN

Guam (U.S.)

MAURITANIA

MALI

NIGER

CHAD

ERITREA
SUDAN

YEMEN

THAILAND

VIETNAM

CAMBODIA

PHILIPPINES

FEDERATED STATES
OF MICRONESIA

SENEGAL
GAMBIA
GUINEA BISSAU
GUINEA
SIERRA
LEONE
LIBERIA

BURKINA
FASO

NIGERIA

GHANA
IVORY
COAST
TOGO
BENIN

DJIBOUTI

CEN.AFR.
REP.

ETHIOPIA

SOMALIA

SRI LANKA

BRUNEI

MALAYSIA

PALAU

KIRIBATI

NAURU

EQU.
GUINEA
SAO TOME
AND PRINCIPE

CAMEROON

GABON
REP. OF
CONGO

DEM.
REP.
OF
CONGO

UGANDA

RWANDA
BURUNDI

KENYA

MALDIVES

SINGAPORE

INDONESIA

EAST
TIMOR

PAPUA
NEW
GUINEA

SOLOMON
ISLANDS

TUVALU

TANZANIA

COMOROS

SEYCHELLES

VANUATU

FIJI

ANGOLA

MALAWI
ZAMBIA
MOZAMBIQUE

INDIAN
OCEAN

New
Caledonia
(Fr.)

ZIMBABWE

NAMIBIA

BOTSWANA

MADAGASCAR

MAURITIUS
Reunion
(Fr.)

AUSTRALIA

SWAZILAND
SOUTH AFRICA

LESOTHO

km 0   1000   2000

mi 0   1000   2000

ATLANTIC
OCEAN

NEW
ZEALAND

ANTARCTICA

FINLAND

SWEDEN

NORWAY

ESTONIA

RUSSIA

LATVIA
LITHUANIA

North
Sea

DENMARK

RUSSIA

BELARUS

km 0 150 300

mi 0   150   300

UNITED
KINGDOM

IRELAND

NETH.

GERMANY

POLAND

UKRAINE

BELGIUM

LUX.

CZECH
REPUBLIC

SLOVAKIA

ATLANTIC
OCEAN

FRANCE

SWITZ.

LIECH.
AUSTRIA

HUNGARY

MOLDOVA

SLOV.
CROATIA

ROMANIA

MONACO

SAN
MARINO

BOS. &
HERZ.

SERB. &
MONT.

BULGARIA

Corsica
(Fr.)

MACEDONIA
ALB.

PORTUGAL

ANDORRA

Sardinia
(It.)

ITALY

VATICAN
CITY

GREECE

TURKEY

SPAIN

Balearic
Islands
(Sp.)

Sicily (It.)

GIBRALTAR
(U.K.)

Mediterranean Sea

MOROCCO

ALGERIA

TUNISIA

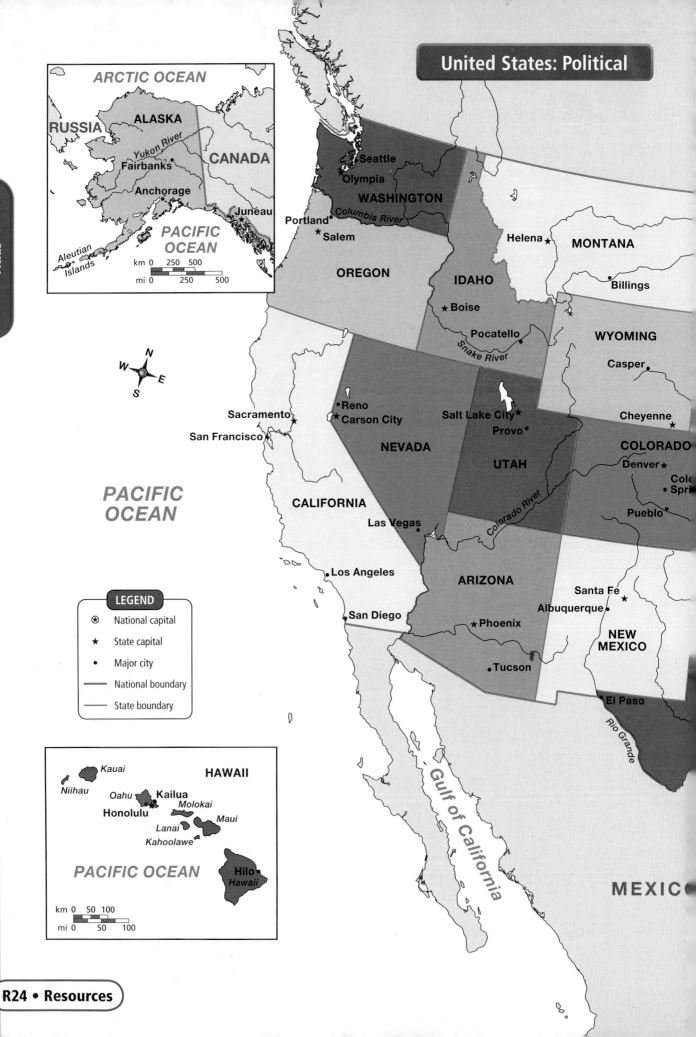

United States: Political

ARCTIC OCEAN

RUSSIA

ALASKA

CANADA

Yukon River

Fairbanks

Anchorage

Juneau

Aleutian Islands

PACIFIC OCEAN

km 0   250   500
mi 0   250   500

Seattle
Olympia
WASHINGTON
Columbia River
Portland
★ Salem
OREGON

Helena ★
MONTANA
• Billings

IDAHO
★ Boise
Pocatello
Snake River

WYOMING
Casper •

Cheyenne

Reno •
★ Carson City
Sacramento ★
San Francisco

Salt Lake City ★
Provo •
UTAH

COLORADO
Denver ★
Col
Spri
Pueblo •

NEVADA

PACIFIC OCEAN

CALIFORNIA
Las Vegas •

Colorado River

LEGEND
⊛ National capital
★ State capital
• Major city
── National boundary
── State boundary

• Los Angeles

San Diego •

ARIZONA

• Phoenix

• Tucson

Santa Fe
Albuquerque •
★

NEW MEXICO

★ El Paso
Rio Grande

Gulf of California

HAWAII

Kauai
Niihau
Oahu   Kailua
Honolulu   Molokai
Lanai   Maui
Kahoolawe

PACIFIC OCEAN

Hilo
Hawaii

km 0   50   100
mi 0   50   100

MEXICO

CANADA

St. Lawrence River

NEW HAMPSHIRE
VERMONT
MAINE
Augusta ★
Montpelier ★
Burlington ●
●Portland
Concord
★ ●Manchester

Lake Superior

MINNESOTA
RTH OTA
k
●Fargo

UTH OTA
ux Falls

St. Paul ★
Minneapolis ●

WISCONSIN
Madison ★

Lake Michigan
Lake Huron

MICHIGAN
Grand Rapids ●
Lansing ★

Milwaukee ●

L. Ontario
Rochester ●
●Albany

NEW YORK

●Boston
Hartford ★
MASSACHUSETTS
●Providence
New Haven ●
RHODE ISLAND
CONNECTICUT

IOWA
Cedar Rapids ●
Des Moines ★

RASKA
Missouri River

Omaha ●
Lincoln ●

Chicago ●

ILLINOIS
Springfield ★

Buffalo ●

Lake Erie
Detroit ●

Cleveland ●

OHIO
Columbus ★

PENNSYLVANIA
Harrisburg ●
Pittsburgh ●

Trenton ★
●New York
Newark ●
Philadelphia ●
NEW JERSEY
Dover ●
DELAWARE
Annapolis ★
Washington, D.C. ⊛
MARYLAND

INDIANA
Indianapolis ★

Cincinnati ●

Kansas City ●
Topeka ★
Kansas City ●
Jefferson City ★

KANSAS

MISSOURI

St. Louis ●

Louisville ●

Ohio River

KENTUCKY
Frankfort ★

WEST VIRGINIA
Charleston ★

Richmond ●

Baltimore ●

Norfolk ●

VIRGINIA

Tulsa ●

Oklahoma City ●
KLAHOMA

Fort Smith ●

ARKANSAS
Little Rock ★

Mississippi River

Nashville ●

TENNESSEE
Memphis ●

Greensboro ●
Raleigh ★

NORTH CAROLINA

MISSISSIPPI

Birmingham ●

Montgomery ★

ALABAMA

Atlanta ★

GEORGIA

Columbia ★

SOUTH CAROLINA
Charleston ●

Dallas ●

TEXAS
Austin

LOUISIANA

Jackson ★

Mobile ●

Tallahassee ★

Savannah ●

Jacksonville ●

ATLANTIC OCEAN

onio
Houston ●

Baton Rouge ●
New Orleans ●

Tampa ●
FLORIDA

Miami ●

Gulf of Mexico

BAHAMAS

km 0 100 200 300 400 500
mi 0 100 200 300 400 500

CUBA

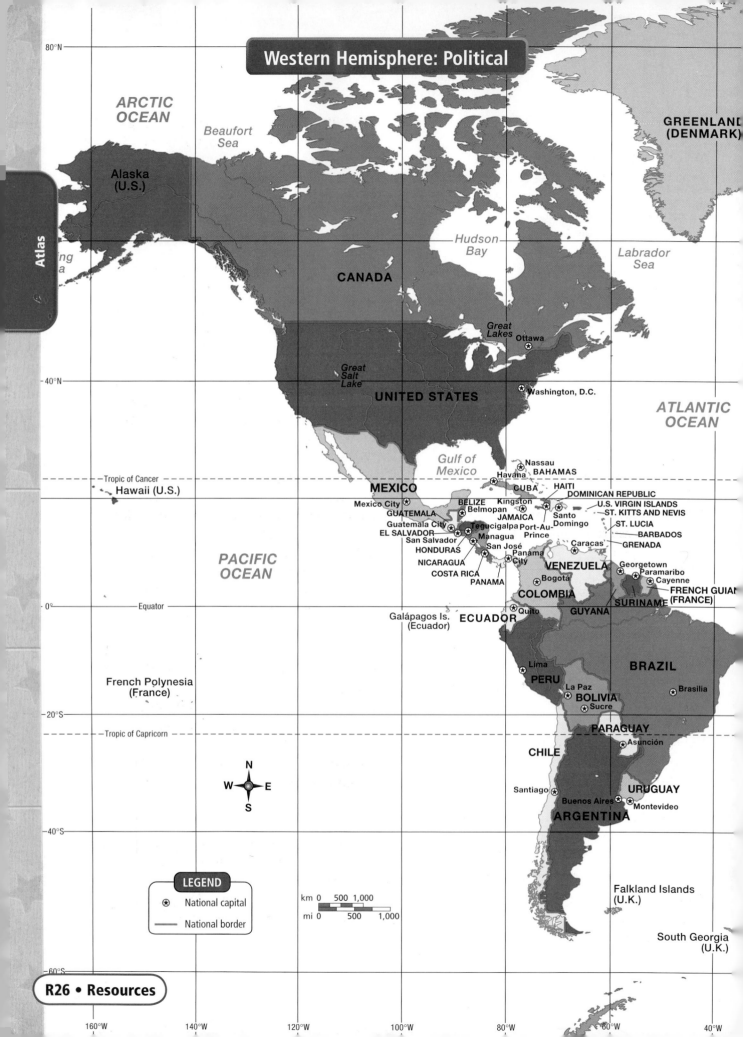

Western Hemisphere: Political

ARCTIC OCEAN

Beaufort Sea

GREENLAND (DENMARK)

Alaska (U.S.)

ing a

Hudson Bay

Labrador Sea

CANADA

Great Lakes

Ottawa ⊛

Great Salt Lake

—40°N

UNITED STATES

Washington, D.C. ⊛

ATLANTIC OCEAN

Gulf of Mexico

— Tropic of Cancer

Hawaii (U.S.)

Nassau
BAHAMAS
Havana
CUBA
Kingston
JAMAICA
HAITI
DOMINICAN REPUBLIC
U.S. VIRGIN ISLANDS
ST. KITTS AND NEVIS
ST. LUCIA
BARBADOS
GRENADA

MEXICO

Mexico City ⊛

BELIZE
Belmopan ⊛
GUATEMALA
Guatemala City ⊛
EL SALVADOR
San Salvador ⊛
HONDURAS
Tegucigalpa ⊛
Managua ⊛
San José ⊛
NICARAGUA
COSTA RICA
PANAMA
Panama City ⊛
Port-Au-Prince
Santo Domingo

PACIFIC OCEAN

Caracas ⊛
VENEZUELA
Georgetown ⊛
Paramaribo ⊛
Cayenne
FRENCH GUIANA (FRANCE)
SURINAME
GUYANA

Bogotá ⊛
COLOMBIA

Galápagos Is. (Ecuador)

—0°— Equator

Quito ⊛
ECUADOR

French Polynesia (France)

Lima ⊛
PERU

BRAZIL

La Paz ⊛
BOLIVIA
Sucre ⊛
Brasilia ⊛

—20°S

— Tropic of Capricorn

PARAGUAY
Asunción ⊛

CHILE

N
W E
S

URUGUAY
Santiago ⊛
Buenos Aires ⊛
Montevideo ⊛
ARGENTINA

—40°S

Falkland Islands (U.K.)

LEGEND
⊛ National capital
— National border

km 0   500 1,000
mi 0   500 1,000

South Georgia (U.K.)

—60°S

160°W   140°W   120°W   100°W   80°W   60°W   40°W

Gazetteer

A

Allegheny Mountains Mountainous eastern part of the Allegheny Plateau in the Appalachian Mountains; extends from north-central Pennsylvania to southwestern Virginia. (41°N, 76°W) page 5

Allegheny Plateau The largest region in the state of Pennsylvania, covering about half the state and consisting of deep valleys, flat-topped ridges, and hardwood forests (41°N, 79°W) page 5

Allegheny River River that runs through eastern Pennsylvania and New York (40°N, 80°W) page 63

Altoona Manufacturing city in central Pennsylvania (40°N, 78°W) page 115

Appalachian Mountains Range stretching from Canada to Alabama (37°N, 82°W) page 5

Asia Largest continent in the world (50°N, 100°E) page 10

Atlantic Coastal Plain Pennsylvania region in the southeastern portion of the state (39°N, 75°W) page 5

Atlantic Ocean Extends from Arctic to Antarctic; east of United States (5°S, 25°W) page 23

B

Baltimore Large city in Maryland (39°N, 77°W) page 104

Berks County Pennsylvania county; location of Pennsylvania Dutch farms (40°N, 75°W) page 164

Boston Capital of Massachusetts (42°N, 71°W) page 53

Bradford City in Pennsylvania (41°N, 78°W) page 150

Brandywine Site of American Revolution battle (40°N, 75°W) page 57

C

Cameron Rural county in north central Pennsylvania; county seat: Emporium (41°N, 78°W) page 163

Camp William Penn Site of the training of African-American soldiers during the Civil War (TK) page 101

Canada Country bordering United States on north (50°N, 100°W) page 49

Cape Cod Popular tourist area in southeast Massachusetts that extends into the Atlantic Ocean (42°N, 70°W) page 185

Carbondale Location of the Welsh festival Eisteddfod (41°N, 75°W) page 165

Carlisle Borough in southern Pennsylvania; site of an 1863 Civil War attack (40°N, 77°W) page 101

Chambersburg Town in southern Pennsylvania that was the site of two Confederate attacks during the Civil War (39°N, 77°W) page 101

Chesapeake Bay Inlet of the Atlantic Ocean between Virginia and Maryland (38°N, 76°W) page 23

Chester County County in southeastern Pennsylvania (39°N, 75°W) page 169

China Country in east Asia; capital: Beijing (37°N, 93°E) page 131

Clifton Heights Town in southeastern Pennsylvania (39°N, 75°W) page 117

Connecticut 5th state; capital: Hartford (42°N, 73°W) page 191

D

Delaware 1st state; capital: Dover (39°N, 76°W) page 24

Delaware Bay Inlet of the North Atlantic Ocean on the east coast of the United States (39°N, 75°W) page 23

Delaware River Flows from New York to Delaware Bay (42°N, 75°W) page 15

E

Ellis Island Location where many immigrants entered the United States in the late 1800s and early 1900s (40°N, 74°W) page 123

England Region in western Europe; part of the United Kingdom (capital: London) (52°N, 2°W) page 27

Erie City in Pennsylvania (42°N, 80°W) page 63

Erie Lowland Pennsylvania region in the northwestern part of the state, bordering Lake Erie, which consists of level, sandy plain (42°N, 80°W) page 5

Europe Continent located between the Atlantic Ocean and Asia (50°N, 15°E) page 10

Florida 27th state; capital: Tallahassee (31°N, 85°W) page 185

Forest Rural county in northwest Pennsylvania; county seat: Tionesta (41°N, 79°W) page 163

Fort Duquesne Important Pennsylvania fort during the American Revolution; the British captured it and renamed it Fort Pitt (40°N, 80°W) page 48

Fort Necessity Important Pennsylvania fort during the American Revolution (39°N, 79°W) page 49

Fort Pitt Formerly Fort Duquesne, renamed by the British during the French and Indian War (40°N, 80°W) page 49

Fort Sumter Fort in South Carolina where Confederate troops attacked Union soldiers, beginning the Civil War (32°N, 80°W) page 100

France Country in western Europe; capital: Paris (41°N, 1°E) page 49

Fulton Rural county in southern Pennsylvania; county seat: McConnellsburg (39°N, 77°W) page 163

Germantown German immigrant settlement north of Philadelphia (40°N, 75°W) page 33

Germany Country in western Europe; capital: Berlin (51°N, 10°E) page 33

Gettysburg Site in Pennsylvania of Civil War battle (40°N, 77°W) page 102

Great Lakes Five freshwater lakes between the United States and Canada (45°N, 83°W) page 74

Great Valley A broad lowland that lies in southeastern Pennsylvania (40°N, 75°W) page 5

Greensburg City in Pennsylvania (40°N, 79°W) page 63

Greencastle City in Pennsylvania (39°N, 77°W) page 107

Harrisburg Capital of Pennsylvania (40°N, 76°W) page 73

Hawaii 50th state; capital: Honolulu (20°N, 158°W) page 131

Homestead Town in southwestern Pennsylvania (40°N, 79°W) page 117

Hungary Country in central Europe; capital: Budapest (47°N, 19°W) page 120

Indiana County County in west-central Pennsylvania; county seat: Indiana (40°N, 79°W) page 169

Ireland Island in North Atlantic Ocean, divided between Republic of Ireland and Northern Ireland (53°N, 6°W) page 33

Italy Country in southern Europe; capital: Rome (44°N, 11°E) page 120

Japan Island nation off northeast coast of Asia; capital: Tokyo (37°N, 134°E) page 131

Johnstown City in southwestern Pennsylvania; site of flood in 1889 (40°N, 78°W) page 123

Lake Erie One of the Great Lakes (42°N, 80°W) page 5

Lancaster Second capital of Pennsylvania (40°N, 76°W) page 73

Lancaster County County in Pennsylvania (39°N, 76°W) page 62

Lehigh Valley Valley in southeastern Pennsylvania with natural limestone resources (40°N, 75°W) page 173

Lock Haven City in Pennsylvania (41°N, 77°W) page 63

Long Island Island in the Atlantic Ocean that lies just off the southeastern part of New York (43°N, 74°W) page 185

Louisiana 18th state; capital: Baton Rouge (31°N, 93°W) page 73

 M

Maine 23rd state; capital: Augusta (45°N, 70°W) page 188

Manhattan Borough of New York City in the southeastern part of New York (44°N, 75°W) page 197

Maryland 7th state; capital: Annapolis (39°N, 76°W) page 186

Massachusetts 6th state; capital: Boston (42°N, 73°W) page 53

Mexico Country in North America that borders the United States to the south; capital: Mexico City (23°N, 102°W) page 164

McKeesport City in southwestern Pennsylvania (40°N, 79°W) page 117

Michigan 26th state; capital: Lansing (46°N, 87°W) page 174

Minnesota 32nd state; capital: St. Paul (45°N, 93°W) page 174

Mississippi River Principal river of the United States and North America (32°N, 92°W) page 73

Monongahela River River that flows through West Virginia and Pennsylvania (40°N, 80°W) page 170

Mount Davis Peak in the Pocono Mountains and highest point of elevation in Pennsylvania (39°N, 79°W) page 5

 N

Netherlands Country in western Europe; capital: Amsterdam (53°N, 4°E) page 33

New Hampshire 9th state; capital: Concord (44°N, 72°W) page 189

New Jersey 3rd state; capital: Trenton (41°N, 75°W) page 24

New York 11th state; capital: Albany (43°N, 78°W) page 25

New York City City in New York state; largest city in the United States (41°N, 74°W) page 184

North America Northern continent of the Western Hemisphere; includes Canada, the United States, Mexico, and Central America (45°N, 100°W) page 10

Northampton County in Pennsylvania; county seat: Easton (40°N, 75°W) page 164

North Pole Northernmost point on Earth (90°N) page 186

 O

Ohio River Flows from Pennsylvania to the Mississippi River (37°N, 88°W) page 48

P

Paoli Site of an American Revolution Battle in Pennsylvania (40°N, 75°W) page 57

Pearl Harbor U.S. naval base on the island of Oahu in southern Hawaii (21°N, 15°W) page 131

Pennsylvania 2nd state; capital: Harrisburg (41°N, 78°W) page 4

Philadelphia City in Pennsylvania; name means "brotherly love" in Greek (39°N, 75°W) page 28

Philadelphia County County in southeastern Pennsylvania; county seat: Philadelphia (39°N, 75°W) page 169

Pittsburgh Manufacturing city in Pennsylvania (40°N, 80°W) page 48

Pocono Mountains Range stretching from the Lehigh River in Pennsylvania to Delaware (41°N, 75°W) page 5

Poland Country in eastern Europe; capital: Warsaw (52°N, 21°E) page 120

Potomac River Runs from western Maryland past Washington, D.C. (38°N, 77°W) page 104

R

Reading Prong Rounded low hills or ridges in southeastern Pennsylvania (40°N, 76°W) page 5

Russia Formerly part of the Soviet Union; capital: Moscow (61°N, 60°E) page TK

S

Schuylkill County County in east-central Pennsylvania; county seat: Pottsville (40°N, 76°W) page 169

Schuylkill River Runs from the Delaware River to the central eastern portion of Pennsylvania (40°N, 75°W) page 23

Gazetteer

Scotland Part of Great Britain; capital: Edinburgh (57°N, 5°W) page 33

South Carolina 8th state; capital: Columbia (34°N, 81°W) page 97

South Mountain Ridge of hills extending about 45 miles in Pennsylvania (41°N, 77°W) page 5

Soviet Union Large communist country that split into separate republics in 1991; capital city: Moscow (61°N, 64°E) page 131

Spain Country in southwestern Europe; capital: Madrid (40°N, 4°W) page 58

Sullivan Rural county in north central Pennsylvania; county seat: Laporte (41°N, 76°W) page 163

Susquehanna River Runs through New York, Pennsylvania, and Maryland, and empties into the Chesapeake Bay (40°N, 76°W) page 23

Sweden Country in northern Europe; capital: Stockholm (62°N, 15°E) page 24

Tinicum Island Capital of New Sweden; now an island in the state of Pennsylvania (40°N, 75°W) page 24

Titusville City in Pennsylvania (41°N, 79°W) page 83

Trenton Capital of New Jersey (40°N, 75°W) page 57

Uniontown City in southwestern Pennsylvania (39°N, 79°W) page 131

United States Country that lies mostly in central North America; capital: Washington, D.C. (38°N, 110°W) page 4

Valley Forge Location in Pennsylvania where George Washington's troops spent the winter of 1777–1778 (40°N, 75°W) page 58

Vermont 14th state; capital: Montpelier (44°N, 72°W) page 188

Vicksburg Mississippi site of Civil War battle (32°N, 91°W) page 104

Virginia 10th state; capital: Richmond (37°N, 81°W) page 23

Wales Part of Great Britain; capital: Cardiff (52°N, 4°W) page 122

Washington, D.C. Capital of the United States (39°N, 77°W) page 101

West Chester Town in southeastern Pennsylvania (39°N, 75°W) page 132

Williamsport City in Pennsylvania (41°N, 77°W) page 63

Wyoming Valley Area in Pennsylvania (41°N, 75°W) page 58

York County County in southern Pennsylvania; county seat: York (39°N, 76°W) page 164

Yorktown In Virginia; site of last battle of Revolutionary War (37°N, 77°W) page 59

Gazetteer

Glossary

A

abolitionist (ah bah LI shun ist) someone who works to end slavery. (p. 94)

adapt (uh DAHPT) to change in order to suit different conditions. (p. 11)

ally (AH ly) a person or group that joins another as a partner in a battle. (p. 49)

amendment (uh MEHND mehnt) a change or correction to improve something. (p. 61)

armistice (AHR mih stis) an agreement to end fighting. (p. 129)

artifact (AR tuh fakt) an object made by human hands. (p. 11)

assembly (a SEM blee) a group of people who come together to make laws. (p. 28)

B

bay (bay) a body of water partly surrounded by land but open to the sea. (p. 186)

boycott (BOI kaht) an action in which people refuse to use or buy certain goods or services. (p. 53)

C

canal (kuh NAHL) a human-made waterway. (p. 79)

candidate (KAHN ih daht) a person who runs for election to a political office. (p. 156)

cape (kayp) a point of land that sticks out into the water. (p. 185)

capital resources (KAH pih tahl REE sohr sez) the tools, machines, buildings, and other equipment that a business uses to make goods or provide services. (p. 192)

cause (kahz) an event that makes another event happen. (p. 134)

charter (CHAHR ter) an official document that tells how something should be done. (p. 26)

checks and balances (syeks ahnd BAH lahns ez) a system that gives each branch of government different responsibilities. (p. 149)

circle graph (SUHR kuhl grahf) a circle that is divided into sections to show how information is related. (p. 166)

citizen (SIH tih sehn) someone who is born in a country or who promises to be loyal to the country. (p. 144)

citizenship (SIH tih sehn shihp) all of the rights and responsibilities of citizens. (p. 156)

climate (KLY miht) the typical weather of a place over a long period of time. (p. 6)

coast (kohst) land that borders an ocean. (p. 184)

coastal plain (KOHST ahl playn) flat, level land along a coast. (p. 184)

colony (KAH luh nee) a settlement ruled by a distant country. (p. 24)

commerce (KAH mers) the buying and selling of a large amount of goods. (p. 81)

common good (KAH muhn guhd) the good of the whole population. (p. 144)

commuter (kah MYOO tuhr) a person who travels between work and home each day. (p. 197)

compass rose (KUM pahs ROZ) a tool on a map that shows direction. (p. 9)

compromise (KAHM pro myz) a plan on which everyone agrees. (p. 96)

confederacy (kahn FEH duh rah see) a union of groups or states that join together for a common purpose. (p. 100)

confederation (kahn fehd uh RA shun) a group of states that together form one country. (p. 60)

conflict (KAHN flihkt) a disagreement. (p. 152)

consequence (KAHN seh kwens) something that happens because of a decision or action. (p. 126)

constitution (kahn stih TOO shun) a document that outlines the laws of a government. (p. 61)

consumer (kahn SOO mehr) someone who buys or uses goods and services. (p. 168)

culture (KUHL cher) a way of life that people share. (p. 14)

debt (deht) money that is borrowed and must be paid back. (p. 26)

democracy (deh MAH kruh see) a system in which the people hold the power of government. (p. 145)

depression (dee PREH shun) a period when businesses fail, prices drop, and jobs are hard to find. (p. 130)

dictator (DIK tay tehr) a leader who has complete control of a country's government. (p. 131)

discrimination (dih skrih mih NAY shun) the act of treating a person or group unfairly. (p. 155)

economy (ih KAH nuh mee) the goods and services that a community uses and produces. (p. 34)

effect (eh FEKT) an event that happens as a result of a cause. (p. 134)

election (ee LEHK shun) the way voters choose people to serve in government. (p. 145)

elevation (ehl uh VA shun) the height of a landform above sea level. (p. 4)

emancipate (ee MAHN sih payt) to free someone from slavery. (p. 101)

enlist (ehn LIHST) to sign up to serve in the military. (p. 101)

entrepreneur (AHN truh pruh nuhr) someone who starts a new business. (p. 170)

ethnic group (EH thnihk groop) a group made up of people who share the same culture. (p. 164)

explorer (ehk SPLOR ur) a person who travels in search of something. (p. 22)

export (EKS pohrt) a product that is sent to be sold in another country or state. (p. 174)

fact (fahkt) information that can be proven true. (p. 76)

federal (FEH duh rahl) something that is a part of the central, or main, government. (p. 100)

foundry (FAHWN dree) a building or factory where metals are shaped into goods. (p. 107)

fugitive (FYOO jih tihv) a person who is running away from something. (p. 95)

governor (GUH veh nehr) the chief executive of the state. (p. 149)

human resources (HYOO mahn REE sohr sez) the services, knowledge, skills, and intelligence that workers provide. (p. 192)

immigrant (IHM ih gruhnt) a person who moves to a new country. (p. 32)

import (IHM pohrt) a product brought in from another state or country. (p. 174)

indentured servant (ihn DEHN churd SUR vahnt) someone who agreed to work for a wealthy colonist for a period of time in order to pay off a debt. (p. 37)

independence (ihn deh PEHN dehns) freedom from the control of another person or government. (p. 54)

index (IHN deks) an alphabetical listing of the topics in a book. (p. 194)

industry (IHN duh stree) a business that makes a product or offers a service that can be sold to people. (p. 34)

innovation (ih noh VAY shun) a new item, idea, or way of doing things (p. 116)

jury (JUHR ee) a group of citizens who decide a case in court. (p. 156)

labor union (LAY bor yew nyon) an organization that tries to improve pay and working conditions for its members. (p. 124)

landform (LAHND form) a certain type of land, such as a mountain or valley. (p. 4)

legend (LEH jund) a tool that explains what the different colors, lines, and symbols on a map represent. (p. 9)

lines of latitude (lynz uhv LAHT uh tood) imaginary lines that measure distance north and south of the equator. (p. 30)

lines of longitude (lynz uhv LAHWN juh tood) imaginary lines that measure distance east and west of the prime meridian. (p. 30)

longhouse (LAHNG haoos) a long, bark-covered building that houses many families under one roof. (p. 16)

Loyalist (LOI ah lihst) a person who wanted the colonies to remain loyal to Britain. (p. 56)

map scale (MAHP skayl) a tool that helps to measure distance on a map. (p. 9)

market economy (MAHR ket ee KAH noh mee) a system in which people are free to decide what to make, how to make it, and for whom to make it. (p. 190)

mass production (mahs pro DUK shun) workers use machines to make many goods in a short period of time. (p. 83)

merge (merj) to combine. (p. 119)

metropolitan area (meh troh PAH lih tahn AHR ee uh) a city and the communities that surround it. (p. 163)

migrate (MY grayt) to move from one place to another. (p. 10)

multicultural (muhl tee KUHL chuh rahl) a population made up of people from many different countries and backgrounds. (p. 164)

negotiate (neh GO shee ayt) to work together to come to an agreement. (p. 75)

opinion (uh PIHN yuhn) a belief or feeling that cannot be proven true or false. (p. 76)

opportunity cost (ah pohr TOO nih tee kahst) the cost of what someone gives up in order to get something else. (p. 170)

Patriot (PAY tree uht) a person who supported the American Revolution. (p. 56)

petition (peh TI shun) a written request for action, signed by many people. (p. 53)

philanthropy (fil AN throh pee) the effort to help people improve their lives. (p. 121)

point of view (poynt ohv vyoo) the way a person thinks about an issue, an event, or a person. (p. 98)

popular sovereignty (PAH pyu lahr SAH vrehn tee) when citizens create the government and have the power to vote and influence laws. (p. 155)

population (pah pyoo LAY shun) all of the people who live in a certain area. (p. 162)

preamble (PREE ahm buhl) the introduction of a document. (p. 148)

primary source (PRY mehr ee awrs) a firsthand account of an event. (p. 104)

proclamation (prah kluh MA shun) an official announcement. (p. 51)

profitable (PRAH fit ah bul) something that makes money after its expenses have been paid. (p. 119)

R

raid (rayd) a surprise attack. (p. 74)

ratify (RAH tih fy) to approve something officially. (p. 61)

Reconstruction (ree cahn STRUHK shun) the government's plan to rebuild the South. (p. 108)

refine (ree FYN) to make a better or more pure form of something. (p. 83)

reform (ree FORM) to change something for the better. (p. 124)

retail (REE tayl) an industry in which small amounts of goods are sold directly to consumers (p. 116)

region (REE jun) an area of land that has one or more features in common. (p. 4)

resolve (ree ZAHLV) to find an answer to a problem. (p. 152)

revolution (reh vah LOO shun) a change in government by force. (p. 56)

right (rahyt) a freedom that the law promises to every citizen. (p. 148)

rural (ROO rahl) an area in the country. (p. 36)

scarcity (SKAHR sih tee) a limited supply of something. (p. 173)

search engine (sehrtch ehn jihn) a Web site that finds other Web sites related to your key words. (p. 194)

secede (sih CEED) to separate from a group or an organization. (p. 97)

secondary source (SEH kuhn dehr ee sawrs) an account of an event that is written by someone who was not present at the event. (p. 104)

segregation (seh greh GAY shun) the separation of people on the basis of their race. (p. 132)

settlement (SEH tuhl mehnt) a small community of people living in a new place. (p. 24)

skyscraper (SKY skray pehr) a very tall building. (p. 197)

specialization (speh shuhl ih ZAY shun) when a business only makes a certain kind of product. (p. 173)

strike (stryk) when workers refuse to work until their demands for better working conditions are met. (p. 84)

suffrage (SUH frehj) the right to vote. (p. 125)

surrender (suh REHN dur) to give up. (p. 74)

tax (tahks) money that people or businesses pay to support the government. (p. 52)

territory (TEHR ih toh ree) land that belongs to a country but has no representation in that country. (p. 73)

textile (TEKS tyl) fabric or cloth. (p. 82)

tolerance (TAH luh rahns) allowing beliefs that are different from one's own. (p. 27)

toll (tohl) money people pay to use something. (p. 80)

tourism (TOO rih zuhm) the business of organizing travel for people. (p. 169)

trade (trayd) buying or selling goods. (p. 34)

transportation (trahns por TA shun) the way people and goods are moved from one place to another. (p. 78)

treaty (TREE tee) an agreement between countries or rulers. (p. 50)

urban (UR buhn) an area in the city. (p. 36)

veteran (VEH ter ahn) a person who has served in the military. (p. 109)

veto (VEE toh) to reject, or not to approve. (p. 28)

W

wigwam (WIG wahm) a small round house made of bark with a dome-shaped roof. (p. 15)

Index

Page numbers followed by m refer to maps. Page numbers in *italic* type refer to photographs, illustrations, or charts.

A

Abolitionists, 92, 94–96
Adaptation, 11, 13
African Americans, 140, 141, 147, 165
  civil rights movement, 132, 133
  in Civil War, 101
  end of slavery in Pennsylvania, 64
  Great Migration of, 123
  during World War II, 131
  See also enslaved people.
Agricultural College of Pennsylvania, 115
Agriculture, 21, 169
  in Appalachian Mountains, 185
  of Archaic Indians, 12
  Civil War and, 107
  in the East, 189
  improvements for, 115
  of the Lenni Lenape, 15
  in Mid-Atlantic region, 198
  of Pennsylvania colony, *36, 37*
  of settlers, 33, 34
  of the Shawnee, 15
  of the Susquehannock, 16
  of Woodland Indians, 13
Algonquian, 1, 16m, 17, 28, 35
  culture of, 15
  French and Indian War and, 49
  language of, 14
Allegheny Mountains, 5
Allegheny Plateau, 5, 6
Allen, Richard, 64
Alliances, 175
Allied Powers, 128, 129
Allies, 49, 128, 131
Altoona, Pennsylvania, 31m, 115
Amendments, 61
American Indians
  Algonquian, 15
  in American Revolution, 58
  conflicts over land, 50
  culture of, 3, 14
  Erie, 16
  French and Indian War and, 49
  Haudenosaunee, 14, 16, 17, 49, 58
  Iroquois, 58
  Lenni Lenape, 1, 15, 17, 28, 35
  Shawnee, 15
  Susquehannock, 16, 23
  treaties with Penn, 28, 29
  Walking Purchase, 1, 35
  War of 1812 and, 74
American Revolution, 54–55, 56–59, 57
Anderson, Marian, 141, 165
Appalachian Mountains, 5, 115, 185, 188
Appomattox Court House, 108
Archaic Indians, 2, 12
Armistice, 129

Armstrong County, Pennsylvania, 169
Arrostook Valley, Maine, 189
Articles, 148
Articles of Confederation, 60, 61
Artifacts, 3, 11, *13*
Assembly of representatives, 28
Atlantic coast, 186
Atlantic Coastal Plain, 5, 6
Atlantic Ocean, 186, 189
Atlatl, 12

B

Baldwin Locomotive Works, 115
Banking, 191, 196
Bartram, William, xx, 38
Battle of Brandywine, 57
Battle of Germantown, 57
Battle of Gettysburg, 93, 102, 103
Battle of Lake Erie, 74
Battle of Yorktown, 59
Bay, 186
Berks County, Pennsylvania, 164
Bessemer, Henry, 118
Bethel African Methodist Episcopal Church, 64
Bifocal glasses, 38
Bill of Rights, 61, *146*, 154
Bills, 149
Biotechnology, 133
Bonaparte, Napoleon, 73
Bonds, 129
Boston Tea Party, 53
Boycott, 53
Bradford, Pennsylvania, 150
Brandywine, Battle of, 57
Bronx, 197
Brooklyn, 197
Buchanan, James, 92, 96–97
Businesses, 169, 170
  buying and selling and, 173
  competition and, 172
  depression and, 130
  development of, 115–117
  in the East, 191, 193
  elements of, 192–193
  in market economy, 190
  population changes and, 163
  specialization of, 161, 173

C

Cameron County, Pennsylvania, 163
Camp Curtin, 101
Camp William Penn, 101
Canada, 175, 184
Canals, 71, 79, 123
Candidates, 156
Cape Cod, 185
Capes, 185
Capital city
  of Pennsylvania, 72, 73, 75
  of US, 184, 196, 198
Capital resources, 192, 193
Capitol building, 147, 198

Carbondale, Pennsylvania, 165
Carlisle, Pennsylvania, 101
Carnegie, Andrew, 112, 119, 121
Carnegie Mellon University, 112, 121
Carson, Rachel, 141, 157
Cause, 134–135
Census, 162
Central Library, 150
Central Powers, 128, 129m
Chambersburg, Pennsylvania, 101, *108*
Charles II (king of England), 26, 72
Charter, 20
Charter of 1681, 26
Charter of Privileges, 28
Checks and balances system, 149
Chesapeake Bay, 23, 186, 198
Chester County, Pennsylvania, 169
Child labor laws, 124
China, 131
Choices, 170–171, 175
Circle graphs, 166–167
Cities, 31m
  government of, 145, 150
  growth of, 34, 36, 186, 191, 196
  immigrant groups and, 123
  of Mid-Atlantic region, 199
  See also urban areas.
Citizens
  government and, 144
  responsibilities of, 142, 143, 156–157
  rights of, 142, 154–155
Citizenship, 156–157
Citizenship skills
  conflict resolution, 152–153
  decision making, 126–127
  point of view, 98–99
City council, 150
City manager, 150
Civil Rights Act, 132
Civil rights movement, 132, 133
Civil War, 90, 92, 93, 100–103, 106–108
Clermont (steamboat), 79
Clifton Heights, Pennsylvania, 117
Climate, 2, 6, 11, 186, 187
Coal, 83, 107, 115, 117, 188, 198
  in Appalachian Mountains, 185
  industry and, 114
Coast, 182, 184
Coastal plain, 184, 185
College of Philadelphia, 21, 39
Colonies, 48–50
Colonists
  Declaration of Independence, 146
  of Pennsylvania colony, 28
  Proclamation of 1763 and, 51
  role in government of Pennsylvania, 28
  taxes and, 52–53
  trade of, 34
  Walking Purchase and, 1, 35
Colony, 24
Command economy, 190
Commerce, 81
Common good, 144, 154
Common Sense (Paine), 55

Commuters, 183, 197
Competition, 172, 175
Compromise, 96
Conestoga wagons, 62, *63*, 78
Confederacy, 100
Confederate States of America, 100–
103, *101, 102,* 108–109
Confederation, 60
Conflict resolution, 152–153
Conflicts, 152–153
  between American Indian groups, 16
  with American Indians over land,
  50–51
  American Revolution, 56–59
  between France and Britain, 48–50
  between Swedish and Dutch settlers,
  25
  War of 1812, 45, 70, 74–75
  World War I, 128
  World War II, 113, 131, 133
Congress of United States, *145,* 147
Connecticut, 191
Constitution, 47, 198
Constitution of Pennsylvania, 44, 72
  Declaration of Rights in, 44, 62, 148,
  154
  preamble to, 143, 148
  rewriting of, 73
  supreme court of Pennsylvania and,
  149
  writing of, 62
Constitution of the United States, 47,
61, 146, 147, *148*
  amendments to, 108
  preamble to, 143
  Supreme Court and, 147
Consumers, 168, 172, 173
Continental Army, 54, 55, 56–59
Continental climate, 6
Continental Congress, 57, 60
Counties, 150
Courts, 147, 149
Crafts industries, 34
Culture, 3, 14
  of American Indians, 14, 15, 16
  diversity of, 164–165
  of European settlers, 22
  of immigrant groups, 33
  of Swedish settlers, 24
Currencies, 174
Customs, 22, 24, 33, 164

 D

Debt, 26, 37
Decision making, 126–127
Declaration of Independence, 47, 54,
55, 146
Declaration of Rights, 44, 62, 148, 154
Delaware (people), 1, 15, 17, 28, 35
Delaware (state), 61, 70, 72, 189, 196,
198
Delaware Bay, 23
Delaware River, 8m, 24, 31m, *56*
Demand, 173
Democracy, 142, 145–147, 155
Depression, 113, 130
Dickinson, John, 53
Dictator, 131
Discrimination, 132, 155

Drake, Edwin, 83
Dutch explorers and settlers, 1, 23, 25

 E

East (United States)
  climate of, 186
  land and water of, 184–186
  natural resources of, 188–189
  plants and animals of, 187
Eastern Woodland Indians, 13, 14
Economics
  entrepreneurs and, 193
  factors of production and, 192
  market economy and, 182, 190, 193
  opportunity costs, 170–171
  price and competition and, 172
  specialization, 173
  supply and demand and, 173
  trade and, 191
Economy, 21, 175
  business development and, 115–117
  entrepreneurs and, 170
  Great Depression and, 130
  Industrial Revolution and, 82–83
  industries and, 168–169
  of Pennsylvania colony, 34, 35, 37
  personal choices and, 171
  railroads and, 81
  steel industry and, 118–120
  of United States, 190
  World War I and, 129
Education, 39, 73, 199
Effect, 134–135
Eisteddfod, 165
Elections, 28, 145, 150, 155, 156
Electric lights, 116
Electronics industry, 133, 169, 190
Elevation, 4, 6
Ellis Island, 123
Emancipation, 93, 101
Emancipation Proclamation, 101
Enlistment, 93, 101
Enslaved people, 37, 64, 94–97
  abolitionists and, 92
  Emancipation Proclamation and, 93,
  101
  voting rights of, 62
Entrepreneurs, 91, 170, 192, 193
Environment, 11, 13, 141
Equal rights, 132, 133
Erie (people), 16
Erie, Pennsylvania, 31m, 63, 107, 169
Erie Lowland region, 5, 6
Ethnic groups, 164–165
Europeans
  culture of, 22, 24
  explorers, 22, 25
  immigrants in Pennsylvania, 32–33,
  35, 120, 122–123
  in New York, 196
  settlers, 24
  World War I and, 128–129
Exchange rate, 174
Executive branch, 147, 149, 198
Explorers, xx, 20, 22, 23, 25
Exports, 174

 F

Fabric industry, 34, 71, 82, 107, 117
Factories, 112, 116, 117
  child labor in, 124
  in the East, 191
  economy and, 169
  growth of after Civil War, 114–115
  mass production in, 83
  textile mills, 82
  waterpower and, 186
  workers in, 84
  World War I and, 129
Factors of production, 192
Facts, 76–77
Family Court Building, *150*
Farming, 21, 169
  in Appalachian Mountains, 185
  of Archaic Indians, 12
  Civil War and, 107
  in the East, 189
  improvements for, 115
  of the Lenni Lenape, 15
  in Mid-Atlantic region, 198
  of Pennsylvania colony, *36,* 37
  of settlers, 33, 34
  of the Shawnee, 15
  of the Susquehannock, 16
  of Woodland Indians, 13
Federal government, 142
  Articles of Confederation and, 60–61
  popular sovereignty and, 155
  rebellions over taxes, 65
  Reconstruction and, 108
  structure of, 144–147
Ferio del Barrio, 165
Festivals, 15, 165
Fire fighters, 150, 199
First Continental Congress, 54
First Defenders, 101
Fitch, John, 79
Flags, 44, 56
Floods, 112, 123
Food processing, 116, 117, 120, 169
Forest County, Pennsylvania, 163
Forests, 115, 189, 198
Fort Duquesne, 48, 49, *50*
Fort Necessity, 49
Fort Pitt, 49, 50
Fort Sumter, 100, 103
Foundries, 107
France
  American Revolution and, 58
  French and Indian War and, 48–50
  Louisiana Purchase, 70, 73
  World War I and, 128–129
  World War II and, 131
Franklin, Benjamin, 38, *54,* 58, 61
Franklin stove, 38
Free School Act, 73
French and Indian War, 46, 48–50
Fries Rebellion, 65
Fugitive Slave Act, 95
Fulton, Robert, 79
Fulton County, Pennsylvania, 163
Fur trade, 24

Index

Gallatin, Albert, 75, 80
General Assembly, 149
Genesee River, *184*
German immigrants, 33, 84
Germantown, Pennsylvania, 33, 57
Germany, 128–129, 131
Gettysburg, Pennsylvania, 31m, 93, 102, 109
Gettysburg Address, 103
Girard College, 132
Glaciers, 10, 185
Goods, 81, 168, 172–173, 190, 191
Government
    Articles of Confederation and, 60–61
    branches of, 147
    of Britain, 53
    census and, 162
    citizens and, 154–155
    constitution and, 46, 146
    Continental Congress as, 54
    local, 150
    market and command economies and, 190, 193
    of Mid-Atlantic states, 198
    of Pennsylvania, 62, 65, 148–149
    of Pennsylvania colony, 28, 29
    by and of the people, 144
    popular sovereignty and, 155
    rights and responsibilities of citizens of, 142, 143, 144, 149, 154–57
    savings bonds and, 129
    state, 148–149, 155, 198, 199
    taxes and, 52, 65, 150, 151, 199
    of the United States, 60–61, 65, 142, 144–147
Governors, 149, 198
    Penn, Hannah Callowhill, 29
    Pinchot, Clifford, 130
    Rendell, Edward G., 140
Gradual Abolition of Slavery Act, 64
Grand Army of the Republic, 109
Granite, 188
Graph and chart skills
    circle graphs, 166–167
    timelines, 66–67
Great Britain
    American Revolution and, 56–59
    Declaration of Independence and, 47
    explorers of, 23
    French and Indian War and, 46, 48–50
    immigrants from, 33
    Proclamation of 1763, 51
    Stamp Act and, 46, 52–53
    War of 1812 and, 74–75
    World War I and, 128–129
    World War II and, 131
Great Depression, 113, 130, 133
Great Law, 28
Great Migration, 123
Great Valley, 5
Great War, The, 128–129
Greencastle, Pennsylvania, 107
Greensburg, Pennsylvania, 63

Half Moon (ship), *13*
Harbors, 186

Harrisburg, Pennsylvania, 8m, 31m, 73, 165
Haudenosaunee, 14, 16, 17, 49, 58
Heinz, Henry John, 91, 116
Hendrickson, Cornelius, 23
Hershey, Milton, 116
Hibernation, 187
Historic sites, 109, 169
Hitler, Adolf, 131
Homestead, Pennsylvania, 117
House of Representatives, 147, 149
Houses, 15, 16, 24
Howard, Liliane Stevens, 91, 125
Hudson, Henry, xx, 20, 23
Hudson River, 196
Human-environmental interaction, 11, 13
Human resources, 183, 192, 193
Hungarian immigrants, 120
Hunter-gatherers, 11, 12, 13, 15

Ice Age, 10–11
Immigrants, 120, 122–123, 125
    as factory workers, 84
    settlement of Pennsylvania and, 32–33, 35, 36
Imports, 174
Income, 171
Income tax, 151
Indentured servants, 37
Independence, 47, 54
Independence Hall, *60*, 61
Indiana County, Pennsylvania, 169
Industrial Revolution, 82–85
Industries, 165, 168
    child labor in, 124
    Civil War and, 107, 108, 109
    in the East, 191
    growth of after Civil War, 112, 114–117
    Industrial Revolution and, 82–84
    natural resources and, 169
    in Pennsylvania colony, 34, 37
    population changes and, 163
    transportation and, 169, 191
    during World War I, 129
    during World War II, 131
Innovations, 116
Integration, 132
Interdependence, 174
Interest, 171
International trade, 174
International Unity Festival, 165
Inventions and inventors, 38, 39
Irish immigrants, 33, 84, 122
Iron industry, 21, 34, 37, 83, 117
    Carnegie and, 119
    Civil War and, 107
Iroquois, 14, 16, 17
    in American Revolution, 58
    French and Indian War and, 49
Islands, 185
Italian immigrants, 120, 122
Italy, 131

Japan, 131
Jefferson, Thomas, 73

Jobs, 133, 169
    African American migration for, 123
    Civil War and, 107
    discrimination in, 132
    entrepreneurs and, 170
    in factories, 117, 120
    during Great Depression, 113, 130
    immigrants and, 122
    in industry, 84
    in Pennsylvania colony, 37
    population changes and, 163
    of settlers, 21
    during World War II, 131
Johnson, Lyndon, 132
Johnstown, Pennsylvania, 31m, 112, 123, 150
Jones, Absalom, 64
Judges, 147, 149
Judicial branch, 147, 149, 198
Jury, 143, 156
Justice, 146, 147

Kelley, Florence, 125
Kerosene, 83
Keystone Bridge Works, 119
Keystone State, 72, 75
Kier, Samuel, 83
King, Martin Luther, Jr., 132
Knights of Labor, 124

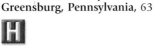

Labor unions, 113, 124, 155
Lake Erie, Battle of, 45, 74
Lakes, 186
Lancaster, Pennsylvania, 8m, 31m, 73, 116
Lancaster County, Pennsylvania, 62, 164, 169
Lancaster Turnpike, 70, 80
Land, 35
    Charter of 1681, 26
    conflict between Britain and American Indians over, 50–51
    conflict between France and Britain over, 48–50
    explorers looking for, 21, 25
    as factor of production, 192
    gained in treaties with American Indians, 63
    as payment to Revolutionary soldiers, 63
    Proclamation of 1763, 51
    Walking Purchase and, 1, 21, 35
Land bridge, 10, 11
Landforms, 4, 11, 185
Language, 14, 33, 164
Lappawinsoe, 1, 35
Latitude, 30–31
Laws, 154, 198
    on child labor, 124
    citizens' responsibility toward, 156
    in Constitution, 61
    of federal government, 147
    of local governments, 150
    of Pennsylvania, 149
    of Pennsylvania colony, 28
Lee, Robert E., 102, 108
Legislative branch, *145*, 147, 149, 198
LeMoyne, Francis Julius, 92, 95

Index

Lenni Lenape

Lenni Lenape, 1, 15, 16m, 17, 28, 35
Letters from a Farmer in Pennsylvania
  (Dickinson), 53
Liberty, 146, 147
Liberty bonds, 129
Libraries, 39, 112, 121
Lincoln, Abraham, 90, 97
  Civil War and, 101
  Emancipation Proclamation, 93, 101
  Gettysburg Address, 103
  as President, 92
Local government, 150
Lock Haven, Pennsylvania, 63
Log cabins, 24
Longhouse, 16
Long Island, 185
Longitude, 30–31
Louisiana Purchase, 70, 73
Loyalists, 56, 58
Lumber industry, 34, 114, 115, 185

Maine, 188, 189
Main Line Canal, 71
Manhattan, 197
Manufacturing, 117
  economy and, 169
  growth of after Civil War, 114–115
  World War I and, 129
Map and globe skills
  review of map skills, 8–9
  use of latitude and longitude, 30,
    31m
Maple syrup, 189, *192*
Maps
  Algonquian and Haudenosaunee, 16
  of battle of 1777, 57m
  cities of Pennsylvania, 31m
  early migration, 11m
  the East, 185m
  exploration of Pennsylvania, 23m
  French and Indian War in
    Pennsylvania, 49m
  Louisiana Purchase, 70m
  of Louisiana Territory, 72m
  population density of Pennsylvania
    in 2000, 163m
  population of Mid-Atlantic region,
    197
  regions of Pennsylvania, 5m
  resources of Pennsylvania, 169m
  roads and railroads in Pennsylvania,
    80m
  state of Pennsylvania, 8m
  of World War I powers, 129m
Marble, 188
Market economy, 182, 190, 193
Marshall, George, 131
Maryland, 189, 196, 198
Mason-Dixon Line, 95
Massachusetts, 189
Mass production, 83
Masters, Sybilla, 38
Mayor, 150
McClellan, George B., 90, 101
McKeesport, Pennsylvania, 117
Meade, George C., 101
Merchants, 37
Merger, 119
Metropolitan areas, 160, 163, 170
  See also cities; urban areas.

Mexico, 175
Mid-Atlantic region, 4, 184, 185m,
  196–198
Migration, 2, 10, 16, 123
Military training, 101
Miller, Lewis, *37*
Mills, 186, 192
Mining, 169
  child labor in, 124
  coal, 83, 107, 114, 115, 117, 188
  in Mid-Atlantic region, 198
  of stones, 188
Money, 174
Morgan, John Pierpont, 119
Morris, Robert, *54, 56*
Mott, Lucretia, 84, 85
Mt. Davis, 5
Muhlenberg, John, 59
Multicultural population, 164
Museums, 165

NAFTA, 175
**National American Woman Suffrage
  Association (NAWSA),** 125
National anthem, 157
National government, 142
  Articles of Confederation and, 60–61
  popular sovereignty and, 155
  rebellions over taxes, 65
  Reconstruction and, 108
  structure of, 144–147
National Memorial Arch, *72*
National Road, 80
Native Americans
  Algonquian, 15
  in American Revolution, 58
  conflicts over land, 50
  culture of, 3, 14
  Erie, 16
  French and Indian War and, 49
  Haudenosaunee, 14, 16, 17, 49, 58
  Iroquois, 58
  Lenni Lenape, 1, 15, 17, 28, 35
  Shawnee, 15
  Susquehannock, 16, 23
  treaties with Penn, 28, 29
  Walking Purchase, 1, 35
  War of 1812 and, 74
Natural gas, 114
Natural resources
  of the East, 188–189, 193
  as factor of production, 192
  industries and, 84, 114–115, 169
  trade of, 191
Negotiations, 75
Neutrality, 128
New Deal, 130
New England, 184, 185, 185m
New Hampshire, 189
New Jersey, 189, 191, 196, 198, 199
New Netherland, 25
New Sweden, 24, 25
New York, 189, 196, 198
New York City, *184,* 191, 197, 199
Niagara, 74
Nix, Robert Nelson Cornelius, Sr., 140,
  147
Nor'easters, 186
**North American Free Trade Agreement
  (NAFTA),** 175

Northampton County, Pennsylvania,
  164

Ohio River, 8m, 31m, 119
Oil industry, 71, 83, 114
Opinions, 76–77, 155
Opportunity costs, 170–171

Paine, Thomas, 55
Paleo-Indians, 2, 11
Paoli Massacre, 57
Paper industry, 37
Passenger wagons, 70
Patriots, 56, 58
Pearl Harbor, 131
Penn, Hannah Callowhill, 29
Penn, William, 20, 26–28, 29, 32, 72
Pennsylvania, 196
  American Indians in, 15–17
  American Revolution in, 56–58
  changes in early statehood, 73
  Civil War and, 101, 106–108
  climate of, 2, 6
  counties of, 150
  economy of, 168–171
  end of slavery in, 64
  enslaved people in, 94
  explorers in, 23
  government of, 148–149, 155
  growth of, 62–63
  immigrants in, 122–123, 125
  industries in, 118–120, 133, 169
  industry in, 82–83, 106, 107, 112,
    114–117
  as Keystone State, 72, 75
  labor unions in, 124
  landforms in, 4–5
  mining in, 188, 198
  as multicultural state, 164
  population of, 160, 162–163, 165
  reformers of, 84–85
  regions of, 5
  state constitution, 62
  steel industry and, 118–120
  tourism in, 161, 169, 198
  trade of, 174–175
  transportation in, 70, 71, 78–81
  War of 1812 and, 74
  in World War I, *128,* 129
  World War II and, 131
Pennsylvania Abolition Society, 94
Pennsylvania colony, 20
  American Revolution in, 56–58
  economy of, 21, 34
  establishment of, 26–27, 29
  government of, 28–29
  settlement of, 32–33
Pennsylvania Dutch, 164
Pennsylvania Railroad, 80, 115
Pennsylvania State University, 115, 121
Perry, Oliver Hazard, 45, 74
Petitions, 53
Pharmaceutical industry, 133
Philadelphia, Pennsylvania, 8m, 28,
  31m, *32,* 80, *150*
  as banking center, 191, 192
  Bethel African Methodist Episcopal
    Church in, 64

boycott of English goods, 53
capture of in American Revolution, 57
Continental Congresses in, 54
electric lights in, 116
festivals in, 165
immigrant groups in, 123
industry in, 115, 117, 169
labor unions in, 124
population of metropolitan area, 163
settlement of, 33
as state capital, 73
Philanthropy, 112, 121
Pickett, George, 102
Piedmont, 6
Piedmont region, 5
Pinchot, Clifford, 130
Pittsburgh, Pennsylvania, 31m, 48, 80, 115, 160
electric lights in, 116
government of, 150
iron industry in, 117
population of, 120, 163
steel industry in, 119, 120
Plateaus, 4
"Pledge of Allegiance, The," 157
Pocono Mountains, 5
Points of view, 98–99, 156
Police officers, 150, 199
Polish immigrants, 120, 122
Pontiac, 50
Pontiac's Rebellion, 50
Popular sovereignty, 155
Population, 162, 165
immigration and, 122–123
of Mid-Atlantic region, 196
of New York City, 197
of Pennsylvania, 63, 160
of Pittsburgh, 120
Preamble, 143, 148
Precipitation, 6, 7
Presidents, 147
Buchanan, James, 92, 96–97
Johnson, Lyndon, 132
Lincoln, Abraham, 90, 92, 93, 97, 101, 103
Roosevelt, Franklin Delano, 130
Wilson, Woodrow, 128
Prices, 172, 175
Primary sources, 104–105
Printing, 34
Printz, Armegott, 1, 24
Printz, Johan, 24
Privacy, 155
Private ownership, 193
Private services, 199
Proclamation, 51
Proclamation of 1763, 51
Products, 190, 191
imports and exports, 174
prices of, 172
supply and demand of, 173
Profit, 119, 190
Public goods, 150
Public services, 150, 199

Quakers, 27, 28, 29
Queens, 197

Raid, 74
Railroads, 80, 81, 83
Civil War and, 107, 108
growth after Civil War, 112, 114
immigrants and, 123
manufacturing for, 115
use of steel, 120
Ratification, 61, 62
Reading and thinking skills
cause and effect identification, 134–135
fact and opinion, 76–77
Reading Prong, 5
Reading skills. See first page of each lesson.
Reading strategies
monitor and clarify, 21
predict and infer, 3, 93
question, 71, 113, 161
summarize, 47, 143, 183
Reconstruction, 108, 109
Reference materials, 194–195
Refineries, 83
Reforms and reformers
civil rights movement and, 132
in labor laws, 124
for women's rights, 84–85, 91, 125
Regions, 4, 5
Religion, 26, 29
freedom in Pennsylvania colony, 28
freedom of, 61, 62, 155
of the Lenni Lenape, 15
settlers looking for freedom of, 21
tolerance and, 27
Rendell, Edward G., 140
Representative government, 145–147
Representatives, 28, 53, 62, 145, 149, 150
Resources, 20
of the East, 188–189
as factor of production, 192
industry and, 114–115, 169
trade of, 191
Responsibilities
of branches of government, 147, 149, 198
of citizens, 142, 143, 156–157
of government, 154
of local governments, 150
Retail businesses, 116, 169
Revolution, 56–59
Revolutionary War, 54–55, 56–59
Ridge and Valley region, 5, 6
Rights
of African Americans, 132
Bill of Rights and, 61, 146
of citizens, 142, 154, 155
Declaration of Rights and, 44, 62, 148
government protection of, 144
of women, 45, 84–85, 91
of workers, 155
Rivers, 11, 186
Roads, 78, 80, 130, 199
Roosevelt, Franklin Delano, 130
Ross, Elizabeth "Betsy," 44, 56
Rule of law, 146, 147

Rural areas, 21, 36, 37, 124, 163, 165, 199
education in, 39
of Mid-Atlantic region, 198
Russian immigrants, 122
Rustin, Bayard, 132

Sales tax, 151, 173, 175
Savings, 171
Scarcity, 173
Schools, 112, 199
Free School Act and, 73
integration of, 132
in Pennsylvania colony, 39
Schuylkill County, Pennsylvania, 169
Schuylkill River, 23
Schwab, Charles, 121
Scots-Irish immigrants, 33
Sea level, 4
Secession, 92, 97, 100
Secondary sources, 104–105
Second Continental Congress, 54
Segregation, 132
Senate, 147, 149
Service industries, 169, 190, 191
Services
of businesses, 168, 169, 190
government provision of, 150, 154
public and private, 199
Settlement, 23, 24–25, 32–35
Settlers, 1, 24–25, 34–35
Shawnee, 15, 16m
Shipbuilding, 21, 34, 37
Civil War and, 107
War of 1812 and, 74
World War I and, 129
Shipping, 186
Skyscrapers, 197
Slavery, 37, 94–97
abolitionists and, 92
Emancipation Proclamation and, 93, 101
end of in Pennsylvania, 64, 65
end of in US, 108, 109
Smith, John, 20, 23, 25
Society of Friends, 27, 28, 29
Soldiers
in Civil War, 101, 103, 106
land as payment to, 63
in World War I, 128, 129
in World War II, 131
South Carolina, 97, 100
South Mountain, 5
Soviet Union, 131
Spanish aid, 58
Specialization, 161, 173
Stamp Act, 46, 52
Stanton, Elizabeth Cady, 84, 85
"Star Spangled Banner, The," 157
State government, 148–149, 155, 198, 199
Statehood, 72–73
State house, 198
Staten Island, 197
State supreme court justices, 149
Steamboats, 70, 79, 81, 83
Steel industry, 112, 118–120, 121, 129, 169, 170, 174

Stein, Gertrude, 180
Stock market crash, 130
Storms, 186
Strikes, 84, 124, 155
Study skills
  primary and secondary source
    identification, 104–105
  reference materials, 194–195
Stuyvesant, Peter, 25
Suburbs, 183, 197
Suffrage, 125
Sullivan County, Pennsylvania, 163
Supply, 173
Supreme Court, 147
Surrender
  of British in War of 1812, 74
  of Confederate Army, 108
  of Germany and Japan, 131
Susquehanna River, 4, 8m, 23, 23m,
  31m
Susquehannock, 16, 17, 23
Swedish settlers, 1, 20, 24, 25
Swisshelm, Jane Grey, 45, 84, 85

Taxes, 61
  citizens' responsibility to pay, 156
  local government and, 150, 151
  price of goods and, 173, 175
  Stamp Act and, 46, 52–53, 55
  state governments and, 151, 199
  on whiskey, 65
Technology, 133, 169, 190, 196
Temperate climate, 186
Territory, 70, 73
Textile industry, 71, 82, 107, 117, 129,
  169
**Thirteenth Amendment to
  Constitution of United States,** 108
Thomson, Elihu, 116
Timelines, 66–67
  See also first of every chapter and unit.
Tinicum Island, 24
Titusville, Pennsylvania, 83
Tolerance, 27
Toll, 80
Tools, 12, *36*
Tourism, 161, 169, 198
Towns and cities
  government of, 145, 150
  growth of, 63, 186, 196
  immigrant groups and, 123
  See also urban areas.
Trade, 34, 174, 191, 193
  among America Indian groups, 17
  Civil War and, 108
  French and Indian War and, 48
  international partners, 175
  in Pennsylvania colony, 37
  transportation and, 81, 169
Trade routes, 22, 23, 24
Trading partners, 175
Trading posts, 23
Transportation, 70
  Conestoga wagons and, 62, *63*
  growth of cities and, 196
  industries and, 84, 120, 191
  as links to other areas, 174
  in New York City, 197
  railroads and, 80, 114
  roads and, 80

  trade and, 169
  on waterways, 71, 79, 170
Treaties
  at end of American Revolution, 59
  at end of French and Indian War, 46,
    50
  at end of War of 1812, 75
  between Penn and American Indians,
    28
  Walking Purchase, 35
Treaty of Ghent, 75
Treaty of Paris, 46, 50
Trenton, New Jersey, 57

Underground Railroad, 95
Unemployment, 130
Union Army, 90, 100, 101, 102, 106,
  108
Unions, 113, 124, 155
United Mine Workers, 113
United States
  census, 162
  civil rights movement, 132
  Civil War, 92, 100–103
  Constitution of, 61
  east coast of, 182, 184
  economy of, 182, 190
  Fugitive Slave Act, 95
  government of, 60–61, 65, 108, 142,
    144–147, 155
  Great Depression and, 130
  independence, 59
  Louisiana Purchase, 70, 73
  slavery in, 94–97, 95
  trade of, 174
  trade partners, 175
  War of 1812 and, 74–75
  World War I and, 128–129
  World War II and, 131
Urban areas, 36, 37, 163, 165
  education in, 39
  immigrant groups and, 123
  industries in, 169
  of Mid-Atlantic region, 196–197
  *See also cities; metropolitan areas;
    towns and cities.*
U.S. Steel Corporation, 119

Valley Forge, Pennsylvania, 58, 59
Vermont, 188, 189
Veterans, 109
Veto, 28, 149
Victory bonds, 129
Vocabulary skills. *See first page of each
  lesson.*
Volunteers, 142, *157*
Von Steuben, Frederick, 58
Voting rights, 62, 157
  popular sovereignty and, 155
  as responsibility, 145, 156
  for women, 84–85, 125

Walking Purchase, 1, 21, 35
Wampum, 17
Wanamaker, John, 116
War of 1812, 45, 70, 74–75

Washington, D. C., 184, 196, 198
Washington, George, 48, 55
  crossing the Delaware River, 56, 57
  French and Indian War and, 49
  in Pennsylvania, 57
  at Valley Forge, 58
Water cycle, 7
Waterfalls, 186
Water power, 186
Waterways, 70, 71, 79, 186
Wayne, Anthony, 57, 59
Weapons, 107
Welsh immigrants, 33, 122
Westinghouse, George, 116
Whiskey Rebellion, 65
White House, 147
Wholesale businesses, 169
Wigwams, 15
Williamsport, Pennsylvania, 8m, 63
Wilson, Woodrow, 128
Women
  Civil War and, 107
  as inventors, 38
  in Lenni Lenape communities, 15
  reformers, 45, 84–85, 91, 125
  work of in Pennsylvania colony, 37
  during World War II, 131
Woodland Indians, 13
Woolworth, F. W., 116
Workers
  in factories, 117
  as factor of production, 192
  Great Depression and, 130
  as human resources, 183, 192
  immigrants as, 84, 120, 122–123
  income of, 171
  jobs available now, 169
  reforms in working conditions, 124
  unions for, 113, 155
  World War II and, 131
World War I, 113, 128–129, 133
World War II, 113, 131, 133
Wyoming Massacre, 58

York, Maine, 192
York County, Pennsylvania, 164, 169
Yorktown, Battle of, 59

Index

Acknowledgments

Acknowledgments

For each of the selections listed below, grateful acknowledgment is made for permission to excerpt and/or reprint original or copyrighted material, as follows:

Photography Credits

Cover and title page Bob Krist/CORBIS. **ii** One Mile Up, Inc. **iii** (bl) BillMarchel.com. (tl) Joseph G. Strauch. (br) britishcolumbiaphotos.com/Alamy. (tr) Tom Brakenfield/CORBIS. (cl) Maier, Robert/Animals Animals-Earth Scenes. (cr) Darwin Dale/Photoresearchers, Inc. **xi** (b) HMCo./Angela Coppola. (bkgd) Photodisc/Getty Images. **xii** (tl) University of Arkansas Museum. (b) Brown Brothers. **xiii** (b) CORBIS. (t) The Granger Collection, New York. **xiv** (b) oldmerthyrtydfil.co. **xv** (t) AP Photo/Jacqueline Larma. (b) Photo by Simon Bronner. **xvi** (b) Joe McDonald/CORBIS. **xvii** (b) Holt Confer/Grant Heilman Photography. **xix** Ray Boudreau. **1** (cr) Historical Society of Pennsylvania/Bridgeman Art Library. (br) Marilyn "angel" Wynn nativestock.com (208)788-0144. (cl) American Swedish Historical Society, Philadelphia, Pennsylvania. (bc) Ingram Publishing/Alamy. **2** (cl) Theo Allofs/CORBIS. (cr) Ohio Historical Society. **3** (cl) The University of Arkansas Museum. (cr) Roman Soumar/CORBIS. **4** National Geographic Image Collection. **6** (cr) Fred Habegger/Heilmanphoto. (b) Holt Confer/Grant Heilman Photography. **9** Ray Bourdreau. **10-1** Archives Charmet/Musee de l'Histoire Naturelle/Bridgeman Art Library. **12** (b) Susie Brown. (t) C.C. Lockwood. (c) Ohio Historical Society. **13** The University of Arkansas Museum. **14** E.R. Degginger/Photo Researchers, Inc. **15** Roman Soumar/CORBIS. **17** Atwater Kent Museum of Philadelphia/Bridgeman Art Library. **20** (tl) Library of Congress, Prints & Photographs Division. (cr) American Philosophical Society. **21** (cl) The Granger Collection, New York. **22** Library of Congress, Prints & Photographs Division. **24** (cl) Cincinnati Medical Heritage Center, University of Cincinnati. (bl) Library of Congress, Prints & Photographs Division. **25** (tl) Bettman/CORBIS. **26** Brown Brothers. **27** Ron Saari. **28** Bettmann/CORBIS. **29** Historical Society of Pennsylvania. **30** Ray Boudreau. **32-3** Byer, Peter/Library Company of Philadelphia. **34** The Granger Collection, New York. **36** Fred S. Prouser/Prouser Photographic. **37** Lewis Miller Sketchbook/York County Heritage Trust. **38** (tr) National Museum of American Art, Smithsonian Institute, USA/Bridgeman Art Library. (bl) The Granger Collection, New York. **39** (cr) From the Collections of the University of Pennsylvania Archives. **44** (cr) Mary Evans Picture Library. (br) Royalty-Free/CORBIS. **45** (cl) Stapleton Collection/CORBIS. (bl) Bluejacket.com. (cr) Minnesota Historical Society. (br) Leonard de Selva/CORBIS. **46** (cr) Bettmann/CORBIS. **47** (cl) The Granger Collection, New York. (cr) National Archives and Records Administration. **48** The Art Archive/Culver Pictures. **50** (t) CORBIS. (b) The Granger Collection, New York. **51** Canadian Institute for Historical Microreproductions. **52** Colonial Williamsburg Foundation. **53** (br) Stapleton Collection/CORBIS. (t) Bettmann/CORBIS. **54** (tl) Bettmann/CORBIS. (tr) SuperStock, Inc./Superstock. **55** Superstock, Inc./Superstock. **56** (b) Art Resource, NY. **58** Bettmann/CORBIS. **59** Library of Congress, Prints & Photographs Division. **60** Photo by MPI/Stringer/Getty Images. **61** (tr) National Archives and Records Administration. (bl) John McGrail/Philadelphiaimages.com. **62-3** (b) Courtesy of the Library of Congress. **64** (cl) Delaware Art Museum, Wilmington, USA/Bridgeman Art Library. (b) Brenton, William L. /The Library Company of Philadelphia. **67** Ray Boudreau. **70** (cr) CORBIS. (cl) North Wind Picture Archives/Northwind. **71** (all) Bettmann/CORBIS. **72** Wm. Baker/Ghost Worx Images/Alamy. **73** Historica American Building Survey, William J. Bulger, Photographer, 1936/Library of Congress. **74** (cl) Duluth Shipping News\Kenneth Newhams. (b) Bettman/CORBIS. **75** Bettman/CORBIS. **76** Bettmann/CORBIS. **78** Bettmann/CORBIS. **79** Bettmann/CORBIS. **82** Bettmann/CORBIS. **83** Bettmann/CORBIS. **84** (br) National Portrait Gallery, Smithsonian Institution / Art Resource, NY Image Reference : ART57671. (bl) Bettmann/CORBIS. **85** The Grange Collection, New York. **90** (cr) The Art Archive/National Archives Washington DC. (br) Photos Courtesy of the Military & Historical Image Bank, www.historicalimagebank.com. **91** (cr) DePauw University Archives and Special Collections. (cl) Bettmann/CORBIS. (bc) Courtesy of Heinz North America. (br) David J. & Janice L. Frent Collection/CORBIS. **92** (cl) Washington County Historical Society. (cr) Bettmann/CORBIS. **93** (cl) MPI/Stringer/Getty Images. **95** (tl) Washington County Historical Society. (br) Louie Psihoyos/CORBIS. **96** (br)Bettmann/CORBIS. (bl) Library of Congress, Manuscript Division, The Papers of Montgomery C. Meigs. **97** Bettman/CORBIS. **99** Ray Boudreau. **100** (br) Mazer Photogrpahy. (bl) Tria Glovan/CORBIS. **101** (t) MPI/Stringer/Getty Images. (bl) Library of Congress, Prints and Photographs divition. **102** (cr) Art Resource. (b) Michele Burgess/Index Stock Imagery. **103** "Hay Draft" of the Gettysburg Address, John Hay Papers, Manuscript Division/Library of Congress. **105** Ray Boudreau. **106** (bl) Tria Glovan/CORBIS. (br) Civil War Treasures from the New-York Historical Society [digital ID, e.g., nhnycw/ad ad04004] http://memory.loc.gov/ammem/ndlpcoop/nhihtml/cwnyhshome.html. **107** (cl) Bettmann/CORBIS. **108** (b) Minnesota Historical Society/CORBIS. (tl) The Granger Collection/New York. **112** (cl) Royal Geographical Society/Alamy. (cr) Courtesy of the Carnegie Library of Pittburg. **113** (cl) The Horse Soldier. (cr) The Granger Collection New York. **114** Royal Geographical Society/Alamy. **115** National Geographic Society Image Collection. **116** (bc) Hershey Community Archives. (bl) Print and Picture Collection, The Free Library of Philadelphia. (br) C.P.Cushing/Robertstock Retrofile. **118** Oldmerthyrtydfil.com. **119** Mary Evans Picture Library. **120** Brown Brothers, Sterling PA 18463. **121** Courtesy of the Carnegie Library of Pittburg. **122** Independence Seaport Museum. **123** Johnstown Area Heritage Association. **124** CORBIS. **125** CORBIS. **127** Ray Boudreau. **128** International Film Service; The Iron Division: The National Guard of. Pennsylvania in the World War, H. G. Proctor; © 2003, The Digital Bookshelf. **130** (bl) The Granger Collection New York. (br) The Pennsylvania State Archives. **131** (bl) Bettmann/CORBIS. (br) The Granger Collection, New York. **132** (all) Bettmann/CORBIS. **133** Photographers Library LTD/eStock Photo. **135** Ray Boudreau. **140** (cr) Congressional Portrait Collection, Prints and Photographs Division Library of Congress. (br) Paul Conkin/PhotoEdit. **141** (cl) Photo by Alfred Eisenstaedt/Stringer/Time Life Pictures/Getty Images. (bc) The Silent Spring by Rachel Carson published by Houghton Mifflin Company © 2002. (cr) Brown Brothers Sterling, PA 18463. (br) Royalty-Free/CORBIS. **142** (cl) Jeff Greenberg/Index Stock Imagery, Inc. (cr) William Thomas Cain/Stringer/Getty Images. **143** (cr) Ron Chapple/Getty Images. (cl) National Archives and Records Administration. **144** AP/Wide World Photos. **145** AP/Wide World Photos. **148** Dennis MacDonald/Alamy Images. **150** (br) AP Photo/Jacqueline Larma. (b) David H. Wells/CORBIS. **151** Jeff Greenberg/PhotoEdit Inc. **153** Ray Boudreau. **154** Photodisc/Craig Brewer/Artbase Inc. **155** William Thomas Cain/Stringer/Getty Images. **156** Ron Chapple/Getty Images. **157** Jeff Greenberg/Index Stock Imagery, Inc. **160** (cl) Richard I'Anson/Lonley Planet Images. (cr) Royalty-Free/CORBIS. **161** (cl) Jeff Greenberg/PhotoEdit. (cr) Photographers Library LTD/eStock Photo. **162** Richard I'Anson/Lonley Planet Images. **164** (tr) Peter Ginter. (tl) Photo by Simon J. Bronner. **165** E.A. Kennedy/The Image Works. **166** Ray Boudreau. **168** Larry Lefever/Heilmanphoto. **170** (all) Ray Boudreau. **171** Ray Boudreau. **172** Bob Krist/CORBIS. **173** (tl) John Colwell/Heilmanphoto. (tc) David Joel/Getty Images. (tr) John McGrail/ johnmcgrail.com. **174** (cl) George Hall/CORBIS. (b) Royalty-Free/CORBIS. **175** (cl) Lon C. Diehl/PhotoEdit. **182** (cr) Elizabeth Hathon/CORBIS. (cl) Miles Ertman/Masterfile. **183** (cr) Jeff Greenberg/PhotoEdit. (cl) Mark Richards/PhotoEdit. **184** (b) Grant Heilman Photography, Inc. **186** Reuters NewMedia Inc./CORBIS. **187** Joe McDonald/CORBIS. **189** Rudy Von Briel/PhotoEdit. **190** Elizabeth Hathon/CORBIS. **191** Tony Freeman/PhotoEdit. **192** (cr) Photodisc/Getty Images. (br) Roy Morsch/CORBIS. (bc) Arthur C. Smith/Grant Heilman Photography, Inc. (bl) Grant Heilman Photography, Inc. **193** David Young-Wolff/PhotoEdit. **195** Chip Henderson/Index Stock Imagery. **196** Alan Schein Photography/CORBIS. **198** Richard T. Nowitz/CORBIS. **0** (br) Victoria and Albert Museum, London/Art Resource, NY. (cr) Bettmann/CORBIS. **R0** (tr) Buddy Mays/CORBIS. **R0-1** (b) Panoramic Images/Getty Images. **R4** (br) The Granger Collection, New York. (cl) Bettmann/CORBIS.

Map Credits

all maps created by Mapping Specialist Limited